GLOBAL
HEARTLAND

GLOBAL HEARTLAND

Displaced Labor, Transnational Lives,
and Local Placemaking

FARANAK MIRAFTAB

INDIANA UNIVERSITY PRESS
Bloomington & Indianapolis

This book is a publication of

INDIANA UNIVERSITY PRESS
Office of Scholarly Publishing
Herman B Wells Library 350
1320 East 10th Street
Bloomington, Indiana 47405 USA

iupress.indiana.edu

The paper used in this publication
meets the minimum requirements of
the American National Standard for
Information Sciences—Permanence of
Paper for Printed Library Materials,
ANSI Z39.48–1992.

Manufactured in the
United States of America

Library of Congress Cataloging-
in-Publication Data

Names: Miraftab, Faranak, author.
Title: Global heartland : displaced labor,
    transnational lives, and local
    placemaking / Faranak Miraftab.
Description: Bloomington : Indiana
    University Press, [2016] | Series:
    Global research studies | Includes
    bibliographical references and index.
Identifiers: LCCN 2015032159 |
    ISBN 9780253019271 (cloth : alk. paper) |
    ISBN 9780253019349 (pbk. : alk. paper) |
    ISBN 9780253019424 (ebook)
Subjects: LCSH: Communities—Illinois—
    Beardstown. | Multiculturalism—
    Illinois—Beardstown. | Immigrants—
    Illinois—Beardstown—Social conditions.
    | Economic development—Social
    aspects—Illinois—Beardstown. |
    Beardstown (Ill.)—Ethnic relations—
    History. | Beardstown (Ill.)—Emigration
    and immigration—Economic aspects—
    History. | Beardstown (Ill.)—Social
    conditions—21st century. | Beardstown
    (Ill.)—Economic conditions—21st century.
Classification: LCC HN80.B43 M57 2016 |
    DDC 305.8009773/465—dc23
LC record available at http://lccn.loc
    .gov/2015032159

1 2 3 4 5   21 20 19 18 17 16

In memory of Farshad-e nazaneen
To maman, Ken, Rahi, and Omeed

CONTENTS

Conclusion: The Global in My Backyard   *209*

PREFACE

I WRITE THESE WORDS IN CAPE TOWN, SOUTH AFRICA, WHERE I AM spending the tail end of my sabbatical leave and where recent days have seen the unfortunate outbreak of violence against poor black African migrants. These attacks, which started in Durban and spread out to Cape Town, have occurred by and large in townships, informal settlements, and areas where poor people live. Nationwide, many African migrants have been injured and killed, businesses have been looted or burned down, and thousands of people have been displaced, forcing them to seek refuge at police stations, churches, and temporary accommodations set up by NGOs. Attackers accuse African foreign nationals of "stealing jobs from citizens"—accusations too similar to those I heard about immigrants in the United States as I did my research for this book.

In the aftermath of these tragic events, I helped facilitate two meetings of African immigrant poor who live in Cape Town's townships, informal settlements, and low-income areas at the invitation of the International Labor Research Interest Group, a local NGO that collaborates with an emerging citywide movement called the Housing Assembly (HA). The Afro-phobic violence, as some call it, spurred the HA to revisit their slogan of "Decent Housing for All" in order to explore how migrants and foreign nationals can be included in the "All" for whom they campaign. These conversations were initiated to overcome racial divisions among the working-class poor, as well as differences over citizenship, and to build solidarity. The plight and pain of migrants as expressed in their powerful testimonials confirm the need for careful and critical study of migration and global labor mobility. This is the area my book explores. Because current global capitalism produces and feeds off intense processes of labor displacement, it is urgent that the social and spatial dimensions of such processes be taken seriously, both locally and globally, and that the instability in categories of belonging based on national, racial, and ethnic identities be acknowledged. Moreover, as I argue and demonstrate in this book, we need to use political-economic structural explanations along with sociocultural ethnographic insights to achieve a relational understanding of what is occurring. For it is through such a relational understanding that we may also help achieve a recognition of commonalities among diverse poor people, even, as the recent violence against African migrants in South Africa reminds us, in the face of potent and volatile differences. With its historical and transnational scope, I hope my book will serve as one step toward bridging national, racial, ethnic, linguistic, and legal differences and building solidarities among the poor and working classes.

May 2015

ACKNOWLEDGMENTS

DURING THE DECADE-LONG RESEARCH AND WRITING OF THIS BOOK, I have been inspired and assisted by many individuals who have shared with me their stories, knowledge, and insights.

First and foremost, my gratitude goes to those who trusted me with their stories in Illinois, in Mexico, and in Togo. While they must remain nameless here, I wish to say to anyone whom I interviewed and whose words I wrote down or recorded, I am tremendously grateful to you. Without you this book would not exist. I also want to give special thanks to my assistants during field work in Togo and in Mexico, who provided invaluable local and trans-national insights. Again, because they are closely linked with my Beardstown interviewees, I cannot name these assistants. But you know who you are. To each and every one of you, interviewees and assistants, I owe an inexpress-ible debt.

I am also grateful to the reviewers of the manuscript and to my friends and colleagues who read all or parts of the manuscript. Their critical comments have sharpened and enriched my analyses and made this book stronger, but of course they are not responsible for its shortcomings. Above all I thank Arlie Hochschild, my mentor and inspiration, for her careful reading of the manuscript and insightful commentary. Her enthusiasm about this project and her intellectual contribution have been indispensable. I am also grateful to the Hochschilds for their generosity affording me "a room of one's own" in Berkeley for a much-needed writing retreat. I thank Lew Hopkins, my esteemed planning colleague, who read the manuscript in its entirety, offered helpful comments, and stressed how the Beardstown story, which is ultimately about placemaking, would be of core interest and importance to planning scholars. For their comments on draft chapters of this manuscript, I am deeply indebted to James Barrett, Charles Piot, David Wilson, Jan Nedervene Pieterse, Matthew Sanderson, Carla Paciotto, Nancy Abelmann, Zsuzsa Gille, Rachel Schurman, Ken Salo, and Zohreh Sullivan, as well as a longtime Beardstown resident who must also remain anonymous. I am also thankful to Zsuzsa Gille, with whom I spent a summer working on our manuscripts daily and reflecting on our day's work every evening. These rich conversations were both fun and stimulating. With Rachel Schurman, I have had many helpful conversations while walking or cooking in Minneapolis or Champaign. Nancy Abelmann's writing workshop and most importantly her critical review of the main ethnographic material used in two of the book chapters were instrumental. Many other friends and colleagues have contributed to this book by focused and stimulating discussion of the project or through informal dinner and coffee conversations. For engagement with my arguments, I thank Betsy Esch, Dave Roediger; James Loewen, Zohreh Sullivan, Behrooz Ghamari-Tabrizi, Dede Ruggles, Terri Barnes, Peter Marcuse, Rochelle Gutierrez, and Eileen Diaz McConnell. With Eileen Diaz McConnell I also conducted fieldwork in Beardstown during 2006, a collaboration that resulted in joint publications, as well as insights cited in this book. Lois Guarnizo and Michael Peter Smith, whose work has inspired this project from the beginning, made helpful comments on an earlier draft of chapter 8. I thank Zohreh Sullivan for her enthusiastic support throughout the project and for responding to my many requests for weighing in on specific points in the manuscript. She never fell short at any dinner gathering with friends and colleagues to remind me and them of the incredible Beardstown story to be told. I am also grateful to my colleagues at the Department of

Urban and Regional Planning and the College of Fine and Applied Arts at the University of Illinois at Champaign-Urbana (UIUC) who enabled me in direct and indirect ways to undertake this project. At UIUC and beyond Daniel Schneider, Marc Doussard, Stacy Harwood, Lynn Dearborn, Betsy Sweet, and Gerardo Sandoval took time to answer my specific questions. I have also benefited from feedback and engagements with the audience in various venues where I have presented and discussed portions of this book.

In the decade-long course of working on this project, I have had the pleasure of collaborating with artists interested in the story of Beardstown as a global heartland. For the Illinois portion of the project I have worked with my artist friends and colleagues, Sarah Ross and Ryan Griffis, who tell a story of Beardstown through videography in three acts. In act three "Moving Flesh" they used professional actors to perform selected transcribed interviews included in this book that I conducted with West Africans, Mexicans, Detroiters, and white locals in Beardstown. Their creative perspective and its synergy with my ethnographic research made my work more enjoyable and offered the outcome a broader reach (see the video at http://regionalrelationships.org/bottomlands/). In 2014, when the artists and activist members of the School for Designing a Society (SDS) expressed interest in adapting portions of the manuscript for a community-based play, SDS members and I met regularly during the spring and summer to create the theatrical expressions and stage adaptation for the core stories and messages of the project. As I revised the manuscript, this artistic exercise enriched and gave clarity to my academic writing. I am inspired by the work of my SDS friends.

For the book cover design, Sarah Ross and Ryan Griffis helped explore design options at an early stage. For the final book cover, I am indebted to Zohreh Sullivan, Behrooz Ghamari-Tabrizi, and Hillary Kahn. Behrooz and Zohreh helped me play around with the title and image and made a much-needed last minute change. Behrooz, as the man of hundred hidden talents, helped to improve on the cover design presentation. Hillary Kahn, offered timely and crucial support when I needed it most.

To Jim Kilgore, I need to offer a range of acknowledgements and thanks. As he read many drafts of this book, he did more than edit the language. He also helped me clarify ideas, remove confusions, and highlight important insights. Thank you, as well, Jim, for your enthusiasm about the project. I am also grateful to Al Davis and Maria Gillombardo, who also reviewed various chapters of the manuscript before submission. Al helped in making the final push with references and bibliographic information.

To afford the time and funding for the making of this book, I have benefited from a number of grants and fellowships. At the University of Illinois, I was supported by the Vice Chancellor's Office for Research Campus Research Board; a College of Fine and Applied Arts Creative Research Grant; the Center for Democracy in a Multiracial Society; the Center for Advanced Studies; and the Illinois Program for Research in Humanities (IPRH). In the context of a collaboration between the Center for the Study of Global Change at Indiana University and Indiana University Press on a project entitled "Framing the Global" (FG), I was awarded a five-year fellowship (2011–2015) funded by the Mellon Foundation. As an FG fellow, I was privileged to discuss my work with other fellows, and the project PI, Hilary Kahn, who closely reviewed and discussed synthesis chapters of my project. I also thank Deborah Piston-Hatlen for making fellows' cyber-space and face-to-face meetings and discussions possible. As guest scholars at the FG project, Saskia Sassen and Gillian Hart engaged with all fellows' work, including mine, and offered me insightful comments on the conceptual architecture of the project. As with the IPRH fellows, the Framing the Global fellows became my intellectual family during the course of this project.

I also acknowledge the important contributions made by my students and research assistants (RAs) at the University of Illinois. Over the years many RAs have helped with this project: Marisa Zapata, Andrew Jensen, Sophia Sianes, Robby Boyer, Shakil Kashem, Djifa Kother, and Samuel Hyde. Special thanks to Shakil Kashem for his diligent work on demographic data used in this volume. I also thank students in my advanced graduate seminar who conducted interviews in Beardstown for their own research: Steve de Santos, Megan Bronson, Wembo Lombela, Jorge Ibarra, Diego Angulo, and Sang Lee. Jorge and Diego were visiting graduate students from the University of Culiacan (Universidad Autónoma de Culiacan). Both while here and from afar, Diego has helped me with the labor data and statistics I include in this volume. His assistance has been indispensable. In 2014, when Jorge returned to our campus, this time as a visiting professor, he helped me track some of the difficult data for Mexican bureau of statistics regarding migration and remittances in Mexico. *Gracias compañeros.* Pastor Guy, a community leader among Congolese in Champaign with extensive links throughout Central Illinois, was instrumental in helping me establish contacts of trust in Beardstown and Rushville and understand the plight of Diversity Visa immigrants in the U.S. Thank you, Pastor.

Much of what drives me in my work is shaped by my family and friends outside academia. As a displaced person living in Illinois, I have felt their love even from afar sustaining me over the years. This is my opportunity to acknowledge their influences at crucial points in my life. My deepest gratitude goes to my family in Iran and in California. The love of my siblings and their families, Farin, Matin, Amin, Sadaf, Sahand, Farshad, and Kousha, Dennis, and Firuze, keeps my soul and body together. My lifelong and transnational friendships with Nasreen, Parnian, Roya, Rana, Ginny, Kjersti, Mooness, Jon Morten, Elisabeth, Eivind, Laila, Helga, Foruzan, Neema, and Cristina have been indispensable in my global journeys of exile. My father and my sister, Farshad, if they were around, would have been pleased to see this book as they helped to shape its inspiration, which is a call for global justice. My beloved sister, Farshad, along with fifty other young girls, was executed by the Islamic Republic at the notorious Evin prison one cold December night in 1982. Her only crime was to seek a just and better world for the working class. It is to her memory that I dedicate this book. My mother, who has been the source of my strength, and my true North to whom I go when I lose my way, is the strongest woman I have known with the biggest heart and soul. I learn from her the love for life and for family. Asheghetoonam. عاشقتونم

Last not least, I would not have been able to write this book if I were deprived of my loving twin sons and my partner: my hope (Omeed), my guide (Rahi) and my companion (Ken). They accompanied me on many visits to Beardstown, met friends I had made there, and took part in West African and Mexican celebrations. As my partner in life who held the forts as I spent time in the multiple field sites of this project in Illinois, Mexico, and Togo, Ken has also been my fiercest critic. He keeps me honest. While no responsibility for shortcomings in this book falls on him, I acknowledge with gratitude Ken's substantive contribution in reflective discussions of my field observations and their conceptual implications. My sons, my joys in life, have been keen to see this book out. My work has been source of amusement and amazement for them: "Mom is still working on Beardstown!" "What is about Beardstown that you like so much?" "Why do you always go there?" I hope they find in this book the hook, the attraction that kept me going back—the story of a global heartland.

May 2015

GLOBAL
HEARTLAND

Figure Intro.1: Cargill billboard outside Beardstown.

INTRODUCTION

The Global Heartland

A WOMAN DRESSED IN A DRAPED, PRINTED AFRICAN FABRIC, WITH one shoulder exposed, and wearing a flamboyant scarlet and gold headdress, locks her parked car and walks toward three men on the sidewalk. The men, who are African in appearance, are engaged in an intense conversation, frequently and effortlessly switching between Ewe and French. One is wearing an off-white *buba* and *sokoto*, traditional African attire made with embroidered brocade; another, slender and tall, wears jeans and a striped blue and white T-shirt; the third man, short in stature, is dressed in a suit and tie and holds a Bible in his hand—he may have just come from a church visit or a Bible study class. At the same moment a crowd of several hundred people are leaving the nearby Catholic Church where the Spanish-language mass has just ended. Many of them stand around on the sidewalks in front of the church and in the parking lot across the street, chatting and socializing in Spanish. A young boy, his hair cut short and neat with the top part greased and swept up to form a peak, is dressed in his Sunday best; he rides away on his bike, ornamented with a small Mexican flag. A man wearing a stiff-brimmed white hat, a belt with a metal buckle that makes his bulging belly even more prominent, and pointy-toed, handcrafted boots holds hands with a young woman with long, black, silky hair, who hardly fits into her too-tight clothes. A little girl of seven or eight runs behind her, yelling "Mama! Espérame!" ("Mommy, wait for me!") as she catches up to the woman and grabs her other hand.

These street scenes, which took place on a Sunday morning in May of 2005, when I made my first visit to Beardstown, Illinois, haunt me to this day, nine years later. I would not have found these scenes unusual were I in Chicago or the university town where I live, Champaign-Urbana. They were, however, astonishing in Beardstown, which had been until not long ago a "sundown town" (Loewen 2005), prohibiting black people[1] from remaining there after dark.[2] Through acts or threats of racist violence, city ordinances, and other means, white supremacist residents of sundown towns kept places like Beardstown white through most of the twentieth century. Once I began my research, I heard from residents about African Americans being chased away well before sunset. Indeed, a few of the elderly white residents recalled their parents taking them to nearby towns to watch "black men being hanged" as late as the 1920s and 1930s. But in a matter of ten years—from 1990 to 2000—the number of people of color living in Beardstown grew by an astonishing 3,200 percent; that is, from 32 black and Hispanic individuals to 1,060.[3] By 2010, when U.S. Census staff were in Beardstown, only three out of every five residents identified him- or herself as being non-Hispanic white; and one out of every five was born outside the United States. Today, of the six thousand residents, an estimated two thousand Spanish-speaking Latinos—predominantly from Mexico but also from El Salvador, Guatemala, Cuba, Puerto Rico, and the Dominican Republic—and over four hundred French-speaking Africans—predominantly from Togo but also from Congo, Senegal, Benin, Guinea, and Burkina Faso—live side by side and among the white residents of Beardstown and the nearby town of Rushville. Since 2007, yet another group has been added to the mix—approximately fifty African Americans from Detroit. One local woman, describing this transformation from a sundown town to a multiracial, multicultural, and multilingual town, observed, "We did not want to go to the world, but the world came to us."

Teaching and living in Illinois's major college town, Champaign-Urbana, I had often driven through typical rural midwestern landscapes—long stretches of cornfields punctuated by road signs that proclaimed pro-life agendas or defended the right to bear arms. I had read about this part of the country—the rural rust belt, abandoned by industries and then by younger residents, who departed in search of jobs and the promise of a better life in big cities. But I had not visited, let alone spent an extended period of time there. As an Iranian who grew up in a bustling Tehran and has lived in many large cities of the world, I was curious to learn about rural midwestern towns. Thus, I made an excursion out of my first visit to Beardstown, which a preliminary demographic review of Illinois immigration had flagged as an outstanding example of demographic change. On my way, I followed road signs from interstate and country highways to small towns that invariably seemed abandoned and forgotten. On the main streets, buildings and shops were boarded up, their exterior walls bearing fading advertisements from decades past; few cars, if any, were parked or being driven along the street; and in some towns, old traffic signs reminded motorists of school zones and crossings, though the schools were gone.

These rural towns posed a stark contrast to Beardstown—both socially and spatially. In Beardstown the downtown businesses were open and thriving. Family-owned restaurants offered Mexican and Dominican fare; grocers stocked foods ranging from cassava to tortillas. A school and library had recently been built. Neighborhoods had been revitalized, as evidenced by the improved and remodeled houses that (weather permitting) displayed flower boxes at the windows and front doors. Even more surprising was that unlike large U.S. cities, Beardstown had no economically or ethnically stratified neighborhoods—there was not a Latino, white Anglo, or black and African neighborhood, no rich or poor neighborhood. The two- and three-story houses of the affluent were situated next to the newly remodeled, smaller homes occupied by immigrants. Trailer homes popped up all over the town, next to well-kept Victorian-era homes as well as in the backyards and front yards of less desirable structures, providing accommodation for a cross-section of the low-income families.

My research confirmed these observations: Beardstown is indeed residentially integrated. It also has a residential integration rate that is higher than that of traditional immigrant destinations like New York or Los Angeles.[4] I learned that in Beardstown there is a high rate of owner-occupied housing units among Mexican immigrants;[5] that the schools have adopted a two-way language immersion program, wherein the curriculum is taught to all in a classroom half in Spanish and half in English;[6] that numerous cultural identity celebrations, such as Cinco de Mayo, are held in the town's public square; and that multiracial soccer clubs play on the town's outdoor fields.

But how did this dramatic change to a former sundown town come about, and in such a short period of time? What brings these diverse people to this part of the country?

The multinational Cargill Corporation, with its local meatpacking plant in Beardstown, is the protagonist that brought about this demographic transformation.[7] On the country road approaching Beardstown, billboards congratulate Cargill workers for "20 years of service" and encourage viewers to "choose job stability" and submit an application anytime, 24/7 (see figure 0.1). The Beardstown plant employs 2,200 people, with an additional 300 contract employees on the site at any time. Each day at this plant, through two shifts of production, about 1,800 workers from more than 30 countries[8] slaughter, process, and pack more than 18,500 hogs. With each 6-month hog weighing approximately 270 pounds, and all collectively weighing about 4.8 million pounds,[9] that amounts to over 7 million 8-ounce servings of pork being produced per day and over a billion pounds per year for over 550 customers serving 16 global markets.[10]

Founded by William Wallace Cargill at the close of the American Civil War in 1865, Cargill is a producer and marketer of food, agricultural, financial, and industrial products and services and has a global reach. Starting with a single grain storage warehouse in Conover, Iowa, the company expanded quickly when Will Cargill's brothers, Sam and James, joined his business venture and bought or built grain elevators along the westward-expanding railways. Twenty years later, the company was handling over 1.6 million bushels of grain and moving into a prominent position in a growing global market. Over the next decades, they added flour mills, salt mines, cattle slaughterhouses, ocean barges, and a vast network of grain trading offices overseas. By the mid-twentieth century, the company had expanded to South America and Europe. Cargill was not only a pioneer in the global marketing game but also an early adopter of information technology, using already in 1957 an IBM 6560 computer to manage its global production and pricing mechanisms.[11] Today, the company's reach extends well beyond the grain business. It has become what Brewster Kneen calls an "Invisible Giant," providing the eggs in McDonald's breakfast sandwiches, the corn syrup in Coca-Cola, the flour in supermarket bread, and the salt in fast-food French fries (Kneen 2002).[12] Cargill is among the nation's top four producers of beef, pork, turkeys, animal feed, salt, and flour. With 140,000 employees in 65 countries, Cargill is the largest family-owned non-publicly traded company in operation since 1865 (Cargill 2013b). In fiscal year 2013, Cargill had net earnings of $2.31 billion, up by 97 percent from the prior year.[13]

In 1987, Cargill bought the Beardstown plant from Oscar Mayer, which closed it after twenty years of operation in the wake of a long and bitter struggle between the unionized workers and management over wages and benefits. That was a difficult time for Beardstown and its residents, as Oscar Mayer was the third major employer to depart over a two-year span, adding to the town's ongoing population and financial losses. Taking advantage of the defeat of the local union, Cargill bought the plant and reopened with an entry-level wage reduced by more than $2 per hour to $6.50.[14] Some of the senior workers were able to change their line of work to better paying jobs and signed up for retraining as truck drivers; some left town; and others, who did not have many options, stayed and waited for the next opportunity to leave. By the late 1980s, following wage cuts, the company faced a labor shortage: workers in the area were not willing to take the lower-paying jobs. This problem was reflected in the plant's high labor turnover rates at the time and was exacerbated when a newly established second shift of operations lacked workers.

Starting in the early 1990s, the plant management turned to recruitment among immigrants and minorities. At first, they sent a team of mobile recruiters to U.S. towns close to the Mexican border and other areas identified as having a high concentration of unemployed minority and/or immigrant workers. Soon after the arrival of each group of immigrant laborers, word of mouth through their social networks began to bring new workers to the plant. Depending on the extent of the plant's labor shortage, employees were sometimes rewarded for this network recruitment with a small bonus (ranging from fifty dollars to three hundred dollars) added to the employee's paycheck. It is important to note that Cargill's hiring practices were not an anomaly; this has been a common trend in the industry since the late 1980s.

In Beardstown, the first round of immigrant recruitment brought Spanish-speaking workers. Some came from other cities within the United States and others directly from Mexico or Central America. Many among this first wave of Latino immigrants were undocumented or held fake papers and had never worked in the manufacturing sector. Indeed, most had been farmers in their home countries or, if they lived in other U.S. cities before their move to Beardstown, had worked in various service or agricultural jobs. By the early 2000s, a few French-speaking West Africans who were laid off from other meatpacking plants in the Midwest also found employment at the Beardstown plant. These workers opened a new channel to a very different group for the Cargill plant's labor supply—namely, highly educated, French-speaking West Africans who gained legal residency and work permits by winning a U.S. Diversity Visa through an annual lottery held in their country of origin. The West African workers I interviewed in Beardstown included an engineer, a veterinarian, a human rights lawyer, and a sociology professor. Despite their background, the fact that Cargill production floor jobs did not require English-language skills was a distinct advantage. These new arrivals needed immediate full-time jobs in order to be able to send for the children they had left behind and to repay the debt they incurred to make the transcontinental journey. In 2007, after an Immigration and Customs Enforcement (ICE) raid, which cost the plant a large number of undocumented workers, yet another mix was added to the workforce as Cargill recruiters turned to Puerto Ricans in Puerto Rico, Cubans in Miami, and African Americans in Detroit in search of so called "legal" workers.

None of these groups of workers received much of a welcome. In 1996, a few years after the Spanish-speaking immigrants had begun working at the plant, violence broke out. After one local man was shot and killed, the perpetrator ran away to Mexico; a six-foot tall cross was burned in the main plaza; a Mexican-owned bar was set on fire; and the Ku Klux Klan marched through town to intimidate what was at that point the only immigrant group, Latinos. To resolve the problems, churches, open-minded white locals, and vocal legal immigrants and immigrant advocates joined forces. Three Mexican nuns were flown in, and bilingual pastors and priests were recruited to local churches. To avoid further turmoil, a few years later when the West Africans were recruited to the plant, they were encouraged to find residences in nearby Rushville. Though also a former sundown town, Rushville did not have the turbulent recent experiences of Beardstown, which "had enough to deal with," as one local close to the management told me when describing this period of time. The last group of recruited workers, the African American Detroiters, did what other African American workers at Cargill plant had done: they commuted to their Beardstown jobs from the larger nearby cities of Jacksonville and Springfield. As I discuss at length in chapter 8, this racialized residential geography of the Cargill workforce was later transformed when all these groups moved into Beardstown, making it the diverse town it is today.

Beardstown's experience is particularly notable not only for its ethnic and racial diversity but also for its social and economic "comeback." Amid other depopulating towns of the rural rust belt, and despite its own population loss of 17 percent during the 1980s, Beardstown both increased its population and combated the shrinking syndrome common to rust belt towns in the last two decades.

One might say the town represents a success story. If so, the narrative would go something like this: Beardstown is a rust belt town that "solved" the problem of urban shrinkage—a common reality for many dying towns of the heartland—by importing an immigrant labor force. Immigrants revitalized Beardstown by fixing up houses, registering their children in the local schools, and spending their money at the local shops and facilities. Some might even be said to have fulfilled the "American Dream." While many small towns adjacent to Beardstown struggle to keep their schools open among boarded up businesses and houses, Beardstown has constructed brand-new buildings for its elementary school and library, offered steady housing markets for home ownership and rent, and fostered thriving local businesses.

In this book I grapple with what is obscured in this congratulatory narrative and seek to understand the broader relationships that produce a place like Beardstown and its revitalization. How is the labor force at the Cargill plant produced? That is, what are the processes, policies, and conditions through which a migrant labor force finds its way to Beardstown? What conditions make it possible for these migrant workers to continue the back-breaking labor of meatpacking—jobs that are known as the three Ds, Dangerous, Dirty, and Difficult, and that their native-born counterparts have largely refused? Furthermore, what happens when a small town shaped through contentious histories of race and labor relations goes through a rapid transformation wrought by global labor mobility? Are these new groups of immigrant workers and their families victimized in this small, single-employer town that traditionally closed itself to outsiders? In what ways do these groups renegotiate the interracial and intersocial divisions that the corporation might promote in the workplace? What difference, if any, does the local context, the place and the politics of place, make in the experiences of the immigrant labor force and the emergent local-global relationships?

JOURNEYS IN THE HEARTLAND AND BEYOND

Ethnographic work for this study began in Beardstown itself. Between 2005 and 2012, I organized focus groups for recent immigrants through their ESL community college classes, participated in community events, and interviewed residents, including native-born locals, recently arrived immigrants, town authorities, and members of nonprofit groups and civic associations.[15] But soon after I started my interviews in Beardstown, I realized that the story of this global heartland could be understood only by following it to the "global elsewheres"—the places from where the workers came, the places to which their transnational families connected them. Thus, I combined my field work in Illinois with travel to the home communities of immigrant workers in Mexico (Tejaro, Michoacán) in 2008 and in Togo (Lomé, the capital city) in 2010.[16] I spoke with workers' children, parents, relatives, friends, and neighbors back home to understand the social, political, and economic processes that motivated them to come to the United States and contributed to their willingness to accept meatpacking jobs in Beardstown. It was only then, with the insights those interviewees offered, that I could piece together a plausible explanation for Beardstown's transformation. As with paintings that can better be seen by stepping back from the canvas, the fuller story of Beardstown was evident once I looked at it from afar. I needed to go away to recognize the global in my backyard.

Another factor influenced my multi-sited methodological approach—the Cargill Corporation and its power over the lives of workers who might share information with me. I could not ignore the risk that talking to me might pose for them, and this awareness set limitations on the kinds of questions I asked. Indeed, our mutual vulnerability became clear to me as a result of two adversarial interactions with Cargill's staff. The first incident occurred in 2006. To inhibit me from interviewing the employees in charge of training

Spanish-speaking and French-speaking recruited workers, the plant public relations staff left me a voicemail message threatening to file a complaint with the Institutional Review Board (IRB) at the University of Illinois.[17] The second incident was in 2012, in reaction to an article published in a local newspaper reporting on an interview with me about Cargill's labor recruitment practices in Beardstown (Rhodes 2012). In this incident, following a complaint to the newspaper by Cargill staff, the offending statements with which Cargill did not agree were removed from the text in the online publication of the newspaper.[18]

These incidents were sobering reminders of the sensitivity necessary in researching and writing about a vulnerable population that is dependent on a town's single employer. In Beardstown everyone and every institution has a relationship to that one multinational corporation. If you yourself do not work at the plant, you probably have a wife or a husband, a son or a daughter, a niece or a nephew who does. One way or the other, "all roads end at the plant." My research in Mexico and Togo, therefore, allowed me to gain perspectives that otherwise might have been difficult in the sensitive context of a company town. Against this backdrop, I have carefully considered the presentation of my material in this book. I chose to identify the town and the company, but took extra care to ensure that all my informants remain anonymous. All names are pseudonyms, and no specific information that can suggest the identity of any informant has been included, unless an individual asked me to include such information or provided me with authorization to do so. Moreover, none of the photographs taken in Beardstown include my research participants.

Since my field research did not take place inside the plant, I rely on the perceptions of workers or former workers as to the dynamics of labor at workplace. I was fortunate on one occasion in 2010 to visit the plant at the invitation of the University of Illinois Extension office, whose staff members were taking a group of local entrepreneurs through the plant for a "show and tell."[19] While my exposure to the plant was quite limited, the overwhelming and overpowering bodily experience of the plant—of the extreme temperatures of distinct sections, of the speed of work and movement, of the sounds and smells—helped me better understand my interviewees' comments about their experiences at work and on a production line in meatpacking, which is the most dangerous of all manufacturing jobs in the United States.[20]

CENTRAL INSIGHTS

This book is a story of diverse, dispossessed, and displaced people brought together in a former sundown town in rural Illinois for work at backbreaking jobs in the meat industry. It is a story of how this workforce is produced for the global labor market; of how workers' transnational lives help them to stay in these jobs; and of how these displaced workers renegotiate their relationships with each other across the lines of ethnicity, race, language, and nationality as they make a new home in Illinois. Beardstown is not an exception but an example of widespread conditions. By focusing on the type of locality that is at the heart of capitalism yet has been largely overlooked in urban scholarship on globalization, which is primarily concerned with metropolitan regions, Global Heartland theorizes global localities beyond "global" and "typical" cities and offers a fresh perspective on place and the politics of placemaking.

The title of the book, Global Heartland, suggests multiple meanings. As an urban scholar I challenge the metrocentrism in both the planning and the globalization literature predominantly focused on "global city" and other metropolitan areas as hotbeds of immigration and globalization. While not a formal region, the heartland has seen different moments of migration, industrialization, and struggle, and its history has stirred much of the country's social, religious, and racial activism.[21] Still understudied and underexposed, the localities of the heartland remain persistently identified with a stereotype of small-town backwardness, as places "left behind by globalization . . . simply withering away."[22] Focusing on localities marginalized by the dominant literature and misrepresented in dominant imaginations of the global spaces, I show the intensity of transnational relations that shape and are shaped by places in the heartland that have seemingly been "left behind" and seek to make a case for understanding these places in their own right. The title Global Heartland is also a play on the complexity of global-local relations. Here, insofar as "heartland" is a metaphor for local, the phrase "global heartland" seeks to engage with critical scholarship that renders "the global" and "the local" problematic categories. Anna Tsing (2005), Michael Burawoy et al. (2000), Zsuzsa Gille (2001), Gillian Hart (2006), and others have critiqued the construction of the global as far and the local as immediate, and of the global as active and the local as passive recipient of global processes. The study of global migration and local placemaking, anchored in the experience of a place in the U.S. heartland, furthers this rich scholarship that retheorizes global-local relations as mutually constituted. "The global" inseparably nestles in the social and economic fabric of "the local." The story of Beardstown as a global heartland, which deepens theorization of local-global entanglements, also reveals the permeability of place as an open entity and a site for the formation and collision of multi-scale processes.

Moreover, *Global Heartland* brings to light and calls attention to the materiality of place and its emergent politics of placemaking. Though place is porous and open and its making needs to be understood beyond its territorial bounds and meanings, place also has specific physical and sociohistorical characteristics, a certain materiality, as I argue in this book, that needs to be taken seriously. *Global Heartland* seeks to open up our imaginations and scholarly conversations to the politics of placemaking beyond those presented by the dominant literature. I engage in a range of tiny everyday actions and practices that take place not only locally but also transnationally and are critically influenced by the materiality of the place in which they occur.

An important goal of this volume is to uncover the global cost of immigration and the resulting processes of local development that we see in Beardstown. To frame the story of Beardstown as one of economic revitalization primarily focused on state agencies, municipalities, or corporate decisions for industry relocation and job creation, or to look at the story as one of immigration and of workers' choices to move for better jobs obscures why people move around the world as migrant workers, as well as the prices paid for local vitality to be achieved. In asking and answering questions about the interplay of the global and the local, we expose the violence involved in processes that produce a cheap labor force, and at the same time the individuality and agency of those displaced workers who, in making a home for themselves, transform their places of destination—what I call "in-placement"—as they cope with their own displacement. The processes and relationships that produce global labor mobility and sustain those workers in their places of destination are interconnected. In *Global Heartland* we learn about processes of dispossession and displacement that dislodge workers from their homes and drive them to labor markets around the world, including places like central Illinois; we also learn how workers cope with low wages in hazardous jobs by temporally and spatially reorganizing familial and community care—what I

call the "global restructuring of social reproduction." Just as the restructuring of production involves contracting out certain of its phases and aspects,
so too, in the realm of social reproduction, certain aspects and phases of care
are outsourced to families, friends, and governmental and nongovernmental
organizations in communities of origin. Stories told in *Global Heartland*,
however, make a critical intervention in understanding workers' social reproduction needs by moving beyond biological care, to include practices and
ideas that provide them with a sense of self and humanity—be it through the
performances of cultural obligations or the sheer imagination of an "elsewhere" where they can be rewarded with respect and dignity.

The stories we hear in this book about displaced labor, transnational lives,
and local placemaking also destabilize certain categories of belonging and
difference based on race, ethnicity, legal status, and citizenship. These are
problematic relational categories that change meaning depending on one's
vantage point. Legal citizenship alone is not adequate to explain the vast
differences in experiences of the white native-born residents, the African
Americans from Detroit, or the non-nationals from Mexico or Togo in the
transformation of Beardstown. Nor is race, constructed as visible skin color
differences, adequate to explain the different experiences of Detroiters
versus those of black African immigrants.

Rather than giving primacy to a "from below" over a "from above" perspective or to an ethnographic over a political economic analysis, I stress framing
relationally—moving between and across vantage points and analytic scales.
Weaving political, economic, and ethnographic insights is not easy. But I am
convinced that this constitutes the only way to braid together the threads
that make for the complex story of globalization in an industrial town in the
rural heartland—a global heartland.

BODIES OF SCHOLARSHIP IN CONVERSATION

Relational Methodologies and Global-Local Relations

This project advances relational methodologies by building on and contributing to several conversations about the study of global processes through
ethnography, including global ethnography (Burawoy et al. 2001), relational
comparison (Hart 2006), and multi-sited ethnography (Marcus 1995). Re-

jecting a mode of analysis that assumes the local to be a preexisting entity and a subject of study only for the purposes of accounting for variation or instances of a global process,[23] it uses ethnography of the local to reveal how the global "emanates from very specific agencies, institutions and organizations whose processes can be observed first-hand."[24] But to detect the friction in globalization, the points of its disconnection and disjuncture about which Anna Tsing (2005) and James Ferguson (2006) remind us, this project studies multiple sites ethnographically and examines relationships across these sites to expose the unequal processes involved in producing the celebrated "global village" in vogue today.

In seeking to understand globalization through Beardstown, I expand the physical sites of my ethnographic study beyond the town in Illinois to Togo and Mexico and highlight the towns position as a nodal point of connection in "wider networks of socially produced space," as Hart's methodology of relational comparison suggests (Hart 2006, 994). But unlike George Marcus's multi-sited ethnography (1995), mine does not follow and stay with the individuals or the movements of a particular group of initial subjects. I start with the relatives of Illinois immigrants in their communities of origin and move beyond the specific practices connecting these transnational families and networks of support to include the broader processes and power structures connecting Beardstown to other global locations. I focus on historical, political, economic, and cultural forces in the world at large and in immigrants' everyday practices, as well as on the imaginations that connect these forces and communities to each other. In effect, I practice multi-sited global ethnography through an interscalar analysis that moves across and between microworlds of specific practices and places and macroworlds of political economic processes and policies.

Industry Restructuring and Migration to New Destinations

An established body of literature shows a dramatic change in patterns of immigrant destinations in the 1990s—a marked shift away from traditional immigrant-receiving states and cities and toward new destinations in the United States.[25] These newer patterns reveal a greater diversity in destinations of new and secondary migrants, not only Mexicans, but also "other Latin Americans, Asian, and non-Asian, non-Latino groups" (Massey and

Capoferro 2008, 44). Immigrants now settle in small towns as well as in large cities, in the interior as well as on the coasts; there is evidence, in other words, of a movement of immigrant labor away from gateway cities on the East and West Coasts to medium-size and small communities in the Midwest and South. While the majority of immigrants still live and work in traditional immigrant-receiving states and cities, as Massey and Capoferro show, California and New York are much less dominant than they used to be in the decades prior to the 1990s. For example, California, Texas, and Illinois used to account for 90 percent of immigrant inflow, but between 1995 and 2000, they accounted for less than half (Massey and Capoferro 2008, 27).

To explain for this demographic shift, the literature has pointed to several factors. A significant one involves industrial restructuring and labor deskilling, particularly in the meatpacking and food industries' rural production strategies.[26] In recent decades, food processing industries have implemented a cost-cutting strategy of relocating urban plants to rural areas, thereby also moving away from the urban strongholds of unions and closer to raw materials. This strategy saves on transportation cost (in the case of Beardstown, from hog farms), and better integrates vertically the production of animals and their feed, the slaughtering of animals, and the processing and packing of meat, while taking advantage of economically distressed rural municipalities that offer tax abatements, along with lax labor and environmental regulations. Recent literature also links the growth of immigrant populations in rural areas and nontraditional destinations, for example in the Midwest and the South, to industry's technological shifts and ability to draw on low-skilled labor among immigrants for its low-pay, high-risk jobs.

Immigrant saturation of the labor market, job displacement, and lowering of wages in Los Angeles and other areas that have traditionally had high numbers of immigrants have also deflected immigrants to new destinations in the Midwest and South.[27] In addition, in view of increasingly stringent federal immigration policies and operations, immigrants, particularly those from Latin America, have moved to areas with less surveillance.[28] At the same time, the amnesty provisions of the 1986 Immigration Reform and Control Act that allowed many formerly undocumented farm workers to achieve legal status also gave them more flexibility in finding jobs in places that previously had few Latinos.[29] For migrant workers, the lower cost of living and the chances for year-round employment in rural areas may be another attraction; a safer environment for raising children and the possibility of a better life in general may be incentives, as well. Then, too, governmental and other resettlement agencies have assisted refugees in making their way to various U.S. destinations. For example, African refugees have been resettled in midwestern cities like Columbus and Minneapolis.[30]

The local dynamics that emerge when employers recruit a minority labor force to nontraditional destinations have been the subject of extensive sociological research in community studies[31] and a small but important research topic in planning.[32] This scholarship by and large agrees that immigration brings activity and business to small-town America and contributes to its revival,[33] but the research diverges on the social dynamics of the process. While some argue that white locals maintain social networks separate from newcomers or never interact with ethnic minorities outside institutions such as church and social work,[34] others see small steps being taken toward a new melting pot or at least interethnic understanding.[35] Regardless of emphasis, what these studies have in common is that they focus predominantly on the relationship between one or several immigrant groups and U.S.-born locals of European descent. They tend not to consider my focus in this book— interracial relations across immigrant groups and the transnational dimensions of their interactions in these new destinations.[36]

Global Heartland thus moves beyond a dual relationship between a single immigrant group and the native-born dominant group. Furthermore, in considering the different kinds of resources available to distinct immigrant groups, along with the constraints and obligations to which they are subject, it can address the question of agency in different immigrant communities.

Crisis of Social Reproduction

More than a century ago, Friedrich Engels (2010[1884]) described how capital transfers certain labor costs to the family, who must take care of the workers for free. Additional scholarship in this tradition has shown that in its urge to maximize profit while minimizing expense, capital underinvests not only in labor but also in collective goods such as roads, housing, health care, education, electricity, and water.[37] In response, the modern capitalist state has intervened through social policies and planning initiatives, which offer labor a safety net and lend capital a hand in covering costs of social reproduction for individuals, households, municipalities, and urban areas.[38] But with the neoliberal restructuring of the capitalist state, and the concomitant reductions in welfare and development programs, the costs of workers' care (collective at urban and neighborhood levels or individual at household levels) became a focal point of struggle.

Many scholars refer to this as a crisis of social reproduction.[39] To cope with this crisis, capital has sought to transfer the cost (and risk) of labor to families and communities, with women at their center, as well as to nonprofit or public-sector organizations, locally, nationally, and transnationally. In the global North, where the public sector had performed some welfare roles in the past, the neoliberal state has largely reprivatized and domesticated care.[40] In the global South, where the state had provided collective goods such as urban infrastructure, the responsibilities of civil organizations and of women have now expanded.[41] In essence, women's and barrio organizations, churches and faith-based groups took over social reproduction at the collective level, increasing their role in the provision of municipal services, infrastructure, and public goods[42] to make the social reproduction of low-income families possible.

Spatial restructuring as a means to ameliorating the contradiction between capital and social reproduction has also been the subject of research in various fields. Agricultural economists who looked at rural-urban connections offered some of the earlier insights.[43] Their work showed that an urban workforce with rural ties transferred some of their social reproduction costs to their networks of support in rural areas.[44] Hence, translocal rural-urban connections spanning across economic zones subsidized urban wages for capital.[45] In considering the spatial restructuring of social reproduction, feminist scholarship has paid attention to the roles of gender, race, and class in the processes and practices that transfer care work to women and to families elsewhere, translocally or transnationally. Feminist historians of the colonial period in Africa, for example,[46] reveal how enslaved women and wet nurses, deprived of their own offspring and families, cared for and raised the children of colonizers and slave masters.[47] Arlie Russell Hochschild (2000, 2012), Pierette Hondagneu-Sotelo (2001), Mary Romero (2002), and Rhacel Parreñas (2001) focus on the contemporary transnational dimension of hierarchically structured care work among women and show how neoliberalism repeats certain aspects of colonial relationships, including displacing caretakers from less affluent families and countries to more affluent families and countries. Whether they become nannies, agricultural workers, or industrial workers, migrants often are absent parents to their own families back home.[48]

In this transnational order, immigration offers new opportunities to governments and people in the global South—in Mexico and Togo, for example—for coping with their own crises of social reproduction. For governments, "exporting workers" and capturing remittances present a means to address problems of unemployment, foreign debt, and provision of collective consumption items such as roads, schools, clinics, sports fields, and infrastructure.[49] For people in the global South, immigration often constitutes an opportunity for effective social and cultural reproduction by reorganizing families and familial care.[50]

The studies of remittances in immigration scholarship, however, have paid more attention to the role immigration plays in social reproduction of immigrants in communities of origin than to its role in communities of destination.[51] We know that immigrants contribute socially and culturally to communities of origin through resources that Peggy Levitt (2001) calls "social remittances," which include ideas, behaviors, identities, and social capital. We also know that immigrants bring with them important social and cultural resources that make a difference in their political integration and economic viability in host communities.[52] But we do not know much about whether and to what extent communities of origin can be at the sending rather than the receiving end of this relationship. We know little about how immigrants' communities of origin might contribute to immigrants' individual or familial care in their destinations. The role of communities of origin in collective social reproduction in communities of destination—that is, in the construction of houses, schools, commercial centers, and so on—often remains obscure.

In *Global Heartland* I move the perspective beyond remittances to detect a range of invisible resources that communities of origin provide immigrant workers within their places of destination. I broaden the definition of social reproduction to include cultural promises and obligations, hopes and imaginations, as well as collective resources that go into immigrants' placemaking in communities of both origin and destination. Recovering the complex relationships between places of origin and destination, this investigation challenges the single story of economic or social remittances as serving to develop immigrants' communities of origin.

Placing Globalization

Decades of superb research on globalization has offered us important insights for anchoring the global movement of capital and labor to a specific place. This research has shifted the level of analysis from global to local and examined the making and working of globalization at the city scale.[53] Sassen's pioneering work on localities that serve as centers of command and control, also dubbed "global cities," has been particularly important. Her work demonstrated that capital cannot function in "spaces of flows," as Castells (1998) conceptualized. Instead, it requires face-to-face interactions facilitated in the global city. As insightful and important as global cities theorization has been for the "placing of globalization," the project of explaining the local social and spatial dynamics of globalization through the experience of large metropolitan areas has also created vast areas of dark, or blind, fields. Or, as Sassen (2011) reminds us, the more powerful the light shed on one point, the harder it is to see what lies outside the illuminated space. Global cities theorization, as critics stress, has created an analytic bias in both the scholarship and the practice of urban development that is harmful and even violent.[54] Upholding world cities as models for cities around the world and theorizing the manifold experiences of urban dwellers through the experience of global cities obscure the realities of the ordinary cities left behind.

In *Global Heartland* I shift the focus outside metropolitan areas to places that have been marginalized by both global cities theorists and their critics. Illuminating the spaces that are not at the center of the dominant literature of globalization, this study reveals the intricacies and complexities in what lies outside the large metropolitan centers that have traditionally received immigrants and been the hub of interracial social and spatial negotiations. How do the dynamics of immigration and immigrant experiences in a place like Beardstown vary from those theorized in global cities? What difference, in short, does place make?

Serious engagement with this question requires an analytic framework that extends beyond the metanarratives of the global as an abstract force that glides over localities smoothly and in uncontested ways. It requires an understanding of globalization processes that does not simply render "place powerless" and "power placeless"[55] and that rejects engagement with localities as passive sites for and recipients of the actions of global forces. In other words, this framework must be able to accommodate the fact that transnational practices are not abstractly located "in between" national territories; nor are they deterritorialized in the sense of being neither here nor there.[56] Rather, they take place within a certain context and locality. This social, historical, and geographical context imposes specific constraints and opportunities that must be examined closely.[57]

In *Locating Migration* (2011a), Nina Glick Schiller, Ayse Caglar, Neil Brenner, and others take on precisely such issues, asking if migration is anchored in places and locations, what difference do these localities make? The answers they arrive at stress the positioning of the localities that draw migrants within global hierarchies of economic, political, and cultural power.[58] The size and the population of the locale, along with its proximity to urban centers, are useful not so much as absolute measures, but as indications of vertical and horizontal connectivity of the given locality in relations of capitalism.[59] Building on this conceptualization, the location of migrants and migration involves "scalar positioning within emerging national, regional and global hierarchical configuration of power."[60] Yet this approach does not pay adequate attention to the materiality of a place—an argument I develop fully in chapter 8 and the conclusion of this volume.

There has been a growing call within planning scholarship to consider the local place as a base of placemaking and urbanism and to understand a community's everyday interactions in our increasingly multicultural world. Spearheaded by Sandercock's now classic *Cosmopolis I & II*[61] discussions of Latino urbanism,[62] as well as intercultural and translocal placemaking,[63] have made important headways toward thinking about the specifics and significance of a local place. Friedmann,[64] inspired by Jane Jacobs, calls it a return to the pedestrian scale to detect the intercultural dynamics that facilitate or frustrate local placemaking. Yet, the bulk of these studies and theorizations reflect on places within large cities and metropolitan areas.

By shedding light on the macroworlds and microworlds of a nonmetropolitan but intensely transnational space in an industrialized rural heartland, *Global Heartland* challenges the prevalent metrocentrism we find in both planning and globalization literature. It uncovers the material characteristics of a locality and the politics it may foster in dynamics of migration and placemaking in a particular context—dynamics that need to be understood in their own right and not as replica or absence of those in metropolitan areas.

ORGANIZATION OF THE BOOK

The story of Beardstown unfolds in four parts. In the first, I take the reader to Beardstown and introduce the local histories of race and labor that have shaped this blue-collar town. Against the backdrop of broader changes in the meat industry's labor composition and struggles, the opening chapters show how Beardstown was transformed from a sundown town to the demographically and ethnically diverse town it is today. Through a fine-grained reading of narratives of distinct groups in the labor force, community surveys, oral histories, and archival research, I highlight the importance of historicizing the local context and the multiplicity of immigrants' experiences.

In part 2, to illustrate the transnational and translocal connections in the story of Beardstown, I take the reader to Michoacán, Mexico, to Lomé, Togo, and to Detroit, Michigan, to hear from the families and friends of those who left for Beardstown. These chapters also weave together political economic and ethnographic material in such a way as to denaturalize global labor mobility and reveal the processes, policies, and conditions that produce the migrant labor force we encounter in places like Beardstown. I draw on interviews conducted with Togolese and Mexican immigrants as well as with African Americans recruited from Detroit to uncover how all these groups are displaced workers, subjects of policies that were designed and implemented to protect and expand the interest of capital across the world. Building on the notion of accumulation by dispossession and displacement, these chapters concern processes that a generic term such as "immigration" obscures.

Part 3, which draws on interviews conducted and relationships observed across the three research sites, unfolds the process I call "global restructuring of social reproduction" to explain what keeps workers in their low-wage, high-risk jobs at Cargill. Immigrant workers with transnational families and imaginations spatially restructure their lives and their families: they leave their children behind and get others to tend to their elderly family members; they sell their labor during their economically active age in one place, but return home for care when they are injured, tired, or not fast enough on the job to be employable. This part also considers how certain transnational practices and imaginations have the effect of subsidizing Cargill wages in such a way as to make them more viable for workers with transnational connections and families than for their native-born counterparts without such support.

Part 4 brings the focus back to Beardstown, Illinois, to stress the importance of the locality and specifics of place in forging dynamics of immigration and global labor mobility. What happens when a global multinational corporation recruits workers whose displacements are produced through distinct sociohistoric processes and then throws them together to work in a small industrial town in the rural Midwest—a town that had remained an all-white enclave through violent histories of race and labor? What are the emerging dynamics of such diverse groups and how are those dynamics negotiated and renegotiated as they try to make a new home in this heartland company town? Framed by the famous observation made by Max Frisch—"We wanted workers, we got people"—the chapters in this part explore how the company manages relationships among diverse people both inside the plant, at the production site, and outside the plant, in the "company's town," as well as how these relationships are renegotiated by the workers, their families, and other residents outside the plant in homes, schools, parks and playgrounds.

The concluding chapter highlights the conceptual and theoretical contributions of the book with respect to (1) the interconnected production and social reproduction of migrant labor; (2) the materiality of place and politics of in-placement; and (3) the unsettled categories of belonging through a perspective that stresses the relational production of difference by citizenship, immigration status, race, and ethnicity. By taking a seemingly isolated, small midwestern town as the locus of this study, *Global Heartland* offers a relational theorization of place and politics of placemaking, and overcomes certain analytic limitations on understanding of global labor mobility.

I hope the voices of people we hear in *Global Heartland* help us recognize the global cost and contingencies of revitalization of local places like Beardstown. Equally, I hope that this book will shine a spotlight on the people around the world who stand behind "local" revitalization plans.

PART I
BEARDSTOWN:
A PLACE IN THE WORLD

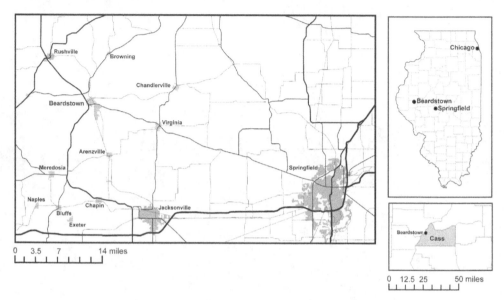

Figure 1.1: Map of Beardstown, Rushville, and Jacksonville, Illinois.

1 ~ WELCOME TO PORKOPOLIS

BEARDSTOWN IS LOCATED AT THE EDGE OF THE ILLINOIS RIVER, 250 miles southwest of Chicago and fifty miles west of Springfield (see figure 1.1). It became a major shipping port and blue-collar industrial town soon after it was founded in 1829. By the mid-nineteenth century, Beardstown was the largest center of meatpacking in the United States and gained its title of the "Porkopolis" (Schweer 1925, 10). From the late nineteenth century to the first half of the twentieth, Beardstown was the seat of several heavy industries, a place where men worked in well-paying union jobs with benefits and security. Today Beardstown locals take pride in being "the watermelon capital of the nation,"[1] the home of Beardstown Ladies Investment Club,[2] and the site of Lincoln's 1858 debate with Stephen Douglas as well as his Almanac Trial.[3] But before looking at Beardstown's history, I would like to take you on a brief tour to introduce the places and institutions that are important for establishing the local context.

When driving westward from Springfield (see figure 1.2), a narrow country road winding through corn fields in the bread basket of the country leads

Figure 1.2: Aerial photo of Beardstown and the Cargill plant located southeast of the town. Courtesy of the U.S. Geological Survey (USGS). Image captured on August 8, 2010, published by USGS.

you to Beardstown. From there, you can take three different routes into town. The first is the "back way," which passes the new middle and high school, built in 2005 at a cost of $22 million (see figure 1.3). Running along the railway tracks, the road takes you past the scars of the town's industrial past—the abandoned manufacturing plants of Allis-Chalmers, a sometime home of agricultural equipment production, Bohn's Aluminum, once a major manufacturer of air conditioning machinery, the Wells Lamont Glove Factory, and the Burlington Northern railroad shop. You will also encounter the boarded-up remains of a movie theater, a bowling alley, and a skating rink. In the 1980s, when corporations closed their factories in the rust belt and relocated to cheap labor sites, Beardstown, like other midwestern towns, lost many manufacturing jobs. The exception was its meatpacking plant, which temporarily stopped operation in 1987 when ownership shifted from Oscar Mayer to Cargill. This back way also passes the few points of interest

Figure 1.3: New middle and high school, Beardstown. Photo by the author.

in the town, including a longstanding newspaper company that, in addition to the weekly *Cass County Star-Gazette*, has been publishing the *La Estrella de Beardstown* in Spanish since 2001. Crossing the railroad and running into the town, the road then passes by *Su Casa*, a Mexican grocery store (see figure 1.4), *La Esperanza*, a taquería, and *La Fiesta Grande*, a Mexican restaurant that is often packed on weekends with locals and visitors from neighboring towns.

The second entry route passes by the newly built public Beardstown Houston Memorial Library, which offers services and books in French, Spanish, and English. After the library come the residential areas. The single detached house dominates the terrain. While there are two mobile-home-parks, one within and another just outside the town, they do not contain the majority of mobile homes nor, are they predominantly inhabited by immigrants or minorities. Indeed, mobile homes are located all over the town, often adjacent to houses (see figure 1.5). Unlike the boarded up manufacturing plants,

Figure 1.4: Mexican grocery store, Beardstown. Photo by the author.

the houses are mostly inhabited; some are fixed up and refurbished, thanks
to the immigrants who have been arriving in town since the early 1990s. In
contrast to neighborhoods in most big cities, neighborhoods here are not
segregated by class or ethnicity. While some blocks are somewhat upmarket,
the distinctions of social status are blurred. Class-wise, Beardstown is a homogenous company town. Most residents are connected to the meatpacking
plant. Although some might be supervisors or senior laborers, management
by and large lives outside Beardstown. Identifying the housing that newcomers inhabit is not hard: they usually have multiple cars parked outside
and Dish Network satellites. Apart from these two giveaways, the housing
stock or the neighborhoods themselves are not signifiers of ethnicity or immigration status. Many of the white, native-born residents live in the mobile
homes; many of the immigrants live in the fixed-up single detached houses.[4]
This contemporary residential development of Beardstown critically impacts
possibilities for interaction outside the workplace between whites and recent
immigrants as well as between Mexicans and Africans, as chapter 8 will

Figure 1.5: Mixed residential landscape: mobile home alongside Victorian homes.
Photo by the author.

discuss in detail. The calculation of residential segregation for Beardstown based on the most recent 2010 census data indicates that the rate continues to be low.[5]

The third way into town is indeed the main entry, the one that welcomes visitors with a sign that declares the town to be the "Site of Lincoln's Almanac Trial, 1858" and the "Home of Beardstown Ladies Investment Club." This entry road passes by the fifty-unit public housing project that used to accommodate only white Americans, but in the last few years has also been renting to a few West African families. Staying on this road, you will go by the Saint Alexis Catholic Church, a significant institution in the lives of Latino immigrants, especially for their transition to Beardstown. The outspoken priest of what had been a diminishing parish was the first to welcome Mexican immigrants to town and receive them with open arms in a weekly Spanish mass. Once hardly having enough parishioners to hold weekly masses in English, and seldom celebrating baptisms or weddings, the Catholic Church revived thanks to the arrival of new Hispanic immigrants.

Continuing along this road, or indeed any other route into Beardstown, you are bound to end up at Art Zeeck Park, in the heart of downtown, where Lincoln made his historic stump speech against slavery in 1858. Located just a block away from the banks of the Illinois River, the city center is thriving economically. On one side of the park is City Hall, the courthouse where Lincoln argued his famous Almanac Trial, and the museum. On the other sides of the park are the town's oldest barber shop, a newer Mexican bakery, a bank, a florist, a café, a newly-established Hispanic-oriented church, and a clothing store covered with Mexican flags, which sells attire for events such as baptisms, *quinceañeras* (birthday celebrations for fifteen-year-old girls), graduations, and weddings.

If you happen to arrive in Beardstown on a weekday after schools are dismissed, or when the plant's shifts change, you will be surprised by the diversity of the town's inhabitants (the latest census declared it to be more than 39 percent non-white, including 32 percent Hispanic). You might see a West African woman with her traditional head dress and clothing side by side with Latino/a parents picking up their kids from school or doing other errands in town. On weekends, garage sale signs and other temporary signage are in three languages: English, Spanish, and French. "Laundromats look more like the headquarters of the United Nations," one of my Beardstown friends joked.

Perhaps this diversity should not come as a total surprise. One could say Beardstown has always been an intensely global place connected to elsewhere from the time European immigrants settled there on Native American land. Indeed, the very formation of the town and the area's agricultural land has been a thoroughly transnational process. The surrounding areas were turned into agricultural land by Dutch immigrants, who brought their knowledge and skills to draining the marshlands.[6] Then came a variety of other European settlers—British, Scots, and Germans. People of color, however, arrived only in the 1990s, when the first immigrants from Mexico were brought in by the local meatpacking plant.

"IT SMELLS LIKE MONEY"

The trade roots of Beardstown rest with its port, which originated as a log cabin built by Thomas Beard to run a ferry service and trade with the local

Figure 1.6: African immigrant and child at park, Rushville. Photo by the author.

American Indians.[7] By 1834 the port was a major shipping hub for grain, hogs, and provisions to the interior of the state and to downriver markets.[8] Until the 1850s, much of the Midwest's meat was shipped down the Ohio and Mississippi Rivers to New Orleans and then distributed throughout the South,[9] and here Beardstown also figured prominently with its chief industry of hog-pens and slaughter houses. In 1833, writes Schweer (1925, 10), as many as seven firms were located in Beardstown. In fact, Beardstown possessed the most extensive pork trade of any city west of Cincinnati. With an average of fifty to sixty thousand hogs slaughtered every spring, an output bigger than that of Chicago, Beardstown earned its nickname of "Porkopolis" (ibid.).

Until the Civil War era, meatpacking was primarily located in midwestern towns that had access to waterways for transportation and to animal supplies, especially hogs. Then, however, the advent of mechanical refrigeration and growth of the nation's railroads resulted in the relocation of large-scale animal slaughter and centralizing packing operations in urban centers like Chicago.[10] For Beardstown, the arrival of the railroad in 1859 and the opening of the Union Stockyards in 1865, just south of Chicago proper, shifted the trade away from its small-scale slaughterhouses (Schweer 1929). Subsequently, Beardstown went into economic decline for several years. But by the late 1860s and early 1870s railroad facilities attracted many other industries, and soon it was said that "For the purposes of manufacturing, Beardstown is not surpassed by any town in Illinois" (Perrin 1882, 108). Indeed, for nearly fifty years the railroad itself was Beardstown's main industry,[11] and it was where engine and train crews from the Chicago, Burlington, and Quincy and the Baltimore and Ohio railroads changed. "Several hundred of roadmen and their families lived and owned their homes in Beardstown," wrote one observer. Over a thousand men, railroad shopmen, were employed in Beardstown, making the 1929 monthly payroll in Beardstown as high as $70,000.[12] The railroad and other industries in Beardstown offered well-paid jobs to its men.

The railroad connection with Chicago also played an important role in labor organizing among Beardstown workers, as well as in providing union-protected industrial jobs. There are several accounts of fierce union organizing among Beardstown's railroad workers during the 1888 "Great Strike on the 'Q'" (that is, the Chicago, Burlington, and Quincy, or CB&Q), the 1894 Pullman strike, and the 1922 railroad shopmen's strike, all of which had national repercussions and significance.[13] Of these, the 1922 strike was perhaps the most tumultuous. At the national level over 400,000 members of six craft unions walked off their jobs, shutting down construction, maintenance, and repair on virtually every major railroad in the country. July and August of that year saw almost daily reports of the bombing of railroad property and workers' homes, the burning of bridges, and the attempted wrecking of trains, as well as riots, assaults, and similar disturbances designed to intimidate strikebreakers (Flynn 1993). In Beardstown, things were no different. Divisions grew among the residents when Greek workers were brought in as strike breakers, and some families took in these "scabs."[14]

In one incident, the sheriff as well as a Greek worker were shot and killed (*New York Times* 1922).

Shortly after this, the railroad company moved its division offices and shops from Beardstown to other towns. Some industries, however, stayed, and new ones opened, continuing to provide well-paying industrial jobs. For example, two major industries that had opened in Beardstown in 1857, the Delta Tanks Manufacturing Company (a General Gas subsidiary) and the Baker Manufacturing Company (a Luria Engineering Company subsidiary), remained in business through much of the twentieth century.[15] Other important new firms and plants opened in the 1960s and operated in Beardstown for much of the twentieth century.[16] This includes Oscar Mayer, which in 1967 built a packing plant in Beardstown and hired more than eight hundred workers, almost all white men from the area.

The 1980s, however, mark a significant turn in the industrial history of Beardstown. This was when most industries in what soon became known as the rust belt began to close. By 1999, only Wells Lamont Glove and one or two other companies remained, apart from the packing plant. Today, Cargill Meat Solutions, known locally by the name Excel, stands virtually alone in town. A division of Cargill Incorporated, this plant is by far the largest employer in town. As noted in the introduction, each day, approximately 1,800 production workers slaughter, process, and pack 18,500 hogs into seven million eight-ounce servings of pork[17] for shipment nationally and to the company's top five global markets of Mexico, Japan, Canada, Russia, and Korea. When you are in Beardstown, you know you are in a packing town. Though the killing floor is located two miles to the southeast, winds carry the smell of the slaughter house through the streets and into the living rooms of this community. The stench of pig excrement and blood may be inescapable, but as one resident reminded me, this is "the smell of money."

RACIAL MAKE UP OF BEARDSTOWN
AND ITS SURROUNDINGS

The location of Beardstown has been important in the formation of its racial and labor histories. At the crossing of a railroad and the northernmost year-round navigable point of the Illinois River, Beardstown has a unique advantage as a site for manufacturing jobs. But being a river town has also brought Beardstown a number of social and environmental anxieties—the threat of repeated flooding (the town was inundated in 1922 and 1926) on the one hand, and the threat of strangers getting off the barges on the other. If the former menace was, to a certain extent, controlled by the construction of a floodwall and levees,[18] the latter has been a more complicated matter.

River towns have a reputation for being "rough and rowdy." For example, while older locals who have lived in the area describe nearby Rushville, an inland farming town, as a quiet town that "kept to itself," they referred to Beardstown as a place where strangers used to come off the barges, go to the local bars, drink, and be rowdy. And in fact, Beardstown always had a steady flow of outsiders—some arriving to have a good time, others intent on finding work, and some brought in by local companies as scabs to weaken labor organizing efforts. The racial makeup of the strangers complicated matters still further: "there were always black people associated with the barges going up and down the river," as one elderly resident noted. Some who ventured off the barges were chased out, while others were told not to leave the barges at all.

Rivals in school sports, Beardstown and Rushville have an intertwined past and present in respect to their economy and their changing social and racial composition. During the economic stresses of the 1980s, when much of the deindustrialization of the Midwest took place, both towns struggled to create employment opportunities for their local residents. By the late 1980s and the 1990s, there were three typical options: gambling, incarceration, or meat processing and packing. Rushville pursued the prison-industrial complex, choosing to house a high-security prison for people with sex offense convictions.[19] Beardstown wooed the Excel Corporation, a subsidiary of Cargill, with lucrative tax benefits to purchase and operate the then-shutdown Oscar Mayer meat-processing plant in town. Of the two industries—prison and meat—it was the latter that changed the racial composition of these two sundown towns.

Historically, both towns had managed through often violent practices to keep themselves almost all-white during most of the twentieth century: Beardstown did so up to the 1980s and Rushville until the turn of this

Figure 1.7: African grocery store, Rushville. Photo by the author.

century. The recalcitrance of Rushville rose to the fore in the mid-1990s, when one Mexican family bought a house in the town. The night before they moved in, the house was set on fire. The local newspapers did not report the motivation, but a few locals retrospectively referred to it as a racially motivated warning sign. Perhaps due to this incident, Rushville remained essentially an all-white town until a decade later, when Cargill recruited French-speaking West Africans to the Beardstown plant and housed them in Rushville.

U.S. Census data for 1890 to 2010, summarized in figures 1.8 and 1.9, confirms this account. The data reveal the overwhelming absence of any group other than whites—in particular the absence of blacks.

By 1990, however, the figures indicate the beginning of a significant demographic shift for Beardstown, which was by no means representative of the area, the county, or the state.[20] While the Hispanic population of Illinois increased from 7.91 percent in 1990 to 15.80 percent in 2010, in Beardstown

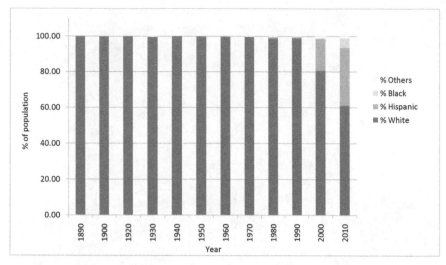

Figure 1.8: Race/ethnicity distribution in Beardstown, 1890–2010.
(See also appendix, table A1.)

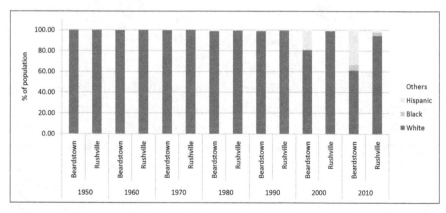

Figure 1.9: Race/ethnicity distribution for Beardstown and Rushville, 1950–2010.
(See also appendix, table A1.)

this group grew from 0.59 percent in 1990 to 32.57 percent in 2010.[21] The black
population also increased significantly during this time, from 0.02 percent in
1990 to more than 5 percent in 2010. The change in the percentage of whites
for Beardstown, from more than 99 percent in 1990 to about 61 percent in
2010 (see figure 1.10) was also astonishing. This was the racial make-up of the
town when I conducted my research.

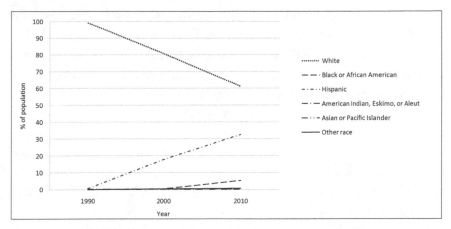

Figure 1.10: Race/ethnicity distribution in Beardstown, 1990–2010.
(See also appendix, table A3.)

"JESSIE OWENS, THERE AIN'T NO HOTEL IN TOWN FOR YOU"

The Star Café is one of Beardstown's most popular spots, frequently receiving the "Business of the Month" award from the chamber of commerce. Since it is conveniently located next door to the Super 8 Motel, where I stayed during my visits, I had been there several times for breakfast but never spoken to anyone other than the waitress, who would frequently refill my coffee cup. I often felt uncomfortable entering the restaurant, not for lack of friendliness by the servers, but because this is a hangout of the local old timers, the white folks so to speak, and I stood out with my darker Middle Eastern complexion and facial features. Despite the integrated residential neighborhoods, not all public commercial or recreational spaces are integrated. For example, while the Mexican restaurant has a mixed and diverse clientele, some of the other eating venues in town have stayed all white. At the Star Café, for example, except for my very last visit in 2012, when I saw one biracial young waitress, I never saw a staff member or a customer who did not appear to be a white native English speaker.

One morning at the Star Café, when I sat alone drinking my coffee and waiting for my order of sunny-side-up eggs, I worked up the courage to break into what seemed to be a closed circle of older locals. By then, I had been traveling to Beardstown for almost two years, and, with patience and persistence, I had gradually found my way into circles of Spanish-speaking Latinos first, and then French-speaking West Africans. I had also spoken to city officials, the chief of police, the Catholic priest, a realtor, teachers, and other local residents in their official capacities, but I had not yet been able to talk to ordinary white residents about the dramatic transformation around them.

I approached the counter where several men in their sixties and seventies sat alongside each other like birds perched on electric wires, and going to the one corner of the counter where no one was seated, I motioned to the waitress. I told her I was a researcher from the University of Illinois, and that I would like to talk with someone who had lived here for long time and could tell me about immigration and changes in the town. This seemed to me the best way to describe my research and to gain her attention. Her reaction made my heart sink. She turned to the row of men, saying, "She wants to talk to someone about Beardstown immigrants." All the men, their eyes shaded by the brims of their baseball caps, lifted their gaze toward her and then toward me, and they all chuckled. After a quick exchange, the waitress pointed at one man (I call him Rob in the interview transcript) and said, "This is your guy. You need to talk to him." Then they all broke into laughter and made some comments in the background that I could not comprehend. Rob, an older man in his sixties, wearing a checkered shirt, jeans, and a baseball cap, got up and walked toward me, coffee mug in hand. "Where do you want to talk?" he asked. I pointed at my table, which was at the far end of the café where I still had my coffee cup. There, I told him about my project. He did not want to be tape recorded, so I resorted to writing quickly.

Rob turned out to be very sociable. He spent over an hour with me sharing his stories about growing up in an all-white Beardstown and telling me a history I had never heard. Others had mentioned that their town used to be all white, but this statement was always presented as a matter of fact: blacks were not in Beardstown because "there was nothing for blacks to do here." Rob, however, offered a different picture, describing Beardstown as a "sundown town." James Loewen (2005), who coined the term, has identified more than a thousand such northern towns that were purposefully kept all-white and enforced segregation by a variety of means ranging from restrictive real estate covenants, stipulating who could and could not buy and rent, to signs warning non-whites to keep out, and acts of violence. Rob recalled that when he was a high school student in the late 1960s, Jessie Owens, the great

African American hero of pre–World War II Olympics who won four gold
medal for the United States against Germany, was brought in by a teacher
to speak at the high school's athletic banquet. "Even someone like the great
world champion Jessie Owens had to leave town at night. . . . It was a huge
deal but I recall after the event he had to go to Jacksonville to spend the night
there." In response to my astonishment, he said, "That's just the way it was.
They [must have] told him we need to take you to Jacksonville because there
ain't no hotel in town for you."

After I first spoke with Rob, many more stories of Beardstown as a sundown town emerged. Two specific incidents in the 1960s stand out. In one
case, a black marine got off one of the barges and went to see a movie at the
theater in town. In another, two black workers, who were hired to paint barns
in the area, went to Beardstown's tavern for a cold drink. In both cases, a mob
of white locals gathered in a matter of minutes. The marine was saved, thanks
to the theater owner, who appealed to the patriotic sentiments of the locals to
let the man in uniform finish his movie before telling him to get on the next
barge out of town. The two painters, however, did not fare so well. After a
mob of white locals rushed to the tavern to drag them out, they were chased
across the park and into the then Park Hotel. Police intervened, and as one
resident recalled, "the cop got inside the door and wouldn't let [anyone] in.
And the black boys went upstairs, crawled out on the porch, jumped off in
the alley, and got in their trucks and rode away." The men were never found,
and they never came back.

These incidents contributed to Beardstown's reputation as a white town
violently opposed to blacks' presence. Indeed, this was well-known within the
black community. For example, a current white resident of Beardstown recalled the experience of a black preacher who was stranded in the sundown
town of Rushville late one night in the 1940s. When he stepped off the bus
he was riding to another town, the driver drove away. The local I spoke with,
who was a young man at the time, working at the Rushville filling station,
recalled that "the poor old man was just terrified, he was really scared . . .
[and kept saying] what am I gonna do, what am I gonna do?" When he offered to drive the preacher to the "safety" of Macomb, a larger segregated city
thirty miles away, "[the preacher] couldn't believe that. . . . I mean, he just
expected . . . that I was gonna take a tire iron [and] hit him on the head. . . .
He was just terrified."

The reputation and fear of these sundown towns generated an effective means of self-exclusion among blacks. This, in turn, gave some locals a way to rationalize and obscure deliberately prejudiced practices: "That is just the way things were"; "There was nothing for blacks to do here"; "It was more a lack of opportunity for them than it was being racist," some older white residents expressed to me.

But what kept blacks out of Beardstown was more than its reputation. The Ku Klux Klan had a presence in nearby towns of Rushville, Havana, and Browning, as well as in Beardstown. In Rushville, for example, "they held [cross] burning parties annually at a farm with about 150 to 300 folk showing up.... One of the wizards from the KKK lived in Chandlerville ... on the way to Beardstown," one longtime resident of the county said. Lynchings were also known to be perpetrated in these towns. As one elderly local recalled, in the 1920s, "when I was little you didn't see any black people. We knew that blacks could not come here, and if they did, they disappeared. We heard all this. A friend of mine saw as a child a black being hung in a neighboring town. Her father took her to watch. Can you believe this! A little child taken to watch that!" Several other locals referred to "hanging of a black man from the bridge between Rushville and Beardstown."

Oral histories recorded in the 1970s to 1980s indicate that there were also signs posted in the area conveying that African Americans could not spend the night or reside in the community.[22] For example, Mr. Hubbard, a black man who worked in construction in Beardstown in the 1920s and 1930s, recalled he had to go back and forth to Jacksonville because he could not live in Beardstown, where there was a sign warning, "Read and run, Mr. Nigger" (Hubbard 1975, 6). A white elderly man born in 1891 and interviewed in 1973, for example, recalls that in the 1920s in small towns west of Springfield, including Beardstown, "there was signs stuck around different places, 'Don't let the sun set on you in this man's town'" (Wright 1973, 5). Also, Mrs. McNeil, born at the turn of the century, was told by her parents that not too long before her time, there were two black men lynched in a Beardstown park (McNeil 1987, 46).

Current elderly residents of Beardstown recall only a few people of color living in the area. They remember Beardstown and Rushville each having a black male cook who worked and lived at the local hotel but was noted to have seldom left the premises. They also recall two non-white children growing up in Beardstown: a biracial boy whose black father did not live with the family, perhaps divorced because of the impossibility of his staying in Beardstown, and a black girl adopted by a local white family.

The locals seldom had any contact with blacks or, for that matter, anyone not white and of European origin. On the rare occasions that such contact was made, it came through sports. A middle-aged local man vividly remembered one such moment in the late 1960s, when an East St. Louis team came to Beardstown to play the high school basketball team. "All players, cheer girls, cheer leaders, they were all black—coming to Beardstown, an all-white town!" For that game, "The gym was packed full. The whole town was there; not one seat was left empty." Most were just curious to see the blacks. What he remembers most vividly is the party after the game. "One of the high school teachers invited all players and cheer leaders on both sides to his house for a party before they left town on their bus. I was not a player but I went along. I recall how curious I was to see them close by. They put the music on and people started dancing. The most amazing experience for me was dancing with a black girl. I am not proud of how I used to think back then. I was not better than others. A lot of our prejudice was from not knowing any better."

Against such racist prejudice and hostility, many of the blacks who worked in local industries lived in segregated neighborhoods of larger cities such as Jacksonville, Macomb, or Springfield. This history is not too far gone. When you walk around Beardstown today, you still come across windows or balconies displaying the Confederate flag (see figure 1.11).

The racial prejudice of sundown towns was not limited to African Americans, although they were the targets of the harshest actions. Nor was this prejudice confined to a distant past. As recent as the late 1980s, a family who hosted a dark-skinned exchange student from Brazil was being pressurized and stigmatized by locals. The father explained, "That we had a Black girl come to live with us . . . was seen as outrageous by the strongly anti-adjustment people [those against the present demographic change in town]. And the fact that this was an exchange student [through the American Field Service program] and not going to be any permanent effect on the community, we thought should have answered . . . questions . . . and with most people it [did, but] there were a few die-hards who resented it and let us know." Following his remark, his wife joined in his nervous laughter.

Despite Beardstown's proximity to Chicago, which in the 1980s had the largest concentration of Mexicans in the United States after Los Angeles,

Figure 1.11: Confederate flag in Beardstown, 2010.
Photo by the author.

the only Latinos in the area was a family of fourteen, whom I call by the
pseudonym Sanchez.[23] The father in this family, a railroad worker from Michoacán and a devout Catholic, had escaped religious persecution and settled
his family in Beardstown in 1920. Strong believers in cultural and linguistic
assimilation, they never spoke Spanish at home. Even their mother, an intro-
verted homemaker, struggled but kept English as the home language. Today
her ninety-year-old daughter recalls her darker complexioned mother and
how seldom she wandered out of the house, even for groceries. But she tells a
story of how her mother nursed a child of a neighbor too ill to nurse the child
herself, and eventually she made some friendships and gained some acceptance. Reflecting on how much the town diversified during her lifetime, she

says "I just wish mother and dad were living, so they could enjoy it. Oh they would have loved this."

MIDWEST MEAT, LABOR, AND RACE

There is a large body of literature that documents the processes by which the meat- and food-related industries have racially and ethnically diversified homogenous rural towns of the Midwest. Industrial packing houses relocated from cities to rural areas starting in the 1960s, but only in the late 1980s did the industry begin to recruit among diverse groups of international immigrant workers. This shift resulted from a series of transformations in the industry and union struggles that shaped its labor relations and ethnic/racial compositions.

The racial and ethnic composition as well as the dynamics of the meatpacking industry have gone through dramatic and rapid transformations over the last century and a quarter. In the late 1800s and early 1900s, the period about which Upton Sinclair wrote in *The Jungle* (1906), meatpacking workers were predominantly European immigrants who settled in neighborhoods surrounding the stockyards (Barrett 2002). The tasks performed by 25,000 workers in the packing plants and allied industries that processed hundreds of thousands of animals in Chicago's Union Stockyards were associated with hierarchically structured ethnic groups. As historian James Barrett explains, "The more skilled butcher jobs were controlled by German, Irish and Bohemian workers, while common labor or low wage, low skill positions were filled by eastern Europeans, creating a distinct color and class structure to the industry and its later emerging labor dynamics" (2002, 46). This line of "ethnic succession" in Chicago meat packing was common in major packing houses in other midwestern cities, including Omaha, Milwaukee, East St. Louis, and Kansas City.[24] The Great Migration of the early twentieth century brought an influx of black workers to industries. Whereas they had been brought in as strikebreakers in the preceding decades,[25] between 1910 and 1920, blacks left strikebreaking behind and took up positions in the ordinary workforce. During that period their ranks in Chicago packing houses rose from 1,100 to 6,510. By 1922 one-third of Chicago's packing house workers were blacks (Barrett 2002, 48–49). Mexican workers entered the industry as well but made up a smaller portion of the workforce. In Chicago packing houses, for example, only 5.7 percent of the workforce was Mexican by 1928. This would change dramatically in the decades that followed (Williams and Ostendorf 2011, x).

Before this period, packing industry owners had used conflict among the white, black, and immigrant workforce as a strategy for labor control. However, the increased presence of black workers—especially in key sectors such as kill floors—meant that the success of workers' organizing depended on support from black workers, and the United Packinghouse Workers of America (UPWA), for one, was able to gain this backing (Horowitz 1997). The unity of white and black workers came about in the 1930s and 1940s through the UPWA's anti-discrimination activities, which addressed the grievances of women, men, blacks, and whites. The consolidated power and insurgent spirit of UPWA made the post–World War II period a heyday for meat cutters. From 1950 to the 1960s the wages in meatpacking work rose from 2.8 percent below the average hourly rate for all U.S. manufacturing jobs, to 15 percent above that average (Horowitz 1997, 276). While meatpacking jobs as a whole were among the best paid jobs in the manufacturing sector, wages began to decline in the late 1960s and 1970s, and by the 1980s, this job status was completely undermined.

The decline of wages, workers' rights, and unionism among meat packers reflected the convergence of several interrelated developments.[26] One involved the restructuring of the industry according to the economics of plant location, production methods, and meat distribution. In the 1960s, technological innovations further mechanized the meat industry, while refrigerated trucks and advanced networks of highway systems allowed for transport over greater distances. This, in turn, facilitated the moves of large-scale meat production and processing plants away from cities to rural areas and the integration of animal farms and feed into meatpacking companies. In addition, by standardizing the sizes of animals, as opposed to having farmers bringing in animals of irregular sizes, companies simplified production to involve more repetitive motions and tasks, thereby making it possible to speed up work and use fewer skilled workers.

One result of these developments was an increase in the rate of work-related injuries for workers.[27] Another was increased output and lower production costs.[28] By depending less on skilled workers, the industry was also able to move away from cities, the strongholds of organized labor, take advantage of cheaper land and labor in rural areas, and ruthlessly battle unions. The first company to succeed in these efforts and substantially bring down its production costs was Iowa Beef Producers (IBP). Subsequently, other corporations had to adopt IBP's strategies to stay in business. As a result, the dominant firms in the industry were reconfigured from the Big Four[29] to the Big Three: Tyson Foods (which bought IBP), Excel (a subsidiary of Cargill), and ConAgra.

As meatpacking plants moved to far-flung rural areas, unions and their negotiating power were devastated. The move brought in a new generation of rural workers who were predominantly white and unfamiliar with union traditions. With the technological transformations that had made the labor turnover rate less damaging to the industry, these workers tended to be unskilled and to receive lower benefits and wages. Roger Horowitz (1997) argues that as packing house workers became more white and more rural, their unions grew more conservative and distant from the militant traditions of UPWA. Meanwhile, as the UPWA had lost its base, the once-powerful and militant union agreed in 1968 to a merger with an old rival, the much less combative Amalgamated Meat Cutters and Butchers Workmen. Then, in 1979, Amalgamated merged with Retail Clerks International Union to form the United Food and Commercial Workers (UFCW), which currently includes meat packers. When the UFCW was formed, meat packers were a dwindling minority in a union of multiple and unrelated trades and thus had little power to organize and unite workers.[30]

Thus, by the early 1980s, the gains labor had made were eroding. Master agreements, which negotiated and fought for all members of the union, including meat packing industry workers as a whole, no longer governed wages and benefits in big companies. In 1983 alone, Horowitz notes, "twenty three unionized plants employing nine thousand workers closed. Cargill and ConAgra used the turmoil to acquire production facilities of other firms and ensure that the new consortium would be predominantly non-union" (1997, 268). By 1990, the unions at meat packing plants were a shadow of what they once were; following the concessions, meat packing wages were brought down by 20 percent below the average for manufacturing jobs (8.73 versus 10.84).[31] Indeed, in terms of real wages, adjusted for inflation, meat packing wages plummeted 30 percent from 1979 to 1990.[32] Thus, whereas meatpacking jobs provided enough income for a solid, middle-class life in the 1960s, by 1990, these jobs paid below average wages. In those thirty years, meatpacking jobs went from being among the best paid manufacturing jobs with the lowest turnover rate—even resorting to waiting lists—to becoming jobs with higher risks and higher turnover (Schlosser 2001).

These processes and forces changed the color of the industry yet again, this time incorporating Latin American, Asian, and African immigrants. Immigrant workers recruited for meatpacking work were brought into a decentralized and relocated industry, whose union organizations were left with no muscle or teeth to fight for the workers. The changing dynamics of race and labor in Beardstown's meatpacking plant, which I will turn to now, was also part of a much broader industry and union restructuring.

In the turbulent 1980s, the whole tone of labor management relations fundamentally changed; and Oscar Myer's Beardstown plant was not an exception. With wages and benefits in big companies no longer being governed by master agreements, and keeping in line with the overall setbacks and concessionary positions that meatpacking unions and Oscar Mayer workers had taken in Iowa, Madison, and Chicago, in the early 1980s the union at the Beardstown plant accepted major rollbacks, including a 23 percent cut in hourly pay from $10.69 to $8.25 and reduced healthcare benefits.[33] As indicated earlier, large companies had closed and hired non-union workers, and Oscar Mayer had also threatened plant closure. To avoid that scenario, workers agreed to these major concessions. But close to the date when this concessionary renegotiated UFCW contract was set to expire in October 1986, an Oscar Mayer vice president, Roger Kinson, who was also a plant manager, announced that the company would close its Beardstown operations.[34] This course of events infuriated many of the Oscar Mayer workers; they had accepted the deal, yet would end up unemployed.

The announcement of plant closure also created tremendous anxiety among workers and their families about employment and the future of the town. At the time of this announcement, the plant employed 620 people—359 Cass County residents and 261 Beardstown residents.[35] Beardstown's mayor announced that the municipality still owed $23,000 on bonds for the installation of sewer lines to the plant.[36] Clearly this was a huge blow to the city, and so the city, the state of Illinois, and the federal government officials responded, all offering their support to the people of Beardstown.[37] State officials put forward a wide array of social programs that would help stabilize the community should the plant leave,[38] and, following union negotiations with Oscar Mayer, the company at last agreed to extend the contracts with UFCW Local 431 for just a few months through April 12, 1987.[39]

In April of 1987, when Oscar Mayer closed down its Beardstown plant, residents had already witnessed the closure of Bohn's Aluminum and Trinity Steel as well as the relocation of Central Illinois Power's administration center to Quincy. All told, these changes cost Beardstown five hundred jobs.[40] With no hope of finding work, families began to leave. The newly elected mayor, Robert Walters, who had worked as a ham boner at Oscar Mayer for eighteen years and served as the representative for the UFCW, reflected the collective desperation of the time when, in a town council meeting, he declared, "I'd negotiate with the devil if I thought it would help."[41]

Shortly after this statement, the local media printed pictures of the smiling mayor signing a contract with the Excel Corporation to take over the plant. Excel was the second-largest meatpacking corporation in America, and a subsidiary of grain giant Cargill.[42] Many concessions were made to get Excel to come to Beardstown, and with downstate Illinois facing rising unemployment, Governor Jim Thompson signed special legislation "waiving the requirement that Excel's parent company, privately held grain giant Cargill Inc., open its financial records before being allowed to locate in a free enterprise zone at the outskirts of town."[43] Cargill received all the economic benefits Illinois had to offer, including a stipend of $215,000[44] to promote local labor force training and a twenty-year tax abatement on its capital improvement.

When Cargill took over the Oscar Mayer plant in 1987, the already weakened union was gone, and the company was able to exact more concessions from workers, including dropping wages that had already been reduced. The new wage schedule cut hourly pay by more than $2 to $6.50 an hour for those with meatpacking experience and $5.50 an hour for those without (Hebron 1987b). It also did not recognize some of the privileges that senior workers had accumulated over their time at Oscar Mayer. Dave, a white former Oscar Mayer worker in his sixties who quit his job at Cargill and moved to another city, explained that one such privilege for more experienced workers was the piece pound standard—a system that tracked workers' production output and paid them above their hourly wages when their output exceeded the plant standard for a set line of work. "Not all jobs had that opportunity," he explained. "But with my tenure, I was able to get one of the jobs that [had this] incentive." Without such incentives and other earned privileges, many senior workers looked for jobs elsewhere. "Some went to construction, some went to truck drivers, . . . just all different fields they chose to go to," one former Oscar Mayer worker stated. Also leaving the back-breaking jobs at the plant that were now paying even less than before, others took advantage of Illinois's Job Training Partnership Act and retrained at the local community college for new types of jobs. As another former OM worker explained, "For example, many of the local workers with seniority retrained as truck drivers. They still [were] working for Excel but not at its production floor." Truck driving, which had traditionally been predominantly white, paid better than floor workers' jobs with their reduced wages. As a result of retraining and absorbing senior workers as truck drivers, labor became more segmented. But in the main, other workers who could leave the plant and the town for better paid jobs with lower occupational risks did so. Consequently, the population of Beardstown went from 6,338 in 1980 to 5,270 in 1990—a shrinkage common to many other deindustrializing towns and cities (see figures 1.12 and 1.13; see appendix, tables A1 and A2, for corresponding data).

Having shed its high-earning senior workers, Cargill gradually built up its operation by training a new labor force from Beardstown and the surrounding communities. But when the corporation initiated a second shift at the plant in 1995, the local pool of laborers was inadequate—inadequate, that is, for the low wages Cargill was offering. This problem soon created a high labor turnover that dogged the plant and made recruitment, training, and retention practices no longer viable. Indeed, by the mid-1990s the plant's labor turnover had reached close to 100 percent.[45] This high turnover rate, combined with the shrinking population of the town and the expansion of production from one to two shifts in 1995 required the corporation to look elsewhere to meet its need for labor that would accept low wages and high risks. Thus, Cargill turned to groups who had less job mobility—first Mexican immigrants and later others. This move drastically shifted the ethnic and racial composition of the plant from what used to be an almost all-white workforce to one that was increasingly diverse. By 2013 the county level data that points to the ethnic composition of workers at the Beardstown plant indicated a labor force that was composed of more than 40 percent people

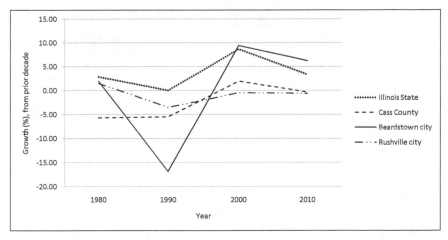

Figure 1.12: Population growth rates (percent change from prior decade) 1980–2010.

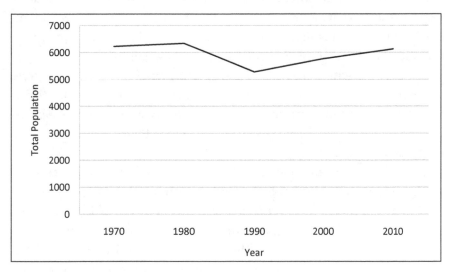

Figure 1.13: Population trend in Beardstown 1970–2010.

of color, that is 25.6 percent Latino or Hispanic, 10.4 percent black or African American, and 2.7 percent Asian.[46]

What took place in the Beardstown plant was not unique. Indeed, its transformation reflects the broader trend wherein meatpacking was no longer a relatively well-paid job for white working-class Americans but a low-wage sector with a greater concentration of immigrants and minorities. In 2006,

Table 1.1. Employed persons by industry, sex, race, and ethnicity, United States, 2014

	Total employed (in thousands)	Percent of total employed			
		Women	Black or African American	Asian	Hispanic or Latino
Manufacturing	15,100	29.3	9.7	6.6	15.8
Animal slaughter and processing	503	34.7	19.6	7.8	35

Source: U.S. Department of Labor, Bureau of Labor Statistics, Labor Force Statistics, table 18 (http://www.bls.gov/cps/cpsaat18.htm; accessed June 2015).

according to the U.S. Bureau of Labor Statistics, the average meat industry wage was 30 percent lower than that of other manufacturing jobs ($11.47 versus $16.77 an hour for all U.S. manufacturing jobs). Figures from 2014 demonstrate that this gap still persists. Mean hourly wages for those working in all occupations within the Animal Slaughtering and Processing sector were 39 percent lower than those working in all occupations in the manufacturing sector. Similarly, those working in production jobs within Animal Slaughtering and Processing were paid 26 percent lower than their counterparts in the manufacturing sector.[47]

The 2014 U.S. Bureau of Labor Statistics figures also reveal the meat slaughtering and packing industry's heavy reliance on minorities (62.4 percent), including 35 percent Hispanic or Latino, 19.6 percent black or African American, and 7.8 percent Asian. This is almost double the total percentage of minorities employed in the manufacturing sector (32 percent overall), including 15.8 percent Hispanic or Latino, 9.7 percent black or African American, and 6.6 percent Asian (see Table 1.1).

Reflecting on this history helps us see the fallacy in the arguments often presented by national media and opponents of immigration that "immigrants took our jobs and pushed our wages down." The change in the racial composition of the meatpacking labor force in rural plants occurred subsequent to the restructuring of the industry. The recruitment of low-skilled immigrant and minority workers into the industry was not the cause but the outcome of the weakening that had taken place in the position of labor vis-à-vis capital in the industry at large. It was the lowering of wages and the increasing harshness of labor conditions that turned the industry to minority and ethnic labor rather than the other way around. This is an important distinction that should bring a more realistic and accurate perspective on the everyday mythology of small midwestern towns and popular media in the contemporary United States.

Figure 2.1: Beardstown street scene on Mexican Independence Day. Photo by Ryan Griffis and Sarah Ross.

2 ~ IT ALL CHANGED OVERNIGHT

A long-standing joke among Beardstown residents is that when Cargill bought the plant from Oscar Mayer in 1987 and reopened, they placed a sign at the Mexican border that read "this way to jobs" and gave directions to Beardstown.

While there was no sign posted at the border, the company did engage in extensive recruitment in Mexico (Walker 2003a). In 1993, Cargill started to offer an economic incentive in the form of a bonus to the few Latino workers who were hired at the plant—a program that continued until about 2008. In 1995, when the plant established its second work shift, the management sent a Cargill nurse, a human resources representative, and a driver of the company van out to targeted locations to find Latino laborers. While the company nurse examined the potential recruits for their health and strength (in particular their wrists and back), the HR person processed the logistics. Lynne Walker's award-winning, three-part series of articles published in the

State Journal-Register documented the process. In one article, she recounted how Cargill sent nurse Lisa Mincy to the Texas-Mexico border "at least 10 times during the eight years she worked at the plant." Mincy administered drug tests and did physicals on "35 job seekers a day during the two-to four-day trips" (Walker 2003a, 7). In addition to mobile recruiting in California, Arizona, and the Texas border towns of Laredo, Eagle Pass, Brownsville, and El Paso, Cargill also placed spots on Spanish-language radio (ibid.).

After the first wave of Mexican workers arrived in Beardstown in the early to mid-1990s, word of mouth became the most effective means of recruiting labor for the plant. With each worker telling relatives, compadres, friends, and neighbors about possibilities for work, Beardstown saw a rapid surge in its Mexican population—what many older residents referred to as an almost overnight demographic shift. One interviewee indicated that in the period of five years from 1993 to 1998, she and her husband brought in about fifty family members to town. Some left more expensive U.S. states for the year-round job security in less costly Beardstown; others relied on the money their Beardstown contact loaned them to cross the border.

This influx of immigrants to Beardstown, which had been losing its white residents, is not unique to this town. Indeed, scholars have documented that immigrants in general, and Mexican immigrants in particular, are increasingly moving to destinations other than traditional gateway states and cities and have identified it as a trend.[1] For example, between 2000 and 2006, the total population in small towns and rural areas increased by only 3 percent, while the Hispanic population grew by 22 percent. Since 1990, the Hispanic population in small towns and rural areas has more than doubled.[2] Several factors account for this, including the border tightening policies of the 1990s that made illegal crossing more risky. Contrary to common assumptions, Massey and colleagues (2002) argue, the border-tightening policies of the last two decades have not halted or substantially reduced the Mexican migratory flow. It is rather the worsening of the U.S. economy in its recent recession that has contributed to a lowered rate of border traffic among undocumented Mexican immigrants. When migrating to the United States with their families with the intention to settle, most immigrants initially prioritize issues like the cost of living and finding a safe environments in which to raise children. They also have a preference for year-round jobs, rather than ones that require periodic relocation. Metropolitan areas, with their higher cost of living and reputation for crime, such as gang activity, are thus not attractive. On the other hand, nontraditional destinations, which have lower concentrations of immigrants, might pose less of a risk of immigrant surveillance.[3]

The Mexicans I interviewed who were among the first wave of recruited labor described their experiences arriving in Beardstown in the early 1990s as traumatic. Not only were they the first group of so called non-whites to enter this former sundown town en masse, but they were also resented and scapegoated for accepting the low wages Cargill paid. One interviewee recalled the bad treatment she used to get at the store. She did not know any English so she could not figure out what was being said around her, until one day, the person who had been behind her at the cash register followed her outside to apologize for the ugly comments the cashier and the others in line had made about her. "I could feel they are saying mean things, but what did I know. . . . I always tried to ignore people . . . just get my stuff and get out." Moreover, the Mexican workers arrived in this potentially hostile environment without the preexisting immigrant support system that those who went to traditional immigrant destinations had. There were no Spanish signs, no interpreters, no bilingual brochures to address their social or commercial needs; no grocer carried their preferred foods. Moreover, no school staff at the time could converse with them about their child's academic placement. If a trip to the clinic became a necessity, there was no Spanish interpreter to help explain the illness or treatment. Even worse, if they were stopped by a local policeman, quite a common occurrence for Mexican workers, language became an instant barrier to resolving the situation.[4]

One of the few bilingual places was the plant, where the Spanish-speaking trainer would show new recruits "the tricks of the trade." The Spanish-speaking trainer also assisted the newcomers in finding rental accommodations. Many of the early arrivals recalled their first housing as the worst of their experiences in Beardstown. They described a town virtually closed to outsiders. Many people who had left in search of jobs elsewhere had boarded up their houses, with no plans to use them for rental purposes. Some residents seized the opportunity posed by the immigrants and set up mobile homes in their yards, but even that was not adequate to accommodate the daily arrival of new families.

Jose, for example, one of the first Mexican workers at the plant, explained that he had to sleep in his car for two weeks while waiting for his first paycheck.

When he did find a place, it was a previously boarded up house that the owner had opened up for rent but had done no upkeep. His wife later confirmed, "It was awful . . . having been vacant for several years, the place was infested by cockroaches and bugs."

"Shortage of housing was severe," the Catholic priest who used to be a point of contact for the new arrivals revealed. "If you found a rental, a lot of people would end up on top of each other there, both for shortage of housing and for saving cost." "Sometimes up to seventeen people [lived] in the same house," the former chief of police recalled. Once one parent had a job at the plant and was settled with a place to live, the other parent and children arrived. This had an immediate impact on schools. The arrival of children who spoke no English and the presence of teachers who spoke no Spanish in a town with such an extreme history of racism and racist practices caused enormous stress for parents. It was "a recipe for disaster," one teacher said.

The profile of students did indeed change dramatically in a short period of time. The number of Culturally and Linguistically Diverse students (CLD) from prekindergarten to grade twelve climbed from 1 in 1993 to 5 in 1994, 85 in 1997, and 290 in 2000. By 2006, of the 1,367 number of students enrolled in school district, 552, or 40 percent, were CLD students. For kindergartners this percentage was as high as 45 percent (see Cottle, Galvez, Starkey, and Úbeda 2007).

A retired nurse who has lived all her life in Beardstown described her "shock and awe" over the speed of change in Beardstown. "I truly mean this, working in a doctor's office, you would see maybe a few [Mexican immigrants], and then you went to bed one night and the next day they were everywhere. I think it was more kind of a shock thing because they came so quickly, in such masses. . . . That's how it seems anyway."

BURNING CROSSES

It should come as no surprise that the rapid transformation of the racial and ethnic composition of Beardstown fueled serious tensions that were often shaped by the histories of race and labor in the area. These tensions arose starkly where jobs were concerned. By allegedly weakening the negotiation power of labor with the company, immigrant workers became targets of white supremacists' hostility, which they justified in the name of unfair competition for "American jobs."

In October 1995, Imperial Wizard Ed Novak and the Klan held a rally in white and black robes. They burned a thirty-foot-tall cross atop a hill about forty-five miles north of Beardstown, just off Illinois Route 136, between the hamlets of Duncans Mills and Ipava in Fulton County. This rally, which drew about two hundred people, was called by the Chicago-based Original Federation of Klans, purportedly to protest the hiring of "illegal aliens" at the Cargill plant in Beardstown. The flyer they distributed—frequently accompanied by a copy of the white supremacist newspaper, *The Truth at Last*—stated, "The only reason that you are white today is because your ancestors believed in and practiced segregation yesterday." In a platform statement, the political positions of the Klan were outlined. Among them were: "protect America's birthright," "protect American jobs," and "close our border." While the Klan was convening on the rural hillside, an anti-Klan rally was being held at the local high school, drawing approximately an equal number of participants. A Methodist minister, Terry L. Clark, from Galesburg stood at the entrance passing out a flyer proclaiming that his church finds it "particularly repugnant that a hate organization built on white supremacy and use of public or subtle violence cloaks itself as a 'patriotic Christian movement.' "[5]

Racial tensions in Beardstown reached a boiling point in August of 1996 with an altercation in which Mexican immigrant Jorge Arambula, who worked at Cargill, shot a white man, Travis Brewer, at the El Flamingo bar. The assailant fled immediately, ending up in his hometown of Monterrey, Mexico, after the incident.[6] The night after the killing, angry whites burned a six-foot-tall makeshift cross in the plaza. The following week, the Mexican tavern where the shooting occurred was torched. The KKK also marched through the town. Some Mexicans who remember the incident mention the overpowering fear it instilled in them. For example, one Mexican now in his late twenties remembering the incident as a child says: "My brothers didn't want me to leave the house. . . . [They] were telling me I couldn't go out, walk home or anything because they were worried that somebody would hurt us. Just the environment of fear. . . . Some people even saw them with their masks, and clothes, and they went around and painted crosses, red crosses where the Mexicans lived. . . . That was kind of a threat or show off that these are the

Figure 2.2: KKK rally against hiring of illegal aliens at Beardstown's packing plant. Norm Winick, "A Gathering of the Klan: A Report of a Ku Klux Klan Rally held Saturday, October 14, 1995 in Fulton County, Illinois," *Zephyr*, Galesburg, Illinois.

houses we are marking that we know you live here, . . . and we are going to burn them down. That's what we thought they were going to do."

This 1996 incident marked a significant turning point in the racial history of Beardstown. The shooting and subsequent events profoundly disturbed the local white community, which was struggling with many different aspects of their changing town. Economically, socially, and racially, there was much to deal with in the context of the rapid transformation over a short span of five or six years. Problems with respect to transition, translation, housing, schooling, and social integration were all acute. For some, the incident solidified their resentment of the immigrants, while others were galvanized to help ease the immigrants' transition. Mark Grey and Anne Woodrick (2005) observed a similar phenomenon in Iowa's rapidly diversifying packing towns and suggest that it followed a "20-60-20 rule" (140), whereby established, native-born, white residents' attitudes toward immigration can generally be divided into 20 percent for, 20 percent against, and 60 percent indifferent. In

the aftermath of the 1996 violence in Beardstown, the fence-sitting 60 percent of the residents rapidly mobilized. It was clear that something needed
to be done. The local whites had to decide either to contribute to a peaceful
transition, or attempt to drag Beardstown back to the sundown era.

A few of the local residents who did not want to see a return to the old
days took a stand and joined immigrants in support of their community's
peaceful transformation. They reached out to a charismatic bilingual advocate of immigrants and civil rights in Springfield, asking him to serve as an
outside facilitator for a community forum they called Beardstown United.
He recalled that when they approached him, his other Latino friends warned
him "it is dangerous to go to these towns, stay away!" Like the other Mexican residents of Beardstown, he was fearful of being in a sundown town at
such an intense and potentially explosive moment. "There were people riding
around town pointing their finger at the Mexicans saying you know, 'You
are next' [making gun gestures with his fingers]. . . . This was pretty big." He
gained courage to go, however, when some of his other friends from another
town agreed to meet him in Beardstown. "I got there and there were about
fifty Mexicans in the room, and the mayor was there, the chief of police
was there, and some of the members of clergy were there, and some of the
concerned citizens. . . . There were still people outside in the hallway as they
couldn't fit in the room." Because the school year would soon begin, people
were worried about the safety of their children. "So the clergy or people there
associated with the clergy volunteered to walk the kids to school, which was
good . . . That was the origins of Beardstown United. And they decided to
start meeting."

The outcome of this forum was not a permanent organization of any sort,
but it did highlight the need for institutional intervention. The Catholic
Church flew three nuns into town from Mexico to help handle the social
problems of the newly arriving Mexican families; the Protestant Church
of the Nazarene hired a bilingual pastor who also served as a translator for
the Spanish-speaking newcomers; a realtor signed up for intensive Spanish
classes in Springfield; and the school district hired a dedicated El Salvadoran
community-school liaison to manage the ever-growing tensions in the relationships between the school and new families.

When the nuns arrived in November of 1999, they were overwhelmed, they
declared, by the rapid increase in Spanish-speaking families and the extent of

the problems of social isolation, cultural alienation, depression, and in some cases poverty. Many of these issues were compounded by a relative absence of social services or any preexisting support networks. Thus, they somehow found ways to function as the food bank and as social psychologists and spiritual guides to give strength to families socially displaced to this town. The church also ran the nonprofit St. Francis Clinic for health care and began offering Spanish-language masses in an effort to revive religious faith as a means of strengthening the displaced families. The bilingual pastor recalled that he frequently accompanied people to medical appointments or on visits to the personnel office at the plant to translate conversations and documents. The Spanish-speaking realtor ran informational seminars in Spanish at the plant on Saturdays, teaching immigrant workers how to apply for a mortgage and buy and fix houses. The role of the school-community liaison, though, was key in many respects because the school was one of the first places that native-born local families most intensely experienced the change. Their children brought with them to the school yard many racist sentiments expressed by their families at home. To ameliorate the initial "shock" of Mexicans' arrival in this former all-white town and prevent the recurrence of a violent incident like the one they were trying to recover from, a range of organizations and individuals had much work to do among both white locals and Latino/Latina immigrants.

DON'T ROCK THE BOAT: RECRUITMENT OF WEST AFRICANS

In the early 2000s, the Cargill plant turned to West African workers, who were legal, educated, and surprisingly willing to take meatpacking jobs. The first few African immigrant workers at the plant came from Senegal and Guinea. They had worked for another meatpacking plant in nearby Moline, Illinois. Since they were familiar with the kind of work involved, Excel readily snapped them up. These workers spread the word about jobs at the Beardstown plant within their network of African friends and relatives. Having lived in the United States for some years and able to switch between English and French languages, one of the early recruits was soon promoted to serve as a human resource representative and trainer for the new French-speaking workers. Moreover, to encourage the existing workforce to recruit new workers within their personal networks, the plant offered an incentive bonus to employees for each successful recruit who stayed at the plant beyond the probationary first three months. The amount of the incentive bonuses varied, depending on the production pressures at the plant and the potential (most importantly legality) of a recruit.

This process brought in African workers from a range of countries: Senegal, Burkina Faso, Congo, Guinea, Togo, and Benin. Regardless of their place of origin, the new French-speaking workers were typically housed in Rushville upon recruitment. Considering the violence against Mexican immigrants that had recently erupted in Beardstown, Cargill management had some concerns about bringing in yet another new group, especially a black one, to the town, according to one interviewee closely linked with plant management and its recruitments at the time. Hence, the new African recruits were given lists of available rental properties in Rushville. Beardstown had a saturated rental housing stock in addition to fresh wounds to heal. Moreover, in the absence of knowledge of racist practices in the area, the African immigrants were willing to move wherever there were units for rent.

Immigrant advocates, predominantly connected with local churches, immediately sought to help facilitate the Africans' settling into Rushville. "We were so scared of poor treatment of black folks in their neighborhoods that we turned extra attentive making sure African immigrants have an easy reception and experience," recounted an ESL teacher and church volunteer. Sometimes helping West Africans transition to Rushville became burdensome, she revealed, recalling how one of the first West Africans complained about not being able to take a rest after having moved in: "he could not take a nap because people kept knocking at his door and bringing him cookies and cake to welcome him to the neighborhood." Marie, a Congolese worker and one of the first I got to know in the region, explained to me how in her case the church members "took her under their wing." She was at the time a single mother and had just moved to Rushville to share a house with a Togolese friend. One Sunday morning she walked through the community looking for a church to attend because, she confided, "I can't live without God and church." When she attended a service, she explained, she was the only black person there, so everyone noticed her and paid special attention to her. "The pastor was particularly nice and welcoming," she noted. After that day, according to Marie, everyone in town who had been at that church knew her. For example, she recalls going to the bank where a teller said, "Oh I know you" and made a note of Marie speaking French. The next time she went to the service she found a French copy of the program for her. "Not sure how they got translation, perhaps [by] computer," she shared with me as she made a facial gesture of pleasant surprise. The church Marie went to that day also helped her find a house for herself and her children, paid the down payment, and then helped to fix it up—an incredible act of kindness in her words. "This house wasn't good at all. It was rundown, but all church, all members, were working here and fixed it nicely so we could move in. . . . What they did was so unbelievable for me." By 2009, in collaboration with the pastor of Marie's church (First Methodist), a Francophone priest arrived in Rushville to hold Bible study groups in French and further assist with the transitioning of the newcomers. In the meantime the African immigrants continued holding informal monthly meetings they had initiated in Rushville since 2003 to support each other, particularly the newcomers. They were further assisted by the Illinois Coalition for Community Services, a Springfield-based nonprofit group that in 2008 hired one of Rushville's French-speaking immigrants as an AmeriCorps volunteer for one year to facilitate the community-transitioning process in the area.

The Rushville church volunteers, ESL teachers, the pastor, and other immigrant advocates were all important to the relatively peaceful settling of Africans in Rushville. The vocal and pro-immigration mayor of Rushville at the time, Scott Thompson, was also crucial in encouraging immigrants' accommodation in Rushville. Unlike the mayor of Beardstown, who would openly wish the immigrants away and the "good old days" back, Thompson in a public forum thanked the West African immigrants for choosing Rushville as their new home. In his moving welcome speech at this forum, he said the immigrants "have given the single most important opportunity to this community—one that I did not have when growing up. . . . I have seen what racial divisions do to communities. This is a wonderful opportunity you have given [to Rushville]!" (personal notes from the Rushville Public Forum, April 26, 2008). In short, established residents of former sundown towns like Beardstown and Rushville recalled the racial exclusivity of their not-so-long-ago-past with both nostalgia *and* fear. Many were determined to avoid repeating that history.

Once the first group of Africans settled in Rushville, other African workers also looked for housing in that town. It is a customary practice that, during their initial transitioning period in a place of destination, newcomers stay with others from their country (be they friends or family, or simply an acquaintance introduced through a common contact). This "cushioning practice" often leads to newcomers settling close to the places where they were first received by their host families and thus accounts for the clusters immigrants and their networks form in their communities of destination.[7]

This practice surfaced in the early years of African immigrants' recruitment to the plant and shaped a new racialized residential geography among the labor force. West Africans workers and their families concentrated in Rushville; Mexicans and other Spanish-speaking immigrants concentrated in Beardstown. But to complete the story, we need to look at African American workers at Cargill. This cohort often had a collective memory of the racism in sundown towns and consequently had continued to live in larger nearby towns such as Jacksonville (thirty miles away) or Springfield (forty-five miles away), which had racially segregated neighborhoods.

But as with many other segregated spaces, this geography was not stable. With the spike in gas prices in the late 2000s, many of Rushville's West Africans moved to Beardstown to be closer to work. This created a West African immigrant community that spanned across the two towns. Moreover, some newly recruited workers—Puerto Ricans, Cubans, and African Americans from Detroit—also started residing in Beardstown, a process that made Beardstown yet more racially and ethnically diverse.

BUSTED BY ICE: HERE COME THE PUERTO RICANS, CUBANS, AND DETROITERS

In the early hours of Wednesday April 4, 2007, Beardstown residents were awakened by a flurry of frantic phone calls—from plant managers to supervisors, from supervisors to workers, from the school superintendent to principals, teachers, and bilingual teaching aids, from immigrants to friends, families, and neighbors—to make known that around 1:30 a.m., the night shift at Cargill was raided by Immigration and Customs Enforcement (ICE) agents. These agents rounded up the cleaning crew at the plant, who worked overnight before the first shift started at 5:55 a.m.[8] and were busy washing the blood, fat, and leftover meat in the machines and on the floors of the plant with boiling water. These workers were employees of an industrial cleaning company, Quality Service Integrity (QSI), a member of the Tennessee-based

Vincit Group, which was under contract to clean the plant. Glenn Karlinsey, general manager of Cargill Pork Beardstown, stated, "No Cargill employees were involved in the ICE action." He declared Cargill had nothing to do with who their contractors hired, but they "take seriously the legal obligation to employ only individuals who are legally authorized to work in the United States . . . [and had] discussed with a number of [Cargill's]contractors including QSI the need to be diligent in hiring practices"(Sander 2007).

ICE arrested sixty-two people, among them fifty-four from Mexico and the rest from Guatemala and El Salvador.[9] The cleaning crew who were left behind informed the arrested workers' closest kin that their family members would not return home in the morning. Cargill reshuffled shifts to keep production going, delaying the first shift by only three hours. Some of the morning shift workers were asked to be at the plant by 4 a.m. to help finish the cleaning. Afternoon shift workers were requested to stay overtime and do the same until they could resolve the issue with the night shift cleaning.

School districts usually get the "heads up" about such raids, in order to cope with the aftermath. Children of arrested parents may not come to school the next morning; others might show up at school, but disturbed and needing consolation or reassurance. In the scramble to deal with the effects of the ICE raid, Beardstown churches, social services, and schools all came together.

This was a difficult day. Responding to an email request for support from a Beardstown friend and resident, I reached out to the Champaign-Urbana community, which had already heard about the overnight raid in Beardstown. Donations in canned food, clothing, and cash were brought over in support of families who had lost their breadwinners overnight, some leaving small children behind without a guardian. The next day my husband and I loaded a van from the University of Illinois's Center for Democracy in a Multiracial Society to full capacity and headed out to Beardstown. We delivered the supplies to the Catholic Church, where the nuns were handling the aftermath of the raid. We even encountered a *Time Magazine* reporter, clad in the mandatory journalist's multipocketed vest with huge lenses and cameras over his shoulder, documenting the town, its immigrants, and the raid. Beardstown featured in *Time*'s next issue[10] as one of the many towns that ICE had raided in recent months.[11] The article noted that U.S. employers ranging from multinationals like Cargill to smaller companies like QSI and individual suburbanites were complicit in supporting illegality, largely because they benefited by paying low wages to undocumented employees. The reporter made a compelling case that undocumented immigrants were in the United States to stay and that granting amnesty was the best policy. He ended his article with a quotation from the vocal anti-immigrant mayor of Beardstown, Mr. Walters, who told the reporter he called the Feds about illegals in his town a few times a month. But in the interview he admitted he was tired of the hassle and ready for legalization. "If I could wave a magic wand, I'd rather have no Hispanics and have this town be like it was in the '50s. But that's just not going to happen," he said. "Amnesty is touchy, but we can't keep doing nothing" (Thornburgh 2007, 42).

After the raid, there was a noticeable drop in the number of Mexican workers on the production floor, by all accounts. This was attributed both to the plant's closer examination of employees' paperwork and employees' self-elimination when they knew that their papers were compromised. Workers who ceased to show up at the plant did not necessarily depart from the town or the Cargill Corporation. Some opted for longer commutes to work in Macomb, Springfield, and Jacksonville. Others looked for jobs in small towns in the area or in the surrounding farms that raise the piglets for Cargill, where undocumented immigrants were less visible. In effect, they shifted their employment from one end of Cargill's integrated industrial processes to the other end of the production chain, where work was more dispersed and less vulnerable to future raids.

The expansion of ICE raids all over the country, most prominently in the meat industry, set off a popular debate on whether undocumented workers took jobs from Americans, which was already a powerful sentiment among many Beardstown residents including Mayor Walters. One Republican presidential hopeful, Congressman Duncan Hunter, said "that the day after the raids, Americans were lined up to get their $18-an-hour jobs back" (Luden 2007). But in reality, no one was lining up to take jobs at the Beardstown meatpacking plants, which paid at the time an average hourly rate of eleven or twelve dollars. To address the drop in the numbers of the Mexican workforce, Cargill had to cast a wider net with a greater likelihood of bringing in citizens and legal residents. They sent mobile recruiters to Little Havana in Miami to recruit Cubans, who are commonly granted refugee status and work permits in this country; to Puerto Rico to recruit citizens from the island's high numbers of unemployed youth; and to Detroit, where yet another pool of unemployed workers had legal citizenship.

Elena, a Cuban refugee with a legal work permit, explained that Cargill recruited labor through advertisements and information sessions in Little Havana. She and a few other Cubans attended one such session at the temp agency where she used to go looking for jobs. "At the information session they told us about the job, the salary and conditions and offered to cover up to $400 to get to Beardstown. We could use it towards bus fare or car; a few of us chose to drive up in one car." When they reached Beardstown, the company had already identified a few rental options for the group, ranging from mobile homes to houses, and a list of vacancies was made available to them. Several lacked funds for a rental deposit so the plant provided the money and deducted these up-front payments from workers' biweekly paychecks. These up-front payments also included the cost of buying some of the gear needed for work, like steel-toed boots.

In Puerto Rico, the company began running advertisements in the capital city, San Juan, then followed up by flying in mobile recruiters to conduct interviews there and in four other towns (Luden 2007). By December of that year (2007), more than fifty Puerto Ricans recruited from the island arrived in Beardstown. "Some got off the plane," said one of my interviewees, "with flip flops in December having no idea what the weather is like in this part of the country." Shelly Heideman, an active member of a nonprofit faith-based group serving the needs of immigrants in Beardstown, said to the Morning Edition reporter she had to expand her efforts to secure donations because the incoming Puerto Ricans needed so many things: "winter clothing, especially for their children, ... They also need[ed] furnishings, pots and pans, linens, towels, sheets, blankets, and almost anything you need to establish a home" (ibid.). Thus, donations from the nonprofit sector and faith-based organizations were important to Cargill's efforts to recruit and relocate workers. We must recognize how such assistance to the new recruits indeed offered a form of indirect assistance to the corporation and subsidized low wages. Everyone who offers assistance to the individual workers, from nonprofit faith-based groups that help Puerto Rican recruits to Catholic nuns and Methodist pastors who help the Mexican and the West African recruits to make transitions to their new lives and jobs in Beardstown, is in one way or another also helping the company. Their offerings make it possible for the corporation to capture a displaced labor force at little cost to itself.

Of the Puerto Ricans who were recruited, however, not all stayed. Some could not tolerate the weather or the harsh work; others could not endure the small town culture or the managers at the manufacturing plant. "Many got into arguments with the line supervisors. . . . They have big mouths and are ready to pick up and fight," one Mexican worker said about Puerto Ricans. "They don't put up with a lot, like we have to." While this worker's comments may reflect some stereotypes, there is a grain of truth in what he said in that workers with legal documentation can be more outspoken and can be more likely to leave, for they have greater job mobility compared to undocumented workers. Not surprisingly, many of the Puerto Ricans left before their probationary period was over.

In Detroit, as in Puerto Rico, the mobile recruitment team was accompanied by a current employee from the recruitment location. Cargill also ran a series of full-page advertisements in the local newspapers. The advertisements and information sessions, combined with word of mouth from those who had moved a few years earlier, brought new African American Detroiters to the plant. As noted earlier, these recruits did not necessarily move to the town. Many of them opted for living in the bigger cities nearby and commuted to the job in Beardstown.

The first African American Detroiters who rented in Beardstown around 2005 indicated that they had a friendly reception from their neighbors. "We had moved with just two garbage bags, and [the] kids. . . . Some neighbors greeted us and one even helped us. [They] brought us blankets," one remarked. But comparing her first impressions with her more recent experiences, especially after 2007 when more Detroiters were recruited, she noted a great shift in white locals' reception: "It wasn't as bad then, because it wasn't as many of us [African Americans] . . . But now that there are more of us and we live walking distance [from each other] where we can walk together things are different." In a 2012 group interview with African Americans recruited from Detroit, several remarked on the "for sale" signs that had gone up around them.[12] They recounted stories that were vivid and painful reminders of the town's sundown town history. "You get the dirty looks, you

walk down the street and they holler 'nigger' out their car door." Other incidents included a Wal-Mart checkout worker slamming change on the counter
top in order to avoid making contact with an African American woman's
hand. Later, a group of young white men pulled their truck over, yelling to
the African American interviewee and her sons, "You know we used to hang
niggers in our back yard. It's gonna be an exception today and we gonna hang
you in the front yard." Some remember a mob of white youth circling a black
girl from Detroit, an encounter that ended in the tragic killing of one of the
transgressors by the white boyfriend of the assaulted girl.

DIFFERENT RECEPTIONS FOR DIFFERENT IMMIGRANT GROUPS

The varied experiences of the immigrant labor force in Beardstown bring
to light the limitations of telling a single story of migration and of migrant
experience in any given place. Just as the same immigrant group can have distinct experiences across different communities of destination in the United
States, so, too, can distinct immigrant groups' experiences vary within the
same local context.

Here, positioning the experiences of the Mexican and the Togolese in the
context of the sundown town history of Beardstown and the more recent
racial experiences of the African Americans from Detroit proves enlightening. The particular timing of these two transnational waves of immigration
is also significant. The West Africans arrived in the area a few years after the
1996 Beardstown violence, and a decade after the first wave of Mexican immigration. One might say Mexicans took the brunt of the effects of Cargill's
labor practices at the plant and the beginnings of ethnic diversification of the
sundown town. As the first wave of migrant workers, Mexicans were blamed
for Cargill's lowering of wages and reduction of other seniority benefits. They
were also the first linguistically, ethnically, and racially different group who
broke into this exclusive residential territory of whiteness. Moreover, having absorbed the first wave of residents' shock and violence, these Mexicans
made the experience of relocation easier for those who followed. But timing
alone cannot completely account for the violence experienced by Mexicans,
as in the cross burning incident, and the very different reception of West Africans, which by all accounts was not marred by the kind of hostility Mexicans

had experienced. African Americans, for example, were the last migrant labor force recruited to Beardstown yet were not spared racist reactions to their presence. Other important factors, such as legal status, education, family structure, and historical migration networks, sociohistoric characteristics of a group and a place can all help explain differences in the experiences of French- and Spanish-speaking immigrants. Most of the French-speaking Africans arrived with legal residency and green cards gained through a lottery visa. They were therefore likely to have a high school education or higher, as this is the requirement for that type of visa,[13] and to be keen to learn English as soon as they could.

Despite these differences, Togolese were in the same boat with Mexican workers when it came to job mobility and other disadvantages relative to white American workers. Running into the bias of U.S. academic institutions, West Africans' college credentials were often not recognized and they therefore had to work as manual laborers.[14] For Mexicans, undocumented status severely limited their options for work and relocation. The French-speaking Africans may not have had concerns with immigration, but most of them had incurred enormous debt just to pay the travel costs to get to the United States. The majority of them also sent money home to support family members. These financial obligations forced them to stay in jobs that, for all their difficulties, at least guaranteed them regular income in a town with a relatively low cost of living.

The community surveys conducted in the area in 2008 offer a snapshot of the diverse groups and confirm my observations in the area at the time.[15] For example, the outcome of the survey of French-speaking Africans in Rushville and Beardstown conducted by the AmeriCorps volunteer indicates that the majority had a high school diploma or higher education (about 54 percent of the 2008 sample group) and that of those who had children, 67 percent had had to leave at least one child behind in their home countries.[16] By contrast, the randomly sampled door-to-door survey conducted by the University of Illinois Extension staff among Spanish-speaking immigrants in Beardstown showed that only 14 percent had more than a high school diploma or some college education[17] and that 84 percent of those who had children had all their children with them. Moreover, the housing survey conducted in 2008 by the Illinois Institute for Rural Affairs in three languages in Beardstown in collaboration with the University of Illinois Extension and the

Francophone priest indicates a much higher rate of homeownership among the Mexican (40 percent), as opposed to the African immigrants they surveyed (8 percent).[18]

—

"WE AIN'T ALL THE SAME"

The differences in the reception of migrant workers in Beardstown are also related to their distinct migration and diasporic histories. Compared to Togolese, Mexicans have long and intertwining contemporary histories of labor and migration in the United States. Many of my Mexican interviewees were the second or third generation of immigrants in their families and already had many other family members living in the United States. This afforded Mexican immigrant workers a much thicker network of support and information within the country[19] and made their transition experience in Beardstown different from that of other international immigrant workers. For example, while many Mexicans were undocumented, sharing a border with the United States enabled them to have their immediate family and in many cases extended family with them in Beardstown. Among West Africans, this kind of familial support system was rare. Beardstown's West Africans formed part of a new wave of migration from Africa to the United States.[20] Many had family members working in other African countries, but few had relatives in the United States or other countries with a favorably convertible currency. This not only thinned their network of support and mobility in this country, but also required them to carry a larger burden of sending money to their families back home.

For the Detroiters who came to Beardstown, the diasporic historical legacies exacerbated their experiences of racism. While legal status, education, and fluency in a European language may have elevated West Africans' position in the racialized social hierarchies of the town, African Americans continued to rank at the bottom. In the collective meeting I had with Detroiters, as I will discuss in length in chapter 5, one expressed how white residents "are often more accepting of [international] immigrants or even black Africans [over them]." Others in the room nodding and raising their hand in blessing supported his perception. To offer an explanation, one jumped in, commenting on the history of racism and slavery in this country: "They lynched us, not them!" one said with conviction. "Yes, we ain't all the same" another whispered under her breath in confirmation.

My conversations with whites, Latinos, and West Africans confirmed this perception that in the racialized hierarchy of Beardstown, African Americans remained at the bottom.[21] Just as West Africans made reference to being different from black Americans, so, too, did whites and some Latinos make distinctions between the "good" blacks and the "bad" ones, with African Americans comprising the latter. As one white woman stated about West Africans, "They are black *but* they are educated. . . . One guy was a doctor in his country. Very respectable." One retired woman in her sixties who had lived all her life in Beardstown working as clerical staff likewise commented on the acceptance of the three groups by the white locals. Referring to West African immigrants, whom she described as walking up and down the alley and standing on her step to get phone signals, and compared to Mexican immigrants, she stated that "people seem to accept them better, they speak more positive of them. . . . I think they have made more of an effort to learn English, maybe it's easier to speak French and switch over, I don't know. But they [the natives of Beardstown] seem to be more positive with them." She then went on to comment about African Americans in relation to the other two groups by saying "there was an influx of colored people several months ago from Detroit, that didn't go well in town. That was the one people were very negative about, they were more accepting to others than them." I have heard variations of statements like this in the narratives of local whites referring to West Africans' efforts to learn English, pursue higher education, and reach professional aspirations in ways that differentiate them from Mexicans and from the African Americans, the latter of whom persist in the imagination of the locals as "the undesired race." One white native-born resident of Beardstown even described African Americans as "the scary ones. . . . [They] look like thugs."

Thus while the color of skin as a visual marker of difference is important, it is not enough, as the different status of West Africans and African Americans in Beardstown attests. Within the "Black-White Paradigm," of racism that dominates American society (Feagin 2002), groups may "Whiten" or "Blacken." Race as sociohistorically constructed category is flexible and dependent on relational positioning with other groups in a specific social and institutional context. Beyond skin color, the status of West Africans and

African Americans in Beardstown was determined in relational terms by education, class identity, and reputation of the two groups.

In terms of class, Beardstown is a homogenous blue-collar town where almost all whites or blacks, Hispanics or Francophones are workers at Cargill or wage earners at nearby agricultural industries, farms or services. But in terms of class identity and imagined class trajectories West Africans are different. While they are all Cargill workers on the production floor and pick up more or less similar paychecks every two weeks, for many West Africans at least when they first start, the Cargill job is a temporary position, a stepping stone toward converting their academic credentials and finding a way to their professional aspirations. Whether this happens or not is beside the point. What is critical is that this difference in background and aspiration distinguishes West African from African American workers at the plant and in town. Comments like "they are black *but* highly educated" are revealing. While Africa may be stigmatized as the "dark continent," the reputation of Detroit—as a rust belt city of "crime and thugs" does not advance the position of African American Detroiters in Beardstown.

Race, as a social and historical construct, is relational and textured within and across racialized groups. It may be that some whites in this former sundown town consider Mexicans, to a certain degree, "honorary whites" and so categorize them higher than African Americans or West Africans in their racialized social hierarchies. However, for many others, Mexicans' dubious legal status combined with their lower education and limited English language attainment can have the opposite effect and contribute to lowering their social status vis-à-vis West Africans. As Eduardo Bolina-Silva (2009) argues in *Racism without Racists*, it is not easy to find people, even in Beardstown, who outright admit to racism. Often language, legal status, and other matters and manners are used as proxies for racist prejudice. For example, as one white American interviewee, a woman in her fifties who works as a receptionist and has lived all her life in Beardstown, said, "I don't have a problem with them living here. But they need to learn to speak English if they are going to live here." Meanwhile, even though Detroiters are English-speaking citizens, they were not spared from the prejudice of this as well as some of my other white American interviewees.

Complex relationships push African Americans farther to the bottom of racialized groups in this town, not only on account of the way they are construed by whites, but also because other displaced groups who seek to elevate their social position may do so by constructing a group yet farther down in the racialized social hierarchy and then distance themselves from that group. The fact is that points of convergence and divergence, solidarities and tensions among diverse racialized and ethnicized groups are not stable, fixed, or constant. They are relational, varying by context, by proximity to others, and by time.

Research by David Roediger and Elizabeth Esch (2012) has shown how the construction of racialized "Others" has historically played an important role in management of labor. This has also been key to the development of Beardstown as an industrial sundown town and today as a company town. Local context also matters. Localities are not passive containers for the working of global forces—in this case, global displacement of labor. In addition to the particularities of each group (for example, with respect to age, education, class aspiration, language ability, and family structure), the broader historically constituted racial structures of a given local context are crucial. In Beardstown, the local histories of race and labor matter to the ways in which different groups are ethnicized, racialized, and classed by dominant white locals, by each other and by themselves. Thus, there can be no single story of migration or experience of inclusion/exclusion, integration/confrontation. Collapsing the distinct groups and their experiences based on skin color, national citizenship, or legal and migration status overlooks critical differences and demonstrates the limitations of such generic categories of belonging as nationality, immigration status, and race.

PART II
DISPLACED LABOR

Figure 3.1: Map of Mexico showing Michoacán.

3 – MICHOACÁN'S LARGEST
EXPORT IS PEOPLE

IN JULY 2008, I DECIDED TO TRAVEL TO MICHOACÁN BECAUSE EARLY on in my research, I had realized that Beardstown was a node in a larger web of closely connected communities. Many immigrants talked about home and how it motivated them to keep working in Beardstown, either because they hoped to return or they feared for what they left behind. I could not understand the transformation of Beardstown without understanding what happened in their home countries. That summer I felt close enough to some of the Mexican immigrants to ask them if I could visit their families back home. I also prevailed on one of them, "Lupita" I call her, to be my travel partner for a journey to Michoacán, a state from where many Mexican immigrants came. Lupita was one of the first Mexicans who moved to Beardstown in the early 1990s and also one of the people I had known since I first started my research. She was not from Michoacán, but grew up in Mexico and knew the country relatively well. Young, outgoing, and brave, Lupita accompanied me on my journey to Michoacán (see figure 3.1).

We arranged to visit Tejaro, hometown for many of the Beardstown immigrants. We also planned to stop over in nearby Numaran. A priest from Numaran had visited Beardstown in 2007 and collected about five thousand dollars to improve the church in Michoacán and celebrate *fiestas patronales,* in honor of the patron saint of the town.[1] Several people we talked to wanted us to follow up on the outcome of their contributions.

To reach our destination, we drove over a long and bumpy road off the highway. This twisting route soon became a simple, one lane dirt road. We passed several villages, some of which we later heard were highly involved with *narcotrafico* (drug trafficking). We parked the car and walked on the stone paved road towards the main plaza. We took a picture of the large clock on the front tower of the church, the prize contribution from Michoacán residents in Beardstown (see figure 3.2).

The church was located at one end of the town's plaza. The weekly open market, *tianguis* was being held at the other end. There were few shoppers, considering this was a weekly effort to bring in buyers from neighboring towns. After taking a few steps in between the neatly organized line of makeshift stands, I heard a voice calling, *"¡Lupita, mujer, ¿qué estás haciendo aquí?!"* ("Lupita, woman, what are you doing here?!"). Lupita turned toward the voice and a fast exchange of chatter and laughter followed. The two women embraced. Lupita introduced me to her friend and explained why we were there. The woman, who was one of the vendors, told those at her neighboring stand that we were visiting from Beardstown. One neighbor exclaimed, "From Illinois! I have visited Beardstown. *Tengo un hermano allá*" ("I have a brother there"). Before long, the daughter of Lupita's friend arrived to help her mother with the stand. A teenager at the time, she had completed elementary and middle school in Beardstown but moved back to Michoacán when her mother could no longer bear the difficult work at the plant. Soon, she was calling to another former Cargill worker who had been injured and left Beardstown to begin a new life selling at this market, and as they chatted and caught up with the news of Beardstown and common acquaintances, a circle formed around Lupita, who explained to them what brought her to Michoacán.

All these people were familiar with Beardstown. Even if they had not lived or visited the town, they were connected to it on everyday basis. This

Figure 3.2: The Numaran church clock provided by Beardstown donations. Photo by the author, 2008.

is profoundly ironic and instructive. For people in this town, thousands of miles from Illinois, Beardstown is a household word, yet I have seldom come across anyone in my Champaign-Urbana community who knows about Beardstown, which is less than 150 miles away. In classes I teach on globalization and transnational global development I often bring up examples from my Beardstown project to challenge students' ideas about the global-local relation and the assumption that people's everyday practices necessarily take place only in their immediate geographic territories. As a starting point to this discussion, I ask the students if anyone knows where

Figure 3.3: Western Union office in Numaran, Mexico. Photo by the author, 2008.

Beardstown is. Only once did a student raise his hand. This student, a white, blue-eyed undergraduate whom I ended up hiring as my field-work research assistant to interview white residents of Beardstown, had grandparents who lived there.

As we made our way toward the car, Lupita and I noticed a Western Union office. All over Mexico and particularly in Michoacán, Western Union out-posts are as ubiquitous as corner stores and are key connecting points in this part of the world. As those I interviewed in Michoacán repeatedly said, "Almost everyone has worked in the United States. . . . Almost every house built in town involves money earned or sent from the United States." Western Union offices are where this money lands (see figure 3.3).

Statistics bear this out. Between 2005 and 2010 Michoacán had the third highest rate of emigration to the United States of all Mexican states, with 7.7 percent of its population migrating there. It also had the second highest rate of child and youth emigrants, sending 8.6 percent of that population group north of the border.[2] The state's economy depends largely on the remittances from these immigrants. While Michoacán represents only 3.8 percent of the total Mexican population, it receives the highest share of remittances in the country—10 percent of the total $21 billion sent to Mexico in 2013.[3] Once many in the region made a living through pig farming, but the rising costs of farming along with falling prices of pork meant a lot of farms had shut down.[4] In recent years Michoacán's economy has been on the decline: by 2012, 54 percent of the population was living in poverty, 9 percent higher than the national average.[5] As a result of this deteriorating situation, large numbers of former farmers have abandoned their communal land holdings to move to cities or cross the border north.[6] Indeed, a *Christian Science Monitor* article reported that by 1995 there were slightly more Michoacános who harvested strawberries in California, picked apples in Oregon, and worked in construction or manufacturing in Illinois—about two million—than the 1.9 million adults who still permanently called Michoacán home (LaFranchi 1995).

TEJARO: "THERE IS NOTHING THERE!"

We arrived in Tejaro mid-morning on a cool but sunny day. To ask for directions to residents in our list of Tejaro families, we needed to find a pedestrian. Yet we found none in sight as we circled the well-paved streets of this town of about four thousand people.[7] Parking in front of what seemed to be a garage converted to a store, we heard the radio from behind the back door as we entered but found no attendant. We called for señor and señora. After a couple of minutes, someone appeared. We bought two bottles of water, got directions to the house of one of the families in the list that she easily recognized—Fernández—and we headed out.

A striking aspect of Tejaro were its empty streets. Entire blocks of town had no people, but there were plenty of barking dogs. The two seemed to go together. To protect the empty houses, departed residents would leave a couple of dogs around to help the neighbor or friend keep an eye on their houses. At first glance, Tejaro looked like a *pueblo fantasma* (ghost town). Yet, an impressive array of public works projects was in place or in progress, including nicely paved roads and newly installed sewage and water lines. Recently built or improved houses lined residential streets, their windows protected by metal grids.

We reached the house of the Fernández family, a humble one-story structure, and rang the doorbell. Mrs. Fernández opened the door. She was a shy
woman and soft spoken. After an awkward suspicious moment, she remembered that her sons had mentioned our visit and invited us in with warmth:
"!Ándale pués!" ("Come on in, please!"). She guided us to a seat at the table
in the entry room, which was also the kitchen, the living room, and the din-
ing room. The walls were covered with pictures of children and grandchildren and other family photos. Mrs. Fernández had on a white flowery apron
(mandíl), a symbol of dedication to family worn by almost all traditional
homemakers—like a sign saying "homemaker at work." Mr. Fernández soon
entered. He was in his late sixties, of medium height, thin, and with a squared
jaw. The lines carved into his expressive, sun-toasted skin told stories. He
wore a cowboy hat and plaid pattern shirt. He removed his hat, pulled up a
chair, and sat down with us. Mrs. Fernández and her sister, who was visiting,
were also at the table. She offered me a soft drink made out of beets—not my
favorite, but anything served cool and with much care and affection is a good
drink. Once the talk about their sons, daughters-in-law, and grandchildren in
Beardstown wound down, it was my turn to ask questions and learn about
their family.

The Fernández's sons, Juan and Pedro, who were working at Cargill's
Beardstown plant, belonged to the third generation of laborers who were
born and raised in Mexico and then exported to the United States at the
peak of their earning potential. Mr. Fernández's father was part of the earliest wave of Mexican emigrants to the United States, who, at the turn of the
twentieth century, built railroads, picked sugar beets, or worked in Detroit
auto factories or Chicago meatpacking plants (García 1996). "He used to
work on the railroads and then came down to be with us and my mother every
now and then," Mr. Fernández recalled. Mr. Fernández himself was among
the second wave of Mexican emigrants who participated in the Bracero Program, the result of a 1942 agreement between the United States and Mexico,[8]
which facilitated the passage of more than four million young and healthy
Mexican workmen to the United States to save its agricultural production
during World War II.[9] He recalled lining up in front of the municipality and
waiting for his name to be called to board the train that took them to the
border and then to el Norte. The work was hard and the separation from his
wife and children even harder. He said that the Mexican government sold

him and his fellow workers to the United States "for fifty dollars," but he added, "I managed to save enough to buy this land and build this house on it." Mr. Fernández was an *ejidatario*, meaning that he held a share of the communal land *(ejidos)* created by reforms following the Mexican Revolution in 1910. As with many others, he could not adequately support himself and his family with the land alone; hence the history of migration in his family.[10]

Mr. and Mrs. Fernández have five children; four were living in the United States at the time and one in Mexico City. They had another child who was tragically killed in a car accident in Chicago. All the Fernández children had moved away. There was nothing for them in Tejaro, Mr. Fernández told us, and went on to explain the turn of events in the 1990s that brought his family to this.

"In Tejaro we used to have a huge production of milk, lots of milk! I had cows that would give me up to thirty liters a day. . . . When Salinas was the president the price of milk went down, because the brother of the president was bringing in dried milk, which sold much cheaper. . . . We wanted to sell the cows' milk at two pesos when the powdered milk was at 1.20 pesos. Everybody started buying that kind of milk. We drove around in our pickup trucks, [but] no one would buy anything. What was left for us to do?" As a result, Mr. Fernández explained, he had had to send his two youngest sons, Juan and Pedro, the only children still living at home, to the United States; and because they knew someone in Beardstown who told them about Cargill jobs, they ended up there. Mr. Fernández's story confirmed what several people in Beardstown had said about Tejaro: *"Alli no hay nada! Te mueres de hambre!"* ("There is nothing there! You die of hunger!")

Seven pyramid-shaped silos stood tall and empty in the town, striking symbols of the diminishing local agricultural production. Once filled with the local harvest of corn, they had been abandoned in 1999, when the National Popular Subsistence Company (Compañía Nacional de Subsistencias Populares, or CONASUPO) was formally dismantled.[11] This organization had been established in the 1960s to protect local farmers in the agricultural market and to subsidize rural consumers in isolated locations. Although it was not perfect and although it had its share of corruption and other problems, the CONASUPO program operated as a "safety net" (Schwartzman 2013, 138). The Mexican government bought corn and other agricultural products from local producers at guaranteed subsidized prices through CONASUPO, and

Figure 3.4: CONASUPO's empty grain silos, Tejaro, Mexico. Photo by the author, 2008.

sold them at state-franchised grocery stores at low prices. To remove market barriers, state reforms gradually dismantled CONASUPO in the 1980s and, at last, liquidated it in 1999.[12] The silos were a sad reminder of the more productive days in Tejaro (see figures 3.4 and 3.5). Mr. Fernández declared, "There is a proposal to use them for murals. I say that is good. . . . At least that would put them to some use!"

Mrs. Fernández offered to take a walk with me to visit one of the silos. I was delighted to have this opportunity to chat with her. As we walked through the neighborhood, I commented on the striking emptiness of the streets and asked if this was because of a special event, time of the day, or day of the week. She shook her head and stated that in the town there were indeed very few houses that were occupied. Most were built by or for immigrants abroad. To protect these houses from vandalism, and for the sake of upkeep, some absentee owners loaned their house free of charge to friends and relatives while they were abroad. Out of curiosity I asked her to indicate the status of

Figure 3.5: Mr. Fernández and his remaining goats, Tejaro, Mexico. Photo by the author, 2008.

each house we passed in the neighborhood. I made a sketch, which revealed that in the sample blocks we walked through, thirteen houses were occupied by current residents of Tejaro (including the interviewee's house), while nine belonged to immigrants who had either left the house vacant, rented it, or left it as a *casa prestada,* or house on loan (see figure 3.6).

Mrs. Fernández did not take the loss of the original owners easily. These were families who had raised their children together and helped each other out. With more of her neighbors gone, she said she felt at a loss. "I feel strange because I have houses next to me but I don't have neighbors. I have no one to ask for a cup of sugar or for a helping hand or to converse with. They are all gone."

It would seem that the global economic policies and treaties that forced residents like Mr. and Mrs. Fernández off their land and livelihood and displaced others, including their sons, to places like Beardstown, also made those left behind feel out of place. Mrs. Fernández experienced loss and a

Figure 3.6: Streets of Tejaro, Mexico. Photo by the author, 2008.

sense of dislocation in her own neighborhood and town—places now very different from what she recalled from her own childhood and when she was raising her children. Thus, both groups, those who physically moved and those whose neighbors around them moved, experienced displacement.

MEXICAN MIGRATION: "THE BORDER CROSSED US"

For the Fernández family, as for other families in Tejaro and in Michoacán, emigration to the United States is not a new phenomenon. The cross-border movements of people across the United States and Mexico were common even in the nineteenth century, after some families were split across the two sides of the newly designated national borders following the end of the United States–Mexico War (1846–1848) and the Treaty of Guadalupe Hidalgo (1848). In effect, the first group of Mexican immigrants in the United

States arrived by default, without crossing any border, when Mexican territories (Alta California, New Mexico, and an expanded Texas) were annexed. "We did not cross the border, the border crossed us," asserts the slogan of a contemporary immigrants' rights movement. This history, to a certain degree, contributed to a sense of entitlement, or what some might call legitimacy, in this group of Mexicans in the United States, especially after the establishment of the Border Patrol in 1924, which not only enforced immigration laws but also initiated the categorization of local residents and workers as legal and illegal (De Genova and Zayas 2003 and 2005). From the point of view of U.S. employers, the border patrol and visa system made it possible to reduce or increase the inflows of workers, as well as to suppress the wages and benefits workers could access or claim. In *Illegal People*, David Bacon argues that "a globalized political and economic system creates illegality by displacing people and then denying them rights and equality as they do what they can to survive—move to find work" (Bacon 2008a, iv).

Historically, the Mexican workforce has been critical to the growth and prosperity of the United States economy. Between 1850 and 1880, for example, when the expansion of cattle ranches in the Southwest and of fruit production in California increased the need for laborers, fifty-five thousand Mexicans fulfilled this need, working on land and ranches in regions that had previously belonged to Mexico (Bailey 2008, 103).[13] Furthermore, the construction of the U.S.–Mexico railroad relied heavily on Mexican laborers. After the United States Civil War, the railroad became a priority in the rebuilding of the devastated country, yet the railroad companies found themselves with a shortage of workers. Blocked from hiring Chinese immigrants following the Exclusion Acts of 1882, they hired Mexicans, who, between 1880 and 1890, made up as much as 60 percent of railway crews.[14] According to Esmeralda Rodriguez-Scott (2002), as the train system in the United States expanded to rural areas and the south, the Irish and German immigrants who had been working in railroad construction chose not to move with their jobs. Consequently, the railroad companies again turned to a Mexican workforce. For their part, railroad workers in Mexico saw such employment as a means to higher wages on the other side of the border. As the construction of the railroad expanded northward, writes García (1996), the Mexican government was repeatedly asked to recruit more workers from the interior.

The resulting influx of migrant labor was substantial enough to enable U.S. employers to keep wages low. Barbara Driscoll (1999) refers to this period in Mexican emigration to the United States (mid–1800s to mid–1920s) as the first and less-documented Bracero Program.[15] U.S. railroad companies, mines, and ranches needed labor, and Mexicans needed jobs.

As noted above, the second wave of the Mexican work force that made a critical contribution to developing the economy and prosperity of the United States arrived as part of the Bracero Program (1942–1967). It was, indeed, largely by the Mexican hand that America became the world's center of agricultural production.[16] During the Second World War, when the U.S. agricultural sector required a young and strong labor force to work on its farms and the U.S. and Mexican governments agreed to recruit guest workers, the resulting Bracero Program contracts were under the aegis of independent farmer associations and the Farm Bureau, and typically were written in English. Consequently, many braceros signed without understanding the terms of their employment.

The end of the Bracero program did not halt the northward flow of laborers. Instead, it just increased the number of those who came without legal status. In fact, the annual average of slightly less than thirty thousand migrants during the 1961–1970 period rose to 395,000 migrants during the 2001–2004 period. Between 1970 and 2004, the population of Mexican origin residing in the United States increased from 5.4 million to 26.8 million (Zúñiga, Leite, and Nava 2005, 32).

The experience of the Fernández family reflects much of this history. Mr. Fernández's father took railroad jobs that Irish and German workers no longer wanted; a generation or so later, Mr. Fernández labored as a bracero for the agricultural producers who needed to protect their crops from loss (not being picked); and in the present era the children of Mr. Fernández have performed the hazardous and low-paid processing and packing jobs that native-born workers have rejected.

However, the changing immigration policies of the United States have greatly affected the conditions under which migrant laborers live. Under the earlier, more lenient border control policy, people like Mr. Fernández and his father were able to go back and forth between Mexico and their jobs in the United States and keep their families in Tejaro. But the passage of the 1996 Illegal Immigration Reform and Responsibility Act, followed by post-9/11 regulations, heightened restrictions on border crossing.[17] With greater risks involved, Juan and Pedro Fernández crossed only once, and then paid *coyotes* to help their families cross the border to join them in Beardstown.

Elaborating on these developments, an interviewee in Michoacán described how when immigrants had families living in Tejaro, "they used to come back or send money to repair and improve houses for their families. They used to come back, paint, fix, build a room. Now all these are *familia completa* [complete families living in the United States], therefore no need to come back and improve.... With economic recession things went from bad to worse *[de mal en peor]*. Now there is less work there and therefore less improvement here." A 2008 *Los Angeles Times* article on Tejaro reinforced the point. In that year, a peak point in ICE raids, deportations, and intensified border control, the daily transactions in the local exchange office fell from seven thousand dollars to eight hundred dollars (Ellingwood 2008).

NAFTA AND THE CREATION OF A MEXICAN LABOR RESERVOIR

What happened to Mr. Fernández and his family in the 1990s is not unique. Many farmers in Michoacán and throughout Mexico also lost their livelihoods when they were pushed out of the market for dairy products and then forced to sell their communal landholding share. Michoacán's chief economic activities are pig farming, agriculture, and dairy production, and with the implementation of the North American Free Trade Agreement (NAFTA) in 1994 and adoption of other neoliberal economic policies by the Mexican state in the 1980s and 1990s, the vulnerable economy of the region came under further stress. The Salinas administration (1988–1994) and the Zedillo administration (1994–2000), in particular, closely followed the blueprint of neoliberal structural adjustment policies prescribed and required by global institutions such as the International Monetary Fund (IMF) and the World Trade Organization (WTO). Salinas drastically cut government social expenditures; devalued Mexican national currency; sold the most lucrative public assets;[18] privatized public companies such as CONASUPO; repealed communal landholdings *(ejidos)*; and signed the NAFTA with the United States and Canada (Vázquez-Castillo 2012). Under NAFTA, the Mexican state lifted tariffs on foreign imports and agreed to cut all agricultural

subsidies and state protectionist interventions, while opening its markets to
North American agricultural products that were heavily subsidized by their
respective governments. For example, from 1997 to 2005, U.S.-subsidized
corn was exported to Mexico at about 19 percent below the cost of production. By 2004, U.S. corn exports had increased twenty-fold since 1993, while
the agricultural livelihoods of Mexican farmers had deteriorated.[19] The reduction of the CONASUPO silos of Tejaro to mere ornamental structures
is a stark indicator of this skewed arrangement.[20] Mexican corn growers
could not withstand the comparative advantages of the U.S. growers whose
produce flooded their market.[21] As a result, 1.3 million farmers were driven
out of business, and the monthly income for self-employed farmers plummeted from 1,959 pesos a month in 1991 to 228 pesos a month in 2003.[22] When
NAFTA was signed in 1994, there were 2.4 million undocumented Mexicans
in the United States. By 2000, the number reached nine million. In 2002 alone,
more than six hundred thousand Mexicans migrated north.[23]

The dismantling of *ejidos* and of CONASUPO contributed significantly
to the production of this migrant Mexican workforce. In 1992, the repeal
of the article that established communal landholdings facilitated the private
sale of individual shareholdings and especially developers' land grabs not
only in the peripheries of metropolitan areas but also in struggling rural
areas such as the highlands of Michoacán. A company with resources to buy
a large number of individual plots cheaply could then reconsolidate them as
large parcels and market them for industrial agriculture, agribusiness, or real
estate speculation. A side effect was the displacement of a large pool of the
rural labor force. The dismantling of CONASUPO, which offered a safety
net for the rural producers and consumers, during the 1990s and its final
liquidation in 1999 also added to this displacement (see Schwartzman 2013;
Relinger 2010;and Yunez-Naude 2003).[24]

Here again the experience of the Fernández family is representative. Having been shut out of the dairy market due to the influx of lower-priced imports, they were courted by private developers to sell their land for cash in
hand. But the cash return was small and lasted only a short while. Subsequently, families became footloose workers, forming a labor pool that could
be nationally and transnationally mobilized to accommodate the needs of
global manufacturing firms such as Cargill. For the state of Michoacán, the
siphoning of adult Mexicans as a cheap labor supply for the United States has

been particularly severe. As one of the locals in Tejaro remarked, "Michoacán's largest export is people."[25]

For Mr. Fernández, as for many others, the long-term impact has been an even more difficult struggle: how to keep a geographically dispersed family intact economically and socially. As we shall see in the next chapter, similar processes, albeit in the context of a very different history and culture, have impacted Togolese, dispossessing them of their sources of livelihood at home and displacing them to destinations like Beardstown abroad.

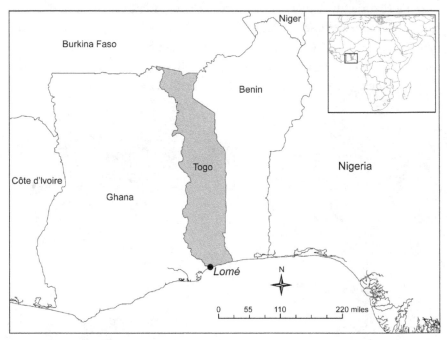

Figure 4.1: Map of Togo.

4 ~ WINNING THE LOTTERY IN TOGO

IN 2010, TWO YEARS AFTER RETURNING FROM FIELD RESEARCH IN Michoacán, I traveled to Togo (see figure 4.1 for map) to interview families and friends of Beardstown's Togolese immigrants in the capital city of Lomé. I was fortunate to have Madam Ellen, a Togolese woman whom I met early in my research, as my companion. She was in her late forties, held an MA in geography, and had been a high school teacher in Togo. When I met her, she was working on the production floor at Cargill, "cutting meat." Back home, she told me, she had never done manual work. Before the Cargill job she had not even cut up a chicken, as she had a domestic worker to assist with cooking and cleaning. In Beardstown, however, she found herself thrown into "the mouth of the giant." Interestingly, of the three people in her Beardstown household, she alone was working at Cargill. Her teenage son, the only child whom she and her husband brought with them to the United States, was enrolled at the local high school. Her husband, who was in his fifties and had been a civil servant in Togo, had not passed the probationary period at the plant. I was told he was too slow.

Madam Ellen was a vibrant character with a contagious laugh. My broken French and her broken English found good company and a bond grew. During each trip to Beardstown, when I paid a visit to her home, I noticed how her English had gotten better, but not my French. We laughed about that as well. When I was ready to embark on the trip to Togo, I sought Madam Ellen's help. She suggested that I go when she was visiting home; she agreed to arrange for me to rent a room on her family's property and to hire her daughter as a field assistant and interpreter. Her daughter was trained as a sociologist at the University of Accra, Ghana, was fluent in English, and experienced in conducting field work. I call her Aku. She helped me interpret local cultural cues and during interviews translated from Ewe, a major language in the southern region of the country as well as in Lomé.

SERENDIPITIES OF FIELD WORK

My flight to Lomé boarded at Charles de Gaulle Airport in Paris. At the gate, only a few West Africans were among those patiently waiting to board our delayed flight. The majority were white expatriates. The extended waits in both Charles De Gaulle and the passport line in Lomé gave me the opportunity to find out more about my fellow travelers. The group included two members of a cargo ship that travelled the west coast of Africa, a team of young and old missionaries who were veterans of the region, a contingent of international development workers, and a well-dressed woman from Benin who was a senior economist at the World Bank's Lomé headquarters. Their varied backgrounds exemplified Togo's myriad connections to the global political economy.

The flight went smoothly. Once I cleared customs, I walked out of the airport building and found a taxi amidst a swarm of people offering transport, currency exchange, hotel rooms, and tourist souvenirs. The smothering May humidity made me feel as if I'd just entered a sauna. Rolling down the window of the un-air-conditioned cab brought no relief. The journey to Madam Ellen's took about thirty minutes, largely along bumpy, unpaved roads. The streets were completely dark; the lights from vehicles and the fast-moving *zamijans* (motorbike taxis) were the only sources of illumination. Street lighting, I would later learn, was a luxury saved for only strategic spots in the city.

At my destination, Madam Ellen and her family members were waiting eagerly, and Aku was on her way. They took me to my room in an adjacent building, a labyrinthine structure comprising a series of additions to the original family home and providing additional rental units for short-term visitors from Togo as well as other parts of Africa. I learned later that some of the funding for this expansion project came from remittances sent by Madam Ellen, and her siblings who lived abroad, in France and on the U.S. East Coast, for at least a decade longer than her. My room was a comfortable space just large enough to fit a single bed and a bedside table.

Shortly after I settled in, the electricity went off. I was stranded, unable to figure out how to get out or to find anyone or anything. Luckily, I had already opened the small window to let in a breath of stifling air. I sat still on my bed and waited in the dark, listening to the rain that was madly crashing on the tin roof. After perhaps the longest ten minutes I have ever experienced, Aku arrived to greet me with a lit candle carefully protected in her hands. She was a thin young woman; her tailored dress clung to her petite figure. Like almost all Togolese women of the urban middle and upper classes, she wore a fashionably styled, straight-hair wig. She had the gorgeous and contagious smile of her mother. Aku told me that power outages were a regular occurrence in the city; at least once or twice a week Lomé's inhabitants expected the electricity to be cut for an average of four hours. She handed me some candles and matches, assuring me that I would need them in the days to come.

With the room brightened by the candlelight, she sat at the edge of my bed and told me her great news. "I won the lottery!" She could see that I was confused, so she repeated, "I won the lottery visa. I played it and I won it!" I had arrived in Lomé to research the experiences of Togolese who left the country for Beardstown by "winning the lotto" (how they refer to winning a lottery visa). Now, after this announcement, my research assistant became a research subject.

LOMÉ MUNICIPALITY: A WINDOW
TO TOGO'S PUBLIC SECTOR

On the second day of my stay, I met the now late Monsieur François, the chief planner of Lomé (see figure 4.2) at his office in the municipality building in the heart of the city. To enter this building, Aku and I passed through a vacant

Figure 4.2: Chief city planner at the entrance to Lomé's municipal headquarters, Togo. Photo by the author, 2010.

lot dotted with several broken-down cars and busses, which turned out to be the repair depot for city vehicles. The municipal building itself showed little sign of recent maintenance. Clearly, looking after the municipal headquarters ranked low on the list of local priorities.

Monsieur François met Aku and me at the entrance. He was a slender man, dressed in a khaki-colored formal suit. We walked through a long corridor that featured enormous printed images of Togo's post-independence presidents (see figure 4.3; see also figures 4.4 and 4.5 for street scenes). These had been recently distributed around the city in honor of the fiftieth anniversary of Togolese independence in April 1960.[1]

Among them was a picture of Sylvanus Olympio, the first president of an independent Togo, in the company of General Gnassingbe Eyadema and his son Faure Gnassingbe Eyadema—the father and son subsequently ruled Togo with an iron fist for almost the entire post-independence history of the country.[2] Their political corruption and oppression was a key reason for the

Figure 4.3: Streets of Lomé: Assembled billboard depicting Togo's presidents during fifty years of independence. From left: Sylvanus Olympio (1961–1963, assassinated while in office); Nicolas Grunitzky (1963–1967, deposed in a coup d'état); Kléber Dadjo (interim president, 1967); Gnassingbé Eyadéma (1967–2005, died in office); Faure Gnassingbé, Gnassingbé Eyadéma's son (2005–present). Photo by the author, 2010.

exodus of many educated Togolese to countries in Africa, Europe, and most recently through the lottery visa to the United States.

After the long walk down the portrait-lined corridor, we arrived at Monsieur François's office, a spacious and well-lit room with a bookshelf holding files and long rolls of city maps and plans. His computer and more paper files and folders sat on his metal desk. Offering us two metal folding chairs, he made himself comfortable behind the desk, turned on his computer, and started looking for files that contain aerial views of the city. "That way," he said, "I can better explain what you need to know about the realities and challenges of the capital city." Speaking of the difficulty of developing an urban infrastructure Monsieur François pointed to the aerial photo now displayed on his monitor and informed us that much of the city did not

Figure 4.4: Author riding a *zamijan* (motorbike taxi) in Lomé, Togo, 2010.

Figure 4.5: Western Union branch, Lomé, Togo. Photo by the author, 2010.

have a sewage system. For much of the city, human waste and sewage were thrown into the canal that runs through the old part of the city and into the ocean.

The most astonishing information he shared with us was the budget for the city. In the 2010 fiscal year, he explained, the annual budget for all of Lomé came to US$850,000—an amount considerably less than half the annual earnings of the football coach at my university. This meager budget translated into no public health care, close to nonexistent public education, and rare instances of paved roads or ongoing infrastructure projects.

I instantly understood not only the decrepit condition of this building, but also how paved roads and street lights were a luxury found only in locations near embassies, international company headquarters, military security zones, buildings that house the World Bank, and the deluxe downtown hotel. To these I should add the residential neighborhood where a British school for expatriates and a boarding school for the rich children of the region were located.[3]

TOGO IN THE GLOBAL ECONOMY

To account for the displacement of the Togolese educated youth to places like Beardstown as manual laborers, we needed to understand the recent history of Togo's political economy and the drastic drop in its position in the global hierarchy. A combination of political and economic changes at the national, regional, and global levels contributed to Togo's economic deterioration and political instability. These, along with new U.S. immigration and visa policies, contributed to the rise of a Togolese diaspora in the United States.

The history of Togo following its independence in 1960 is an intriguing one. Whereas in the colonial transition period from 1956 to 1965, "Togo had the lowest economic growth rate of all twelve French ex-colonies" (Decalo 1976, 91), from the late 1960s to the mid-1970s, Togo's economy boomed, having an annual growth rate of 5 percent from 1966 to 1970, and 7 percent from 1971 to 1975 (ibid., 108–109). While in its heyday during the early 1970s, the century-old entrepôt of Lomé was the jewel of the region and the trend-setter in fashion, but its economy was in decline by the late 1970s (Heilbrunn 1997). By 2010, Togo—a sliver of land with thirty-five kilometers of coastline and some 550 kilometers of interior land and a population of four million—was one of the poorest countries in the region. In 2010 Togo ranked seventeenth lowest in per capita income of the world's 218 nations.[4]

Togo's economy relies heavily on an agricultural sector that employs 65 percent of the labor force and exports primarily coffee, cotton, and cacao. In addition, Togo is the major world producer and supplier of phosphate, a mineral used in making fertilizers. The 1974 nationalization of the Togolese phosphate mines and the subsequent phosphate boom contributed to the country's economic prosperity and relative stability. When the world market prices for phosphate quadrupled in 1974, Togo's terms of trade virtually doubled, and so did government revenues (Toporowski 1988, 18). With ambition fueled by record phosphate prices, the government set to realizing its long-harbored desire to establish Togo as "the Switzerland of West Africa" by developing banking, tourism, and other services.[5] In 1975, however, phosphate prices and volume slumped, and by 1977, the phosphate market collapsed (Heilbrunn 1997, 477). This led not only to economic deterioration but also political instability. Nonetheless, the government continued its expenditures, resorting to large-scale foreign borrowing on commercial terms to cover costs. While economic growth was initially boosted by vigorous investment, the activity was slow to show any returns. Instead, by the end of the 1970s, debt had grown to be a severe problem. Between 1975 and 1980, public and government guaranteed debt rose by a factor of six, reaching US$975 million, or 86 percent of Togo's gross domestic product (Toporowski 1988, 19).

With debt accumulating alarmingly, the government turned to the IMF, which made loans with the usual conditions, thereby forcing the government to cut back its expenditures by almost 20 percent in nominal terms but over 30 percent in real terms in 1979 (Toporowski 1988, 19). In 1983 and 1984, even more stringent financial "stabilization" plans were adopted. In return, the IMF provided two stand-by arrangements, and the World Bank negotiated structural adjustment programs in 1983 and 1985. As in many other African countries, the loans and the ensuing austerity measures made Togo's economic and social conditions worse (Akyeampong 2000, 204). Its draconic austerity program did not deliver promised financial achievements. Unable to make payments between 1979 and 1986, Togo had its external debt rescheduled six times (Toporowski 1988, 19). In the meantime, General Gnassingbe Eyadema (1967–2005) maintained his corrupt and oppressive regime and stayed in power until he died in office and his son Faure Gnassingbe took over.

The shifting economic realities of the country were compounded by Togo's reconfigured geopolitical position. While many West African countries had flirted with the Soviet Union during the Cold War era, Togo stood on the other side of this ideological divide. Because of General Eyadema's un-wavering support for the West, Western powers favored the country, and major donors made considerable contributions, representing 40 to 80 percent of real gross domestic income (Kohnert 2011, 4). Subsequently, however, the fall of the Berlin Wall diminished the geopolitical importance of Togo. In the absence of a Soviet threat, Western governments increasingly sup-ported multiparty movements in Togo and in the region. Such movements had spread rapidly on the African continent and promoted the opening of democratic spaces. Now, General Eyadema's political abuses would no longer be overlooked. After his rigged election in 1993 and the violence that broke out in the streets of Lomé in protest, most international donors stopped ex-ternal aid flows. The U.S. Agency for International Development (USAID), for example, which had funded multimillion dollar development projects in Togo, closed its Lomé office (Piot 2010, 30). Following bursts of street protest and political repression in 1991–1993 and 2000–2005, the World Bank ceased its projects in Togo.[6] Although France continued its relationship with the country, France dropped its aid package to Togo from 200 to 50 million francs per year in 1994) and devalued the currency of Togo (the CFA franc) by 50 percent (ibid.).

In this new world order, General Eyadema survived, but "the Togolese state nevertheless became a shadow of its former self" (Piot 2010, 3). The country's annual GDP growth rate, for example, consistently declined from 5 percent in 1985 to minus 15 percent in 1994; in the following decade, it was able to improve only by 1 percent in 2005 and close to 3 percent in 2010.[7] Similarly the per capita GDP dropped from 440 CFA francs in 1986 to 320 in 1994.[8] By 2005 the public debt of Togo, a quarter of which was domestic, reached 115 percent of GDP, and in 2006 its stock of foreign debt reached US$1.8 bil-lion (IMF 2007, 5). Real GDP in Togo, however, declined 1 percent per year from 1990 to 2007.[9] In September 2005 Togo was rated as the seventh most taxing nation of 155 worldwide with which to do business, according to the World Bank (Kohnert 2011, 23). The country's per capita GNI went down

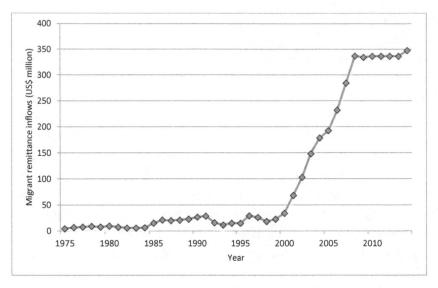

Figure 4.6: Trends of migrant remittance inflows ($ millions) to Togo. World Bank staff calculation based on data from IMF Balance of Payments Statistics database and data releases from Central Banks, national statistical agencies, and World Bank country desks (World Bank, n.d.).

from $430 in 1990 to $300 in 2000 (Oduro and Aryee 2003, 4). As poverty worsened in the 1990s both in depth and severity and political instability and violence escalated,[10] an increasing number of people turned to emigration.

By the mid-1990s, in the absence of government policies for addressing the unemployment problem and the continued limited space for political expression, one could say that the Togolese fashioned their own public policy: exit and remit support to families back home. While some crossed the border to other African countries to buy goods and bring them home for sale, others moved to sites on the continent, in Europe, or North America. Selling their labor power as displaced workers, they sent their wages back home. The economic value of this labor force displacement is captured in remittances. In 1975, annual remittances stood at just $5 million. By 2000, the figure had escalated to $34 million and by 2013 to a staggering US$337 million (see figure 4.6).[11] In 2009, indeed remittance inflow counted for more than 10 percent of Togo's GDP (World Bank 2011, 37). By the end of the last decade the country's economic center of gravity had shifted outside its national boundaries.

PLAYING THE "LOTTO"

It is in this context that educated Togolese like Aku decide to emigrate. In 2009, for example, 36 percent of emigrants from Togo were among the highest educated citizens, many of them holding college degrees, a trend that was clearly accelerated. Previously, from 1996 to 2004, the percentage of Togolese, aged twenty-five and older, who had advanced degrees and were living in Organization for Economic Co-operation and Development (OECD) countries had increased from 13 percent to only 16 percent.[12]

Traditionally, many Togolese traveled to other African countries and to Europe. For those who had a certain level of education, Europe was the ideal destination, especially France and Belgium, where their fluency in French would stand them in good stead. Immigration to the United States by Africans in general and by Togolese in particular began in the late 1980s. In the entire period from 1901 to 1960, African immigration averaged only 767 people per annum (or total of 45,306 for that period).[13] Over the past fifty years, however, the number of African immigrants in the United States has increased more than forty-fold, growing from 35,355 in 1960 to almost 1.5 million in 2009 (McCabe 2011). Almost half of these Africans have arrived since 2000.[14] "More have been coming here annually—about 50,000 legal—than in any of the peak years of the middle passage across the Atlantic," reported a New York Times article in 2005, and "more have migrated here from Africa since 1990 than in nearly the entire preceding two centuries" (Roberts 2005).

Although both women and men from a range of backgrounds have emigrated to the United States, the overall demographic consists of highly educated elite from West Africa (Terrazas 2009). The Migration Policy Institute reported that as of 2009, 41.7 percent of African-born adults aged twenty-five and older had a bachelor's degree or higher, compared to 28.1 percent of native-born adults and 26.8 percent of all other foreign-born adults (McCabe 2011).

Togolese immigrants in the United States are part of what Paul Zeleza (2009) refers to as "contemporary diasporas;" theirs, in particular, is a "structural adjustment diaspora" (36). These Togolese are refugees, traders, and professional elites who emigrated to the global North as a result of the worsening economic conditions and political conflicts in their country.[15] A Togolese Cargill worker who was an engineer back home told me he had a job and earned good money but the political situation drove him away. Another interviewee in Beardstown explained her reasons for leaving Togo in terms of corruption: "You need to have the right political connections; your education is not going to serve if you don't know the right person or family." Still others are under pressure to leave due to the possibility of persecution for their political views or activities. The ESL teacher in Beardstown, who has taught many freshly arrived West Africans in her classes, describes the political trauma that often preceded many of her students' arrival: "They come here for bare life" she said. She sees her students as being in political and economic exile, no matter what kind of visa brings them over.

The African immigrants find their way to the United States through a range of legal and semi-legal visa acquisition strategies. Lottery visas constitute a main avenue. In 1991 the U.S. Department of State established a quota system for immigration by underrepresented groups, referred to as the Diversity Visa (DV), and implemented it in African countries starting in 1995.[16] Through this visa category alone, about 185,900 Africans (an average annual number of 18,594) migrated to the United States between 1999 and 2008.[17] In Beardstown, for example, almost all Togolese arrive with work permission acquired through the DV and obtain legal residency.

The Togolese acquisition of DVs is a complex process, as Aku describes based on firsthand experience. To qualify, the applicant must have either a high school education or skills in specific fields listed by the U.S. Labor Department. Despite the large number of applications submitted each year, the lottery visa is open to a very narrow range of the population. Applicants who meet visa qualification requirements must maneuver complex submission policies and embassy interviews and be able to afford the cost of the visa application processes as well as the expense of travel. A range of factors influence the success of an applicant whose name is drawn through the lottery system, but as a general rule, those with higher education and skills of greater need in the United States have a better chance to pass the interview at the U.S. embassy. Despite their name, lottery visas are not conducted blind, but involve a screening to yield "the cream of the crop" among Togolese.

In his ethnographic research in Togo, Charles Piot (2010, 2013) documents the range of strategies Togolese use to improve their chance of winning the lottery and making the journey over with their family. Some hire specialized consultants to submit their DV application on an annual basis, help them navigate the U.S. embassy requirements, and even help them fake marriages with the DV winners. To increase their clients' odds in the lottery, a sophisticated industry has emerged to manipulate identities and documents as well as kinships—what Piot calls "kinship by other means" (2010, 79). For instance, in a case like that of Aku in which a single woman wins the DV, she would be considered by many aspiring visa applicants as extremely attractive because she could include a new addition to her family, and hence to her visa, by marriage or the birth of a child. In such a hypothetical case, a Togolese immigrant in Beardstown might cover the cost of travel for a Togolese DV winner like Aku if she were to carry a fake birth certificate or back-dated marriage documents. Aku would then become the vehicle of exit for the child or the spouse whom the Beardstown Togolese left behind in Togo. Production of such fake documents to prove marriage or child birth after an applicant submits a visa application is now an established industry. Marriages of convenience or, may I say, marriages of visa, are no longer a rarity or secretive strategy. In this process and over time since the inception of the DV in Togo, the visa applicants/winners have become more savvy in faking "visa kinships," while embassy staff have become better at detecting them (Piot 2013).

Membership in an imagined global community and having an imagined future therein are critical to the production of a globally mobile Togolese labor force. These can also take a bizarre turn. In his ethnography of Togolese visa aspirants in Lomé, Charles Piot (2010) describes a series of protests that started in April of 2008. Hundreds of Togolese whose lotto visas were denied took to the streets in red T-shirts representing their bleeding hearts; many formed a red-shirted crowd that took part in sit-ins in front of the U.S. embassy for ten months—despite several appearances by the U.S. ambassador to Togo on prime time national TV to explain the conditions of the visa and dispel false accusations and expectations. The events of 2008 remind us of the intensity with which Togolese, even prior to immigration, feel a sort of membership in an imagined global community and an imagined promise of a global future (Piot 2010). For many highly educated young men and women, the lottery visa is the vehicle to leave Togo for the United States, which, they imagine, will bring a better future for themselves and their children.

Many, however, do not have a clear idea what they are getting into when at their final embassy interview they list their place of destination as Beardstown. In a focus group I held in the Beardstown area in 2008, for example, a recent African arrival stated: "I thought here is the El Dorado." Another interviewee who had come to Beardstown to join a friend of his friend, who had assured him that he was guaranteed a full-time job in Beardstown, said: "When I arrived it was dark and I woke up in the morning, looked out the window and thought my friend has brought me to a wrong place. This could not be America. I don't know what I thought. I just knew this couldn't be it. There must be a mistake."

Those ending up in jobs below their education and skill level, like my interviewees in Beardstown, see their work at Cargill as a stepping stone to better opportunities. They need the jobs at Cargill to learn the language, pay their debts,[18] and bring their family over. The transition to a real profession for which they are educated, however, may take much longer than they think, or it may never happen. Their college degrees are not recognized in the U.S. academic system. They have to start from undergraduate education, for which they do not have funds, and scholarships are rare. Furthermore, Cargill workers do not have time off to travel to bigger cities in search of jobs, and in Beardstown there are no other employment options. The heaviest burden however, is that of the debt they incur in order to get the Diversity Visa.

BROKEN CHAINS AND WASTED BRAINS

The story of Kossi, whom I interviewed several times over the period of 2009–2011, is illustrative. He is a tall, well-built young man who holds a Master's degree from the University of Lomé, and was working at a reputable international nongovernmental organization with a monthly salary that amounted to $250 and was good by Togolese standards[19]—better than what public or private sector employees could expect. He told me he submitted an application for emigration to the United States through the Diversity Visa because his salary was not enough to live on or make a better future for his newborn child. When his name was drawn in the lottery in 2008, he decided to take the leap of faith that the future would be brighter in the United States.

He left his job in Lomé and headed for Beardstown in the hope that he could continue his education, ultimately get a PhD, land a job, and be able to reunite with the wife and child he left behind.

When I interviewed him two years after his arrival in Beardstown, he was still working at the plant. He shared some of his frustrations with me. His college degrees were not recognized by U.S. universities. He worked full time, sometimes six days a week, which made it hard to look for any other job, especially given Beardstown's distance from other urban centers. He explained that he needed the full-time job at the plant because he had to pay the debt he incurred to make the journey to the United States and to support the family he left behind, including contributing funds toward the education of his brothers. He told me he felt stuck in a cycle that was hard to break and that sometimes he wished he could return home. When I asked what stopped him, he referred to the shame of failure and returning empty-handed; moreover, he incurred too much financial and social debt to be able to return. But then he also said that he was not sure he would want to return, knowing that there would be no livelihood for him in Togo. So he preferred to stay despite the fact that his current employment was wasting a hard-earned education.

Kossi put me in touch with Mr. Kofi in Lomé, whom I interviewed during my time there. Mr. Kofi was the relative who received and distributed the remittances Kossi sent home. He was a charismatic person who commanded instant respect. His simply furnished house contained only a sofa chair, coffee table, and an old wooden buffet. He offered me a glass of water, and we started right into our conversation. I learned that Kossi's departure had been a big blow to him. On one hand, he was glad for Kossi and felt more secure for his own old age because of Kossi's remittances. On the other hand, he explained that Kossi's emigration "breaks the chain" of mentorship that has functioned for so long in his family. As a university-educated elder in his extended family, Mr. Kofi had followed a well-charted path, moving to Lomé from the family's ancestral village and being housed and looked after by an uncle. Once he completed his university education, he got a job and settled in Lomé and reciprocated the uncle's favor by hosting other youth in the family who were in situations similar to his. He noted that this was common practice among many families since small towns and rural areas do not offer adequate educational opportunities. Mr. Kofi has hosted and mentored many of his relatives through high school and at least seven through to college. He had thought Kossi was the next in line in his family to become the host and mentor of youth, including Kossi's two brothers, who moved from the village to Lomé and were at the time housed with Mr. Kofi. But with Kossi gone, the chain was broken. Referring to cycle of hosting and mentoring youth in his extended family Mr. Kofi laments, "I feel I am in an eternal cycle that won't end."

The departure of people like Kossi not only deprives his extended family of a valuable asset, but also dispossesses a society of its brilliant minds and educated members. Steven Sampson (2002), working in the Eastern European context of the Balkans and post-socialist global integration, refers to a somewhat similar process as "decapitation" whereby a whole elite educated group is lifted off from the body of society. In the Balkans, Sampson argues, NGOs and international multinational organizations decapitate the society in the sense that for the elite who work for foreign projects, "their entire world is externally focused" (310). While for many the ultimate strategy is emigration, for others who do not physically emigrate, their ideals, their imagination, and livelihoods are linked to the West or to foreign projects. In the Togolese context, it is indeed the U.S. lottery visa that facilitates this "decapitation" process.

When bright individuals like Kossi are siphoned out of local communities to perform manual jobs like those at the Beardstown plant, not only is the community robbed off its educated youth, but a tragic loss of resources is taking place and is aptly referred to as "brain waste" not "brain drain"(see Gwaradzimba and Shumba 2010; Zeleza 2009).[20] One highly educated and idealistic Togolese who had returned home from the United States to serve his country told me in an interview that the contemporary African brain waste was a modern version of slavery. "Our nation is forced to be an emigrant nation," he said. "The lotto visa has a purpose: to take from this land our brains and to take over there to work for their free slavery." After this play with words "free" and "slavery," he continued. "The result is a vicious cycle. People go to debt to go over there, then they have to work to pay debt and pay for needs of those left behind. . . . It is constant firefighting."

In the stories of Togolese immigrants, as in those from Mexico, we see the close connection between the dispossession of people's livelihoods and the displacement from their communities in search of a better alternative. For the Mexican farmers whose agricultural economy was assaulted under globalized, market-driven policies such as NAFTA, the privatization of *ejidos* paved the path for farmers to abandon or sell their land and move away in search of livelihood. In the Togolese scenario, the establishment of the U.S. Diversity Visa created a controlled exit path for the displacement of the educated population of working age, now dispossessed of a promising future under the neoliberal political economic order.

5 – DETROIT

"The First Third World City of the U.S."

HERE I TURN TO ANOTHER DISPLACED GROUP OF MIGRANTS WHO supply cheap labor to the Cargill plant in Beardstown: a small cohort of African American workers from Detroit, Michigan. Although they have not crossed any international borders, they have crossed many deep social and cultural borders to take jobs at Cargill. Like Togolese and Mexican workers, they arrive in Beardstown as a result of historically produced processes that dispossessed them in their community of origin.

We begin, however, in Beardstown in the aftermath of the 2007 Immigration and Customs Enforcement (ICE) raid, when Cargill focused on recruiting Puerto Ricans on the island, Cubans from the Little Havana area in Miami, and African Americans from Detroit—this last group a surprising choice, given Beardstown's sundown history. Because of this history, the few African Americans who worked at the Cargill plant before 2007 lived in neighboring towns and cities like Jacksonville and Springfield and commuted to work. Upon arrival, most of the new African American workers from Detroit soon opted for a similar commuting strategy, though a few took up residence in Beardstown. Despite their presence in town, I had difficulty securing an interview with any of them. On more than one occasion, other Cargill workers arranged interviews for me, only to have the interviewees fail to show up. Then came a serendipitous moment in a local fast food place in July 2012.

I was with a Beardstown friend ordering coffee when a black woman emerged from the back kitchen. She briefly said something to the people at the register about an order. I noticed from her accent that she was not a West African but an African American. Gathering my courage to ask the cashier if I could have a word with her, I was able to speak with her briefly and to explain my project—that I was writing a book about immigrants in Beardstown and wanted to include stories of African Americans as well. I left her with my business card and asked her if she would call me after work. Although she looked at me suspiciously, she kept my University of Illinois card and said "I'll see."

She called me that afternoon after her shift ended, and we met shortly thereafter in a quiet corner booth in the local Mexican restaurant. Angela was in her early fifties, a tall and fit woman, with hair cut very short. Until recently, she had lived all her life in Detroit where she had worked in restaurants and hospitals. Her grandmother, she told me, "used to pick cotton. . . . She worked and cleaned up the white people's houses, . . . and helped raise their kids." Her mother moved to Detroit from the South when Angela was little. Angela moved to Illinois in 2008 with her partner of four years, Alex. She had four sons from a previous relationship. Alex had three sons and a daughter. Seven of their children were of working age; all were employed at Cargill except for one son, who had moved to Beardstown couple of weeks prior to our conversation and was hopeful that his Cargill application would be accepted. Angela worked at the plant for about a year and her partner for about nine months, but they both had to quit for health reasons. He developed problems with his blood pressure and asthma, and at the time was seeking disability assistance. She had difficulties with her feet and gave up the backbreaking routine at Cargill for a fast food job.

Like most Mexicans and Togolese, Angela relied on social networks to guide her in the transition to her new life.

> First my aunt got here, and her daughter. . . . But before that it was some friends that stayed around the corner from me in Michigan. They came, when she came, she stayed with them. And then, when I came, I stayed with her, and then I moved with another friend of mine,

because her house was too crowded already with her family, and then that's when my partner came down and brought my youngest son. And then . . . [his] son came, and then we just got [his] other son down here, and then my other son came, and we are all here! And we all stayed in one house . . . maybe twelve people in one house, until everybody . . . got enough money to find their own places.

Coming from a big city, Angela and Alex did not stay long in Beardstown. Once they had secured jobs, they rented a place in a black neighborhood in Jacksonville, about thirty miles away. Before their lease was up, however, they had to pack and leave in a hurry. Some guys—black guys, she explained— "jumped my son real bad in Jacksonville, like thirty guys. . . . They jumped him because all the girls was hollering at him because he had just bought a new Charger, brand new blue Charger, and was working at Cargill. . . . We moved almost overnight in a hurry back to Beardstown and then we rented this place close to the other Detroiters."

Angela estimated that there were about eight families or perhaps fifty Detroiters living in Beardstown, almost all connected to each other by blood or by life-long friendships and neighborhood roots in Detroit. They all lived within walking distance of each other.

"Most weekend all our friends come over," she said. "We got a pool in the back. . . . We buy ribs and chicken or whatever and we put it on the grill. . . . We have a good time." Then she went on to say "but we [also] have a lot of problems with that a lot of times. . . . It's always somebody call the police and say that the music be loud, which it don't be loud." Nonetheless, Angela was glad she had found a safe place to live and was determined to make Beardstown her home:

In Detroit, I used to carry a gun. It was so rowdy. You go on the corner, you got people bumming, begging, trying to rob you, you know it was just, it was crazy. I carried a gun everywhere I went. [For that] I went to jail a couple of times. . . . But I love it down here. . . . It's peaceful, I don't mess with nobody, they don't mess with me . . . I can sleep with my doors unlocked. . . . I go in Family Video or Save A Lot, I leave my keys in the car and it's there when I come out. [The only] problem [is] with couple of people that might want to call us niggers or "go back home niggers" but I look over that. . . . [I tell my children] . . . as long as they don't spit on you or put their hands on you, they can say whatever they want to say. . . . I just act like I don't hear them . . . Cause we ain't back in slavery days no more and ain't nobody hanging no niggas cause we ain't letting them hang us today.

Two of Angela's sons who now work at Cargill finished high school in Beardstown, a point of pride for her:

School district is great down here. They really take the time, the schools, they call you when your kids don't come to school, if they miss a day, they call that same day, my son had missed school for a whole month in Detroit, and I didn't find out until a month, and then they come and want to send Protective Services to my house. Here? You miss one day, they calling you. They wanna know why your child wasn't in school. I love the school system. And the teachers, they just great. They send the progress reports home, let you know how your kids are doing in school. . . . I never want to go back to Detroit. . . . I never had this much peace in my life.

When I finished my interview with Angela, I thanked her and told her it would be great if I could talk to more African Americans about their experiences in Beardstown. Leaving the restaurant, I got about two miles down the road when she called. "If you still want to talk to more folks from Detroit," she said, "you need to come to my place right away. They want their stories to be in your book." Excited by the opportunity, I made a U-turn and drove to Angela's house. Angela was waiting for me in front of a neglected but once elegant two-story house. She took me in through the back door. The backyard had a large plastic pool and a grill, as she had told me. Some lawn chairs and water toys were scattered on the dried-up grass. Following her into the house, I met one of her sons and the wife of another; she was white and had an infant holding on to her tightly. They made way for me and directed me toward the living room. It was a steamy and sticky July evening, typical for central Illinois that time of the year. An air-conditioning window unit was working hard and loud to cool down the room. Angela's partner, Alex, was seated on the sofa. I told him that I had already learned some of their story from Angela and was looking forward to hearing him speak about his experience of their move to Beardstown. "Oh yes, you will hear a lot tonight. We all want our stories to be in your book," he said.

I explained a bit about who I was and what I was doing in Beardstown. Angela finally came to join us. She pointed to her cell phone in her hand, indicating a recent text or voice message, and told me that another couple, Carol and Aaron, would be there in a second.

Aaron and Carol arrived; the others joked about their dressy clothes, saying that's why it took them long to get there. Carol was wearing a wig to look presentable, and she was made-up for the occasion. Aaron was wearing a black beret with a red pin on the front. I couldn't tell what the pin symbolized. The couple pointed at me with a laugh. "We are going to be in her book, we must look good!" Aaron said. Even joking around, he had a powerful presence.

He sat down and began to tell his story. Now in his sixties, Aaron was a native of Detroit who raised his children, married, and remarried in his hometown. In his younger years he was a unionized auto worker. He worked a couple of years at Ford and another few at Chrysler. Like many others in Detroit, he saw jobs dry up, and when the automobile factories closed down or reduced production, decimating the backbone of the local economy, other industries began to fail or left the area, which henceforth became part of the rust belt.

Carol was at least a decade younger than Aaron, who had several adult children from previous relationships. Together, Carol and Aaron had five children, ages nine to twenty-five. Their oldest daughter moved to the area with her family and was working at the Cargill plant, while two of Aaron's sons were working at the Ford plant back in Detroit—jobs that were scarce and hard to get. When they mentioned these sons, they both nodded in admiration: "They have good jobs!" Carol had never worked in the manufacturing sector before she came to Beardstown. With Detroit shifting to jobs that serviced financial enterprises, Carol's opportunities were rather in the service jobs, like the one she had with a local hotel.

She told me how they ended up in Beardstown. It was a spring day in 2005 in Detroit, when Aaron saw a full-page advertisement in the *Detroit News* that read: "Relocate to Excel- Beardstown, IL." "Excel was what it [the plant] was called then," he explained to me. "I was like where is Beardstown? . . . But I grabbed the newspaper and showed it to Carol and told her I'm gonna go and get this interview here and see what they're talking about." Aaron had just lost his night shift Wal-Mart job, and Carol worked at a hotel. Struggling to find and hold on to jobs in Detroit, they were attracted by the advertisement, and the next day, Aaron went to Cargill's promotional meeting at a temporary hiring agency downtown. Cargill recruiters said that full-time jobs were available and that the company would pay for bus tickets, as well as providing one thousand dollars to help the new workers get started, with all advance payments to be deducted from pay checks later on. "[They also told us] how they were such a good family business, and they would relocate us, how we would have a nice, laid back life," said Aaron. "I come back home, and

I told her . . . we could relocate, and maybe do better, because in Michigan . . . everything was real bad with the recession, everything was closing down."

So they went through the company's routine of a urine test for drug use and a medical exam to make sure they were strong enough to endure the work. Once all was cleared, "we packed and moved."

Carol also told me that she took stacks of the applications back to her friends, neighbors, nieces, and nephews, all of whom were suffering from lack of jobs. I asked her why she did this and if she was paid. She said, "I did it because I felt we were blessed with a job here in Beardstown and I wanted others to have the opportunity." It was only later, in 2007, that the company sent out a worker originally from Detroit with the recruiters. She estimated that through word of mouth, company advertisements, and mobile recruiters, over one hundred people from Detroit were brought into the plant.

But not all the migrants continued to work at the plant nor did all stay in Beardstown. Some, explained Aaron, could not handle the job because it was too hard on their health: "They try to work you into the ground." Others quit because of chauvinist or racist attitudes on the floor. But when migrants from Detroit stopped working at the plant, Aaron said, they might still stay around, especially if they had moved to Beardstown as part of a group and others in their family continued to work at the plant. However, as Carol pointed out, some Detroiters found moving from a big city to a small town and from almost all-black inner city Detroit to almost all-white rural Illinois very difficult. They had to make many adjustments, ranging from coping with the lack of amenities and entertainment to dealing with the prevailing racist attitudes of people who still did not want African Americans living among them.

Carol and Aaron explained how racist attitudes pushed them first to try to live in Springfield: "Cause we're from Detroit. . . . It felt more like our city," said Aaron. "It felt more like, you could buy barbeque if you wanted to, she could go to the beauty shop, the mall was right up the street, the movies was right down the street, you know?" Carol continued, "The kids could go skating, or bowling or whatever, and it wasn't no problem. There was things to do. . . . Here there's nothing to do."

Angela's partner also lamented the limitations of small-town life. "The food was closing down at ten at night until McDonalds started staying open all night. You gotta go out of town to eat." Aaron added, "You start thinking if I gotta keep driving there for everything I might as well live there." Hence both couples had tried living outside Beardstown to be closer to bigger cities. But they moved back to Beardstown for different reasons. Whereas the attack on their son had prompted Angela and Alex to do so, for Carol and Aaron, the reasons were economic. They could not afford to live in Springfield after gas prices rose, Carol explained. "Gas was real bad that summer, as a matter of fact, it was the first time that we had started missing work. It seemed like every Wednesday night, we didn't have no gas. One time, we couldn't even get here on payday cause we didn't have no gas. . . . So [by summer of 2011] we decided we had to come back down here to Beardstown."

Away from their urban neighborhoods, lifestyle, and culture in Detroit, African Americans in Beardstown were "out of place" much like international migrant workers. The culture shock that they experienced in Beardstown, and the almost daily racist harassment by some residents and the police, were a constant reminder of the borders they had crossed to get to jobs in the rural Midwest.

This was not the first time that blacks who had been displaced to small midwestern towns had to negotiate rural-urban differences in conjunction with their racialized histories and experiences. Nearly a century and a half ago, some recently freed slaves migrating north saw small rural towns as in-between spaces or alternatives to big cities like Chicago and Detroit. During the Great Migration era of 1910–1930, rural towns in the Midwest served as places for cultural acclimatization of African Americans who were transitioning from a rural life to an urban one (Blocker 2008). Now perhaps the acclimatization is the other way around. It is inner-city African Americans who need to negotiate the transition from industrial cities to small towns in rural areas and adjust to their cultural practices and norms.

BEARDSTOWN BURNING

My conversations with Aaron, Carol, Angela, and Alex continued well into the night, with some of their adult children joining us and cans of beer opened and countless cigarettes lit up as they recounted their experiences. At one point, Aaron asked me, "Do you have a name for your book?" I made a facial gesture that indicated I had not decided. He said, "You should call it 'Beardstown Burning.'" He took a drag of his cigarette. "Do you want me to tell you like it really is? Or like you want it to, because I tell you the truth." I moved slightly forward to the edge of my seat at the sofa, looked at him and the others in the room and said, "Please tell me things as they are."

With this invitation everyone's stories began to unfold. Almost everyone offered an example of the difficulties they face in Beardstown. They told me how almost every day they "get the dirty looks," how "you walk down the street and they holler 'nigger' out their car door." Their children got ticketed by the police for jay-walking when there was no sidewalk and all the kids were walking on the road to school, but only the black children were ticketed. Other stories emerged: of the Wal-Mart checkout worker who slammed change on the counter top in order not to make contact with a black hand; of the police who broke into a Detroiters' wedding reception with the excuse that under-age people had been served alcohol; of enjoying barbeques, only to have the police come around, as if they had done something wrong.

The police were a particular target. "The police," said Aaron with all his passion, "is the worst in this town. They are like Nazis, they are Gestapo!" He pronounced this with emphasis. "See, they preying on us every week. . . . You see, you can't keep pushing people like us cause, see, we all from Detroit. . . . If you keep pushing, we gonna push back. And then this town will burn. You see what I'm sayin?" In other interviews with residents of Beardstown, many immigrants, especially, concurred with Aaron on problems with the police.

The Beardstown police force is an all-white, English-speaking force. The lack of diversity and the limited training officers receive have been repeated sources of complaint among immigrants and their white advocates in town. Given that the town's political institutions and officials, such as city hall and aldermen, are comprised completely of white, English-speaking U.S.-born citizens, the chief of police and the mayor are, to say the least, not sympathetic to immigrants. All advocacy falls on deaf ears.

The group at Angela and Alex's house explained that not all whites were racist. Indeed, they said that they all had good friends who were white, as well as Mexican and Puerto Rican. At the time of the interview, they were excited about attending the wedding of their close friends in town; the couple was Puerto Rican and white. Of their seven adult sons, Angela and Alex remarked, several were dating white girls. I had already met the white mother of their granddaughter. Another son had married a Mexican.

When asked about interracial dating, Alex replied, "Locals don't like that their white girls like our boys. . . . Every time they go to the bar, somebody call them a nigger." Their girlfriends get called "nigger lover," too. "They go from one bar, to another bar, to another bar. It ain't no matter where you at. . . . They fighting back this way, but see when the police come, they be the ones that get locked up." Carol continued, saying they were "just tired of the racists. . . . It's not only with the whites, it's also with the Mexicans. And we don't want nobody going to jail. Cause eventually somebody is gonna get hurt really bad. Somebody is gonna do some jail time."

A pregnant pause filled the room. I imagined that in their minds, they were seeing their children locked up, as I was at that moment. I asked if they could see themselves staying in Beardstown or if they wished to go back to Detroit. While their views of Beardstown differed from one another's, they agreed that returning to Detroit, with its lack of jobs, was not an option. "There is nothing for our youth but trouble," Aaron added. "When you're young and you're in the inner city Detroit, there's nothing you can do but pick up a gun or a bag of dope and stuff, and sell it." Carol continued, "You know in Detroit . . . if you a felon you can't even work for a temp service. . . . Everybody in Detroit is a felon. Everybody, maybe except for the elderly people. . . . It's crazy." Alex added, "In Detroit people get shot every day, ... they stabbing the teachers, they shooting the teachers. . . . See we're all minorities. We all came here for the same reason, which is Cargill. We came to get a job. To live better than where we were." Then Alex paused and said that, while he didn't want to return to Detroit, he was hopeful of moving to another town in the Midwest, somewhere a bit bigger, a bit more open, with a bit more African Americans. When I asked where would that be, he did not have an answer. He knew that he did not want to go back to Detroit and that he did not want to stay in Beardstown, but where the next stop might be depended on jobs.

DETROIT OF BOOM AND BUST

The decision of people like Aaron and Carol to relocate from Detroit to Beardstown did not start with the attractive advertisement Cargill placed in that local Michigan newspaper, or with the company's promotional recruitment session in downtown Detroit. The roots of their relocation lie in the complexities of the recent history of Detroit, a classic case of urban boom and

bust. In its golden era of the 1950s, Detroit's population was nearly two million. The city housed famed automobile, steel, machine tool, and other heavy
industrial facilities. From 1930 to 1960, Detroit was a bastion of employment
for African Americans escaping the Deep South and leaving behind jobless-
ness, poverty, and virulent racism. In the 1950s black men could realistically
expect secure industrial employment, but they faced a different world in the
decades that followed (Sugrue 1996).

Aaron experienced the end of this boom during his early days as an auto
worker, but in the "different world" that emerged during the 1960s, opportunities dried up for him and his contemporaries. During the last four decades
of the twentieth century, Detroit went through an extraordinary deindustrialization accelerated by the forces of globalization.[1] Factory after factory
was boarded up or sold for scrap. Whereas during World War II, Ford's leg-
endary River Rouge plant complex employed between ninety thousand and
one hundred thousand workers, in 2004 it employed six thousand (Freeman
2004). Overall, by 2003, the remaining auto plants employed 36,523 workers,
a reduction of 61 percent since 1960 (ibid.). By the end of the century, more
than a quarter of Detroit's population, which by then had fallen to below
a million, was living in poverty. Just three years later, unemployment had
reached 22.5 percent in the city, nearly double the average for the United
States (Borchert 2004, 106). Once the jewel of industrialization, Detroit became what a *New York Times* editorial called "The First Third World City of
the U.S." (Chafets 1990a).

In an era when global manufacturing capital was relocating to low-wage,
low-regulation sites, Detroit's strength turned out to be its fatal flaw. The
fixed capital of heavy industry was an albatross around the neck of the city.
Factories continued to close down, urban tax revenues plummeted, and
public services went into freefall. Detroit became an economic nightmare,
especially for its most vulnerable sector, the African American working class.

A vast body of literature has documented the demise of Detroit and processes leading to creation of the rust belt. The technological innovations
that created the assembly line and the means for mass production in the
auto-industry, dubbed "Fordism," laid the foundation for the flourishing
of Detroit. But these very same processes also made the decentralization
of production possible. Thus, by the 1950s, certain aspects of automobile
production were moved to locations where costs—whether in terms of the

fixed capital of land and the plant or the variable capital of the labor force—
were lower. Many industries moved entire plants or large portions of their
production. Some relocated to the suburbs where white workers had moved
to fulfill their dream of homeownership; others shifted to smaller southern
towns where labor was not only cheaper but also less organized. Later, some
industries outsourced sections of production to other countries with lower
cost of fixed and variable capital as well as fewer regulatory constraints. With
the combined processes of automation and decentralization, the number of
Detroit manufacturing workers plunged.

Diminishing jobs were aggravated by racial discrimination, which operated not only in the workplace, but also through spatial segregation (Feagin
2000; Thomas 2013). Spatial segregation in this period created a ring of white
suburbs around the black inner city. Excluded from the suburban dreams and
possibilities of the 1950s, blacks were concentrated in the downtown and
city proper. Patterns of segregation worsened in the 1970s and 1980s, when
white flight still would have happened if middle class blacks moved to the
suburbs (Sugrue 1996). With the few plants remaining in Detroit operating
at far below capacity, black youth were increasingly unemployed and concentrated in the ghettos of Detroit's city center. It is important to stress here that
blacks did not have residential mobility (ibid.). While whites moved to where
jobs relocated, blacks' movements were constrained by racial barriers. The
relocation of factories from the city to the suburbs and southern towns, and
later across the border, reduced economic opportunities for Detroit's blacks
more seriously than for whites.

Young black people like Aaron, who came of age in the late 1960s, became increasingly more alienated and more severely affected by the city's
shrinking job market in which they could not compete with whites for jobs.
Persistent discrimination in hiring, combined with spatial segregation, and
a shift to deindustrialization of the city made the prospect of employment
for blacks in metropolitan Detroit increasingly dim. Many gave up searching for jobs, and the number of adults wholly unattached to the urban
labor market or engaged in criminal activities steadily grew. With tenuous
connections to the labor market, and with spatial entrapment in inner city
neighborhoods, the black people effectively turned into a volatile surplus
population, which subsequently became a labor reserve for companies like
Cargill.

The Detroit of no jobs, poverty, and violence was the environment in which Angela carried a gun, fearing for her life if she walked the streets unarmed, in spite of being charged with carrying a concealed weapon. This was also the environment in which Aaron and Carol refused to raise their children, preferring racist harassment by police and others in Beardstown to life-threatening street violence and decaying schools in Detroit.

—

ACCUMULATION BY DISPLACEMENT

These stories of Detroiters, along with Mexican and Togolese migrants to Beardstown, call attention to processes of displacement within and across national borders. Contrary to a common approach in migration studies, which focuses on immigrants' experiences at the point of arrival in communities of destination such as Beardstown and naturalizes "immigration flows," I attempt to problematize the normalization of such movements. Through the stories of immigrants in the communities of origin and of destination, the conditions that produce both migration and a migrant labor force are exposed. The stories of the Fernández family, of Kossi, of Angela and Aaron help us understand that the arrival of a diverse work force in towns like Beardstown has not been incidental, innocently caused, or driven solely by the desires of immigrants for upward mobility—a narrative that presents global movement of people and families as natural and inevitable occurrences, just like flow of water determined by a law of physics: water flows to the lower plain; people move to places with higher likelihood of jobs. Naturalizing international immigration falsely assumes a certain innocence in the project of globalization and mobility of labor and capital. By contrast, I am concerned with the systematic creation of these movements. The creation of this internally or internationally displaced labor force has been in the making for decades through policies that devastate the sources of livelihood for disparate communities and cause the expulsion of people from what had been their lives and their being forced into places not of their choosing. These processes and policies turn migrants' communities of origin into a labor reservoir serving the interests of multinational corporations. Uprooted, displaced, and relocated, they are racialized as workers of color, forced into a subordinate social position, and subjected to low-wage, high-risk work, as well as being criminalized by their legal/illegal status. With limited employment mobility, workers of color are paid lower wages than whites for the same or similar work. "Like the enslaved African Americans on southern plantations," writes Joe Feagin, most racial and ethnic minority workers "have been super-exploited by white employers" (2002, 972). This super-exploitation, Feagin argues, is a source of "racial surplus value," which by no means accrues to the workers. On the contrary, it is extracted from them precisely due to hierarchical racialization of labor, as well as by criminalization of immigrant status.

The expansion of capitalism has its roots in the interconnected processes of dispossession and displacement that occur at multiple local, regional, and global spaces and scales. In the seventeenth, eighteenth, and nineteenth centuries, the creation of colonies by dispossessing indigenous peoples of their land and resources gave European capital a jump start for accumulation. Through colonial-era dispossessions, capital enjoyed free or extremely cheap labor. This early form of accumulation, which Marx called "primitive accumulation" or "the original sin of capital," was not a onetime occurrence, argues David Harvey (2005), building on Rosa Luxemburg's critique. The contemporary neoliberal policies of privatization continue this original sin through processes that dispossess people from their communal goods and assets—be it privatization of communal land or of municipal services. In such instances, capital accumulates by taking assets from the public. Harvey calls this "accumulation by dispossession." If the colonial dispossessions allowed capital to enjoy free displaced labor through enslavement, the contemporary processes of accumulation by dispossession allow global capital to enjoy displaced laborers as "wage slaves."

Conditions in Beardstown, Illinois, in Tejaro, Mexico, in Lomé, Togo, and in Detroit, Michigan, are intimately connected to each other and need to be understood relationally. Capitalism, for its continued accumulation, produces and relies on uneven developments at multiple scales: across urban spaces, across regions within the country, and among regions and countries across the globe. Uneven capitalist developments that produce local, urban, regional, and global inequalities also produce conditions for labor migration and displacement. Corporations rely on surplus labor produced in one location to recruit for their high-risk jobs in another location, each time at lower costs to the corporation. The stories of farmers like Mr. Fernández, urban educated youth like Kossi, ex-industrial workers like Aaron, or people like Angela who have barely held onto temporary employment as well-paying job opportunities became scarce, are all about the production of surplus labor found among people of color uprooted from their homes.

When Mr. Fernández, could no longer compete with prices of milk, corn, and other agricultural products imported under the unfair trade policies of NAFTA and the dismantling of CONASUPO, he had to put up his *ejido* for sale and send his sons Juan and Pedro to the United States as migrant workers in hope of the small remittances they might send back. "We have no other way to support ourselves," he told me. The policies that devastate the markets for local producers serve the interest of U.S.-based agribusinesses not only by expanding their opportunities in a global market, but also by producing a reservoir of cheap labor for their operations. Thus, when Juan and Pedro Fernández lost their rural livelihood to midwestern agriculture, they had no alternative but to sell their labor to Cargill—that is, to the very kind of midwestern multinational that foreclosed economic opportunities for people like Juan and Pedro in their home countries and used their labor for staking out and reaping profits from global markets.

While economic and political policies of global capitalism created a surplus population among Mexican youth thirsty for employment, the implementation of Diversity Visas opened a floodgate to supply potential labor force in another location. The educational and vocational terms of the visa accelerate the emigration of skilled and educated Togolese. In Togo, the process of accumulating global capital involves dispossessing a society of its educated citizens. It "decapitates" a community, a society, and a nation in the present, by removing the knowledge and skills of youth like Kossi, and in the future, by preventing them from assuming traditional mentorship roles, and it displaces them as legal subjects to supply labor for rural industrial jobs that American workers are reluctant to take.

Although the Detroit workers in Beardstown did not cross national borders, they, too, are displaced laborers, and they have had to negotiate historically, socially, and spatially constituted internal borders. Displacement of Detroit African Americans has also been in the making through decades of policies that facilitated uneven development at multiple scales to sustain global capitalism. In Detroit, deindustrialization led to the relocation of the city's previously well-paying unionized jobs across the country or the border, local policies spatially segregated the workforce into white suburbs and a black inner city, and neoliberal policies of "leaner meaner government"[2] drastically cut urban spending for education, transport, health care, and jobs. Thus, through "interconnected forces of race, residence, discrimination, and industrial decline" (Sugrue 1996, 271), Detroit's unemployed black workers effectively became an apartheid-style labor reservoir for capital to tap into at times of labor shortage and ever-diminishing wages—just as Cargill did at the Beardstown plant.

By studying migration at its inception points, in Michoacán, Togo, or Michigan, we can see how systematic policies and processes produce cheap and subordinate labor for capital. While processes which create a displaced migrant workforce are distinct in each context, there are parallels. In each instance, the heart of the process is the dispossession of people from viable local livelihoods and their conversion into a cheap labor supply for global markets, their transformation into workforce that is racialized, displaced, criminalized as illegal and has limited recourse to organizing. These diverse and displaced people arrive in Beardstown leaving rapidly diminishing assets and opportunities behind in their communities of origin. They have no real home to which to return.

PART III
OUTSOURCED LIVES

Figure 6.1: Walls of transnational families, Tejaro, Mexico. Photo by the author, 2008.

6 – GLOBAL RESTRUCTURING
OF SOCIAL REPRODUCTION

In 2012, a university reporter interviewed me for an article which quoted my argument that immigrants' families in distant locations contribute to the development of the heartland in places like Beardstown. This article was then picked up and reprinted by *My Journal Courier*, a newspaper in the Beardstown area with a large local readership (Rhodes 2012). The article grabbed the attention of different people for different reasons. Cargill's management, for one, objected to my description of how the company recruited immigrant laborers and offered bonuses to workers who helped the company by recruiting through their personal networks. Mike Martin, identifying himself as the plant's director of communications,[1] made a call to the journalist who wrote the piece protesting the report, and subsequently the statement was removed from the online version of the newspaper. This report also gained traction among some of local residents and workers at the Cargill plant, who posted their comments online in response to the article.

One reader, who described herself as a Cargill worker and Beardstown resident and signed in as "Ashley," reacted to the article with disgust and disbelief. She did not understand how, with all the money immigrants send home with their paychecks, I could still argue their communities of origin helped the development of Beardstown. She wrote to the journalist who reported on my findings:

> Your article starts out by telling how immigrants line up at the post office to send their money home then proceeds to tell us how this BENEFITS us in Beardstown? . . . Who are you kidding? They [immigrants] all live here and pay taxes, . . . they shop here, buy there [sic] food here but then the extra money is going back to support there [sic] country. Do you realize how many AMERICAN BORN citizens have moved from this town BECAUSE of all the immigrants? If there were more Americans and locals getting the jobs that they are giving to the African community, then that would be even MORE of a help to our economy and community, because NO money would be leaving the states. . . . . Personally I don't care if your [sic] illegal or not illegal, makes me furious that people want to support sending money out of this country. (Online comment, no longer available)

Another reader, who signed in as "ron6103," responded to her:

> The reason Cargill recruits internationally is because they cannot find enough local workers. If enough people that needed jobs in the community were willing to work at Cargill (at lower wages than they are perhaps used to, I do recognize that), then others would not need to be brought in. Secondly . . . it's THEIR money, not "OURS." They earned it working, and can do with it as they please. Get over this blatant racism. Immigrants aren't destroying this country, they're keeping it afloat. If not for the immigrant community at the Cargill plant, Beardstown would be shrinking like most other smaller Illinois communities. (Online comment, no longer available)

This exchange captures the diverging points of views expressed to me by many native residents whom I interviewed. Many agree with "ron6103" that without immigrants Cargill would not exist. And without Cargill, Beardstown would be just like the other towns in the area struggling with depopulation and economic decline. On the other hand, many like "Ashley" resent the amount of money that immigrant workers send home, seeing it as a siphoning of resources out of Beardstown. One interviewee I spoke to in Beardstown, a white female longtime resident in her fifties, described her observations of immigrants sending remittances home as follows:

> You can see it every day when you go to the post office. They are lined up to the door for money orders, and send money home. In fact one of the other guys . . . asked the gal at

the counter how much money do you think goes outta here, like to Mexico or Africa or wherever? And she said you wouldn't believe. And he said oh yeah I would. Well there they come here and work and don't spend their money here and that doesn't help us, there is something wrong with that picture.

It is fair to say that, no matter on which side of the immigration debate they fall, most commentators and interviewees recognize Beardstown is closely connected to other places around the world. But how is this connection created? What kinds of relationships connect Beardstown and other places in the world? And what range of resources flows across these places? The answers to these questions are not adequately understood.

Whether they are advocates or opponents of the immigrants' employment at the plant, most locals see the international connections through a single lens: other places send us workers, we send them remittances. This construction misses and hence makes invisible another flow of resources across immigrants' communities of origin and destination. Instead, the economic flow of resources is almost always conceived as a one-way street: resources are generated in Beardstown and sent away as remittances that support development and the livelihood of people and communities across the globe. Even the academic literature on immigration often fails to move beyond this model.

Although there is some debate about the kind of development and dependency created through the processes of international immigration,[2] the literature focuses predominantly on the flow of remittances from the global North to developing countries.[3] In this context, at issue is whether the economic resources sent home through remittances bring development and economic growth or social inequalities and dependencies to immigrants' communities of origin in the global South. Seldom, however, is a reverse development flow studied or suggested.[4] Rather, the dominant conceptual framework takes the global North as the center, the place from which power radiates to the periphery, and the global South as simply a recipient in this relationship (Mahler 1998). Accordingly, scholarly debate focuses mainly on assessing how immigrants' communities of origin in the global South are affected—positively or negatively—by the remittances sent home in what Gillian Hart (2006) critiques as an "impact model."

What these constructions of globalization and immigration leave out is the reverse flow of resources—in material and in kind, in exchange value and in use value—that contributes to the development of places like Beardstown in the U.S. heartland. The extent to which the communities of origin subsidize the livelihood of immigrant workers in communities of destination has received limited attention from researchers, policy makers, and popular media. The idea that it may be the "poor" communities of the global South—the very same poverty-stricken families and networks that immigrants leave behind—that might be contributing to the flourishing and development of towns like Beardstown is incomprehensible for most Illinois residents, including "Ashley," the online commentator cited above.

To engage with this commonplace discourse, we need to work through a series of related questions. First, is there, as these commentators suggest, only a one-way flow of resources between Beardstown and other communities across the world—namely, that of remittance immigrants send home? If not, what other resources flow in the other direction? Second, why should Cargill rely on an immigrant workforce? No one whom I interviewed suggested that the white local workforce was lazy or that the nature of meatpacking made it unfit for native-born populations. After all, the very same hard work had been done by local, predominantly white workers prior to the 1990s. Clearly, the issue comes down to whether the work is worth doing for the wages offered. So if this explains the reluctance of local populations to take the Cargill jobs, then why do these wages seem more viable for an international immigrant workforce than for native-born workers including African Americans?

Through the stories that follow in this chapter, I seek to answer the above questions by focusing on transnational practices, connections and imaginations that tie international immigrant workers to their communities of origin. I highlight how these connections involve not only remittance transfers, but also multidirectional flows of less visible resources, as well as the hopes, obligations, and imaginations of transnational immigrant workers.

FRAGMENTED HOUSEHOLDS AND OUTSOURCED CARE WORK: INVISIBLE SUBSIDIES TO CARGILL WAGES

Sena was one of the many Togolese Cargill workers with whom I spoke in Beardstown and Rushville. She and her husband, Dodji, were in their late forties. In Togo, Sena did occasional dress tailoring while Dodji trained as an agricultural engineer, had struggled to stay employed. When they won the lottery visa in 2002, she said, they headed out to Rushville and stayed with their Togolese friend who had told them about the Cargill jobs. After obtaining their social security cards and getting their first pay checks from Cargill, they moved to a place of their own around the corner. The couple had a seven year old son, George, born in Rushville, who spoke Ewe and French at home and English at school. Three other children were left behind in Togo because Sena and Dodji could not afford the travel expenses for the entire family. The couple was barely able to scrape up enough money from family, friends and other sources to pay for two travelers. They faced the heart-wrenching decision that many Togolese confronted when coming to Beardstown: to leave all or some children behind.[5] In their case, it was all three—sons Elipklim and Mawutor, at the time six and nine years old, respectively, and daughter Emefa, then fifteen—to be cared for by Sena's mother.

I visited Sena's family in 2010 when I traveled to Lomé. By then, the youngest was in his teenage years, and the older son had moved to Ghana in search of a job. "He was just desperate hoping there might be something for him to do, so he is gone to see what he can find," said his sister, Emefa. Twenty-three at the time, Emefa had her own family with a man named Djidonou who had three children living with him from a previous marriage. Together, they had a five-year-old daughter, and Emefa was pregnant with another. When I visited, the grandmother, Sena's mother, was very ill and lying on what seemed to be her death bed. Four of Djidonou's cousins and four of Emefa's cousins from the villages of Maritime, the state where Lomé is located, were also part of the household. Taking in cousins and youth from villages was quite common for Togolese families, who sought to help out school or job opportunities in the city. Emefa's seventeen-member household rented three shoddily constructed rooms in a larger structure consisting of other groups of rooms and shacks rented by several other families. Emefa's family's rooms were located at a corner at the end of a row of rooms, which gave them an additional semi-outdoor living space. This was where the grandmother slept and where several other household members would make their beds at night. The room where they received me was the main one of the three they rented. It was dark and windowless.

I was surprised to see how this young couple had taken an additional eight young boys into their household on top of the two Sena had left behind. Such arrangements do not emerge only as a result of transnational migration. Traditionally, raising children is not exclusively done by the immediate family. Charles Piot (2013) explains that kinship is not constructed merely through

blood relations but also through practices of care. Those who take in and raise
a young person, for example, consider the young person kin, independent of
blood relations. This cultural practice, combined with the uneven developments of rural-urban areas, means that youth from villages are often sent to
stay with family members or friends in the city in hopes that they will find
educational or employment opportunities. The fact that this is a typical arrangement does not make it any easier, especially for families like Emefa's,
who survive on minimal incomes.

Like thousands of other unemployed men and women in Lomé who did
home-based work as a *coiffeur* (hairdresser) or a tailor, Emefa was a hairdresser. The best that she and others like her could hope for was that from
the network of other poor and unemployed people around them, they could
earn the equivalent of one or two dollars a week. Her husband, Djidonou,
carried cargo at the Lomé port for about one thousand CFA francs ($2) in a
day. Port authorities also let him salvage discarded or unclaimed items from
the port with the intention of reselling them at some point. For example, in
the room where the family received me was a rusted mini-refrigerator, three
stereo systems and an oversized boom box in various states of disrepair, and
many other discarded items waiting for buyers.

With this insecure family income, they had to come up monthly with thirty
thousand CFA francs ($60) for housing and utilities and forty thousand CFA
francs ($80) for food, the most expensive item in a budget that their low in-
come could not cover. When I spoke with them, they were distressed because for
over a year, Sena had not been able to send the one to two thousand dollars that
she had sent regularly per year to help with food expenses and the boys' school
fees. Dodji had become ill and lost his job, and her wages went mainly to their
own living expenses, with only a small surplus for her mother's medication and
her son's schooling. As if to dispel any hint of complaint or suggestion of Sena's
lack of care, Emefa made sure to stress that Sena helped when she could: "We
pray that Sena's condition gets better, so our condition gets better here too."

At the end of the interview, Emefa stepped out of the room and then came
back with the help of two of the boys, bringing in bowls of *akume* (mashed
corn) and *fetri de see* (okra stew), which they had prepared in our honor. I
was embarrassed by their generosity. They insisted that they would not let
Aku and me leave without feeding us. Having just gone over their household
budget, I knew their dire situation. Yet again I was reminded of what life has

taught me: the less people have, the more they give. I knew that there was not enough for all seventeen household members and was uncomfortable consuming what was for them a precious commodity. Aku, however, whispered to me that according to good Ewe manners, we needed to finish all the food on our plates or else risk insulting the family by suggesting that we did not like what they had served us. As we parted, repeatedly thanking them for their hospitality, they asked if it was now the time for them to bring out their suitcases. Emefa said with a smile on her face, "We have them packed and are ready. We thought Sena sent you after us to take us with to the United States." I was not completely sure whether the statement was made in jest or if those bags really were packed. I never found out.

That summer when I returned home, I took the pictures and stories of my visit with her family to Sena in Rushville. Aku, who by then had come to the United States and continued to help me with the project, came with me. Sena had made an impressive spread of food to receive us and was thrilled to see us, for, as we say in Farsi, "We carried the scent of her sons and daughter" to her. Sena started looking through the photos I had brought one by one. When she got to the close-up portrait of her youngest, now with a suggestion of facial hair above his lips, she turned her head away, so that we would not see her agony. I gazed at the floor and waited for her to guide the next moment. She pulled herself together and pointed at the food on the coffee table. "Why don't you help yourselves?" she said.

Once the emotions had subsided, I asked Sena if she expected to see her children one day. She explained she had not gone to visit them and that instead she was saving to pay for them to come to her when their paperwork was in order. In principle, she should have been able to take care of the visas for her children earlier by becoming a citizen as soon as she qualified. She could have filed for family reunion as soon as she was naturalized. But in practice, most immigrants like her were unable to get through these procedures so quickly. Lack of information was one reason. As Sena put it, "We don't know the language, we don't know who to ask, where to go. So it all takes us longer." The other was financial. To procure visas for family members, Sena had to come up with the money needed to process all papers and cover medical exams, flights, and travel expenses. Meanwhile, her husband had been out of work for over a year, and she had her own debt to pay back, plus she tried to send sustenance for the family. They had spent almost six million CFA francs ($11,000) for the two of them to come to the United States, raising the money by selling her land and borrowing from family, friends, and a lender who demanded 100 percent interest, and while they had repaid almost all debts, their living was still precarious. Sena shook her head: "You see I have to work, have to keep going, I must." I asked if her health was ok. She responded, "No! I have pain everywhere," then repeated with emphasis, "ev-reeee-where, but must be going to work, how could I not?"

In Beardstown, I interviewed many Togolese families who faced the same pressures as Sena, having also left behind members of their nuclear family. In Togo, I spoke with more families who took care of Cargill workers' children and other relatives. Marie was another one of the latter. A single mother of a two-year-old, she had also been taking care of her brother's baby since he and his wife left for Beardstown. When I visited Marie almost a year after their emigration, she was breast-feeding her brother's baby while talking with me. Though he and his wife were sending her what amounted to $30 monthly, Marie felt deeply how hard it had been for them to leave their newborn behind. "They wanted to be able to both work as soon as they got there so that they could provide for the child . . . and pay for money they owe. If they took the baby, that would have been difficult. . . . It was hard. It is hard."

This strategy of restructuring households and performing care work transnationally plays an important role in the ability of an immigrant workforce to raise a family on Cargill wages. One might say that in these scenarios, the care work for Togolese workers at Cargill is outsourced to their communities of origin, where the work is performed at a much lower cost. By raising Cargill workers' children, Emefa, Djidonou, and Marie were in effect subsidizing Cargill wages and by extension the Beardstown economy. Indeed, there is an army of people in the immigrants' communities of origin, with women at the center, doing the care work for Cargill's Togolese workers. But their contribution is invisible to the public and seldom noted in remittance-focused discourse of immigration.

GLOBAL CRIB AND INFIRMARY: RE-SPATIALIZING LIFE-CYCLE STAGES

To cover their families' expenses, groups of immigrants use different strategies. Among Mexicans workers, the likelihood of having their nuclear family with them is greater than among West Africans. Of the Mexicans sampled in Beardstown, 84 percent of those who were parents had all their children with them, as opposed to 33 percent of West Africans.[6] Nonetheless, Mexican workers have also restructured and outsourced aspects of their care work to their communities of origin.

I return here to 2008 and my visit to Numaran with Lupita. We had been walking around the plaza for a few minutes that morning when we came across a group of older men talking under the generous shade of a ficus tree (see figure 6.2). When I told Lupita that I was wondering whether some of them had worked in the United States, she set off to find out. "*Señores! Perdonen me!*" she said as she approached. Being young and attractive probably helped Lupita get their attention, and when she explained what I was doing, they happily agreed to answer my questions.

Of the ten men in the group, nine raised their hands when I asked if any had worked "el Norte." The one who had not, they said, was a *cacique,* the name for a member of the agrarian elite who are known for political corruption; their intimation was that a *cacique* did not need to emigrate to earn a living.

The men who had worked in the Unites States told me that they had done so for most of their adult lives but had had to return to Michoacán because they could no longer find jobs in the competitive U.S. labor market. In addition, one man's hand had a tremor, what seemed to be symptoms of early Parkinson's disease; another explained that he hurt his back in construction work and could no longer do what he used to do. For the most part, they all agreed, they were no longer competitive in the day laborers' market. "No one would pick us up," one said. When I asked if any of them planned to move back to the United States, one smiled and said, "*Ya no nos querían*" ("they wouldn't want us anymore"). He was standing next to a young boy who was perhaps eleven or twelve years old. He placed his hand on the boys' shoulder and said, "It is now his turn."

Another man pointed at the youth and said, "He will also go to el Norte and come back like us when he is old. Give him another two or three years, he will be gone." I invited the man who made this statement to tell me a bit more. He referred to the high school in Morelia, capital of the state, and explained: "High school is the training ground for border crossing. That is where they learn where to cross, where not to; which coyotes to trust or not to; how much to pay; how to pay. . . . They seldom finish the *segundaria* [high

Figure 6.2: Men at the Numaran plaza, Mexico. Photo by the author, 2008.

school], and why should they if there is no work for them? . . . Long before that they are gone to the other side."

That day in Numaran, as I walked away from this conversation, it was hard to avoid thinking of their reality as one in which care work in the course of the life cycle is fragmented, outsourced to distanced communities that function as these workers' "global cribs and infirmaries." While the care work required in the beginning and the end of the life cycle is performed in Mexico, they spend the most productive of their laboring years in the United States. As the men pointed out regarding the young boy, he was raised and cared for in Mexico until he reached a point that he was strong enough to cross the border. But then, I thought to myself, like the other men at the plaza, when he is discarded by the U.S. labor market he will be back in Michoacán—perhaps under the same tree at the plaza where the older fellows had gathered that day. He too, I thought, would most likely bring back, his injured, old, tired, or slowed body to be cared for in Michoacán. I refer to this process as "respatializing life-cycle stages."

BEYOND ECONOMIC RATIONALITIES OF TRANSNATIONAL
LIVES: PRIDE, GUILT, AND THE RITE OF PASSAGE

These stories uncover the invisible transnational resources involved in the social reproduction of the Cargill workforce. Individuals and collectives in Togo and Mexico temporally and spatially reorganize care work activities to make Cargill wages viable. Immigrants who leave their children behind in the care of relatives and spouses—or return home to their relatives and families when they are old or injured—outsource the responsibility for care work for the segments of their life cycle that can be considered periods of "down time." This means they perform the care work at one stage or another for one member or another elsewhere, at a site where that care work can be performed at lower or no cost. I call this the "global restructuring of social reproduction." Just as the restructuring of production involves contracting out certain phases and aspects of production to cut costs, so in the realm of social reproduction, the performance of certain aspects and phases of care work by families and institutions in the immigrants' home countries cuts costs to Cargill and reduces its burden to ensure that wages cover the costs of social reproduction. In this scenario, in addition to public and nonprofit institutions, a network of friends, neighbors, and family members invest their free or minimal-cost care work—namely childcare at one end of the life spectrum, and elder care at the other. This effectively subsidizes the wage Cargill pays for its high-risk, low-wage meatpacking jobs.

But the global restructuring of social reproduction does not rely *only* on the ability to transfer costs by "outsourcing" care to individuals and families in workers' home communities. Nor should we reduce the transnational relations of care work to its economic utility. Social reproduction involves far more than maintaining, feeding, and housing oneself and one's family. In addition, it includes the ability to sustain a sense of self and dignity, to maintain a cultural identity and meaning—in literal terms, to keep body and soul together. A complex set of imaginations and expectations, affect, and obligations tie the lives of transnational immigrant workers to their families and communities of origin abroad.[7] These ties also play a role in how workers like Sena, Kossi, and Juan and Pedro Fernández, assess the worth of their wages—a worth that cannot be reduced to its monetary value.

While walking through the empty neighborhood and lamenting the loss of her neighbors, Señora Fernández helped me recognize not only the kind of obligation she felt toward the neighbors who left, but also the kind of obligations that made many of her neighbors, in particular their youth, embark on the journey north. For many young men and women who have to witness their families struggling to get by, she explained, taking the risk to cross the border and provide for one's family has become a rite of passage. For boys, it serves to prove their manhood and masculinity; for girls, it serves to prove their commitment to family. To illustrate, Señora Fernández invited me to imagine "a male or female youth who sees the neighbor next door has food on the table, not them, and knows it is because one or more of their children took the risk to cross the border." They feel inadequate, almost betraying their families, and a sense of shame, she explained, if they do not risk crossing the border for improvement of their family's lives.

I had heard similar sentiments about guilt, shame, and pride associated with emigration and work abroad when I spoke with Togolese immigrants. Seeing themselves through the eyes of those in communities of origin, they stay in meatpacking jobs at least for a few years despite their education, legal status and upward aspirations. Kossi is one example. I interviewed him in a hot and humid summer day at his home in Beardstown. I recall he was complaining that the small apartment's window air-conditioning unit was not working and that he had not been able to sleep the night before. He had informed the landlord but to no avail. While he was wiping beads of sweat from his forehead, his cell phone emitted ring-tone signals several times in what he explained was a routine practice of "flashing," in which the caller wants the cell phone to register his or her number and hangs up before the phone is answered and the caller is charged. Kossi said he would return the calls later that day, but already knew what they would be about—"asking for contributions and help."

During that interview, Kossi talked about a mixture of guilt and responsibility that made him respond to those calls. Being able to assist made him feel good about himself, but the pressure and need, he explained, were just too much. Sometimes, he confided, he regretted having left his professional position in Lomé to come to the United States. But he did not see going back as an option, not only because of the enormous debt he had incurred but also because of cultural expectations. As an Ewe, Kossi, upon his return, would need to build a home in his village of origin and perform ceremonies for his ancestors who passed away while he had been gone. This, along with a further series of cultural rituals, would be quite costly.[8] Regardless, fulfilling cultural expectations were important to his sense of pride and honor.

Kossi detailed the fear of giving in to the temptation to return home, a recurrent thought for a man who had never done manual labor and found the work at the plant excruciating. Should he succumb, he knew he would bring shame to his family and be ridiculed by all—"by the same ones who flash me and flash me and always ask me for contributions for this and for that," he explained to me, "the same ones will make fun of me if I go back without enough money." When I spoke to Kossi's uncle in Togo, he confirmed this assertion, noting the shame that would result for the family if the immigrant was to come back without enough money to perform the acts of a home-coming king. In effect, the expectation to be a good Togolese Ewe created additional pressures to keep Kossi in his job far away at the Beardstown plant.

Hence, the contradictory feelings of shame and guilt on the one hand, and pride and honor on the other, constitute an emotional nexus that drives the migrant worker to endure the daily grind of high-risk, low-pay jobs. Among Mexican immigrants in Beardstown, the ability to fund a celebration of a daughter's sweet fifteen, or *quinceañera,* was such a force, as was the ability to contribute to the celebration of a proper *quinceañera* back home. Both created an additional incentive to continue working to satisfy cultural norms and expectations.[9] For these workers, taking the risk to migrate and do hazardous work at the plant was not only a means to provide school fees for their siblings or loved ones, or security for their aging and ailing relatives, but also a strat-egy for reclaiming their honor and dignity. While in part expressed through performance of obligations toward individuals, this identity and pride is also claimed through their ability to perform cultural rituals and obligations. Thus, for example, in Tejaro, thanks to U.S.-based Tejarans, including those in Beardstown, the celebration of Tejaro's *fiestas patronales* had extended from a two-day-long celebration to three days, and when I was visiting, there was speculation for a future fourth day (see figure 6.3). Beardstown immigrants took great pride in being able not only to sustain existing cultural traditions but also to leave their own unique mark on events in their community of origin.

Figure 6.3: Announcing *Fiestas Patronales* to be held in Tejaro,
Mexico. Photo by the author, 2008.

ON FAMILY OBLIGATIONS AND DEBT

In understanding what motivates Sena, Kossi, and the Fernández sons to take
the jobs that many of their U.S. born counterparts have walked away from
over the past three decades, we need to pay attention not only to what real or
perceived conditions stretch their wages in a material and nonmaterial sense,
but also what conditions constrain their mobility. Among Mexican workers, employment choices and job mobility are limited due to a legal system
that criminalize them as illegal aliens and poses threats of physical violence,
detention, and incarceration. West African interviewees, whose legal status

and education provide a certain freedom, are constrained by the less tangible chains of debt and family obligations, as well as being exacerbated by transnational fragmentation of their households, which further lock West Africans into dependencies and obligations.

I had a most illuminating conversation in 2007 with Mr. Yao, at his home in Rushville. A shy, soft spoken, tall man in his thirties, Mr. Yao was a mechanical engineer back in Togo and now was cutting meat. "I worked and earned good money," he said, "but it was not paying enough to care for the many around me. . . . [Moreover] the political situation is not good," he added. "I was not in politics and stayed away from politics, but still the country is not safe because of political troubles, because of uncertainty with government members." So he played the "lotto" three times, winning on his third attempt, and managed to pull together the resources to travel to the United States. He left with his wife in January of 2004, going first to Maryland, where he knew a Togolese, and worked there for seven dollars per hour in a restaurant. A friend who was a cab driver in Chicago had a Togolese friend in Rushville, who had told him that Cargill paid eleven dollars per hour and needed workers. "He told me about it and said, 'You can pay your debt faster.'" So Yao and his wife moved to Illinois, stayed in Rushville with this friend of the Chicago friend for a few months, and then got their own place once they passed the plant's three-month probationary period.

I asked him, "So did you pay faster?" My question clearly struck a strong chord with him. He was suddenly quite animated and almost sprung out of his seat at the kitchen table. He fetched two shoe boxes. One was filled with neatly organized receipts. He grabbed one bunch of the receipts and a piece of paper that was in the box and said, "See this. Just this weekend we sat down and went through our receipts to calculate how much we have sent home." Clearly, he was excited about the opportunity to share this information with me. I was a witness to something quite important to him. The receipts were for money orders for each payment that he had wired home. "We still have to calculate from January 2006 till now. But from May of 2004 to January of 2006 my wife and I sent a total of seventeen thousand dollars home!" I quickly calculated: "That is about a thousand dollars a month over seventeen months," I said. "You are right!" He responded "Every day they call, because they need money to survive. In Africa we live together." As I launched into multiple related questions about debt, family obligation, purpose, why, and how, he relieved me by going to the heart of the matter. "We are a large family, many things go wrong. Different things are needed. We had some money but we also borrowed money. Some of it we had to pay quickly to avoid interest, some of it was borrowed from family who were good to us to give us what they had." Then he went to the other shoe box, which was not neatly packed. These were the more current receipts and they had yet not gone through them. He grabbed the top receipt accompanied by a handwritten note. "For example," he said,

> the money I sent last week was fifty thousand CFA francs [approximately $100] to my mother: . . . you know is my job to do it, I pay for health, food, everything for her. Another fifty thousand CFA francs was to my older sister: she lives with her husband and children. Her husband works but money is not enough. I also paid thirty thousand CFA francs [about $60] to my younger brother: he got sick, this money I sent was for health care and hospital bill. Then last I paid eighteen thousand CFA francs [about $35] for school fees of my other younger brother. Last week alone I sent home 148,000 CFA francs [or $300]. By my living here I send money and it is a bit easier for them but not enough because the same time I sent this for four people I received three other calls—another brother his wife got sick and her son who has to go to high school. Another call from a friend again who got sick for hospital bills. Third person was a friend he lost his job so I have to support. He helped me when I needed help.

In trying to better understand his situation, I wondered if like some of the West Africans I had spoken to he and his wife had polygamous fathers and hence a larger number of siblings and half-siblings to look after. Sena, for example, had told me that her husband's father had twelve wives and fifty-one children. Her husband's father was a state nurse. "He traveled to villages and had wives in many villages. . . . Some gave birth to six, some to eight, some to one or two kids." But in the case of Mr. Yao and his wife, I learned that there were no multiple wives or marriages involved. Mr. Yao had two sisters and four brothers and his wife had two brothers and three sisters—a large family by U.S. standards but not exceptionally large for Togolese. He and his wife took turns paying for their families.

In further conversation with Yao, I learned the importance of his observation: feeling obliged to support a friend because the friend had helped him. Relatives and friends, who emptied their small jars of savings to help a lottery visa winner go overseas, wove fabrics of responsibility and expectations that obliged the immigrant to return the favor—a reciprocity that was a condition of life and gave meaning to one's actions.

While transnational families subsidize Cargill wages through their free or underpaid care work, those who are immigrants bring with them familial obligations, financial and emotional weights that inhibit job mobility. As one interviewee explained, he wanted to retrain himself and move on to better jobs, but the job at Cargill was exhausting. For months in a row he would work six days a week, leaving him no time to take classes or look for any other work, especially since Beardstown was not close to big cities. He always needed to take time off from his current work to look for other work in big cities and every hour off the clock cut into his capacity to carry out familial responsibilities. Hence, despite their legal status and education level, familial obligations and debts tie West African workers to their meatpacking jobs in Beardstown.[10]

IMAGINATION OF AN "ELSEWHERE"

In addition to the sense of pride, guilt, and cultural identity, an important force in the dynamics of transnational immigration is imagination of an "elsewhere"—a place where one could retire or retreat, where risk could be transferred or averted. Immigrants decide to migrate for more than simply survival or selling their labor power. As discussed above, they also take into account the promises of migration in social and cultural terms—the respect they might receive by leaving or the shame they might be subject to by returning; and the ability to perform cultural rituals. How a worker might perceive the viability of a wage is also influenced by the imagination of a promised elsewhere, a place to go to in times of difficulty, a place where one can go and be set for life, a place that promises a better future and hence provides an incentive to endure the risks of a meatpacking job for Cargill.

Below, I will discuss the stories of Bruna, the Garcias and Magnolia as a way to unpack the complexities of the "elsewhere" in the migrants' lives.[11]

Bruna is one of the women whom I met in Michoacán's informal market with Lupita in 2008. After working at the Beardstown plant, she moved back to Michoacán with moderate savings when her body started to pay the toll for the physically demanding job. She had become just too slow for the work on the line. She expected that her savings would set her up in a long-term business venture. The reality was she felt lucky to make it back with just enough to cover the smallest of capital outlays—a rack of clothes for resale. She explained that she traveled to the Texas border to buy the clothing (mostly Chinese), and then sold the items at the local market. I asked her if she earned well. She shrugged and made a hand gesture of "more or less" accompanying a prolonged "ok."

While Bruna's savings from Cargill work provided her with "a way out," others who managed to compile more savings still experienced difficulties. The story of the Garcias is a case in point. I interviewed this family in Beardstown and in Michoacán in 2008. The extended family of fourteen had gradually moved to Beardstown over the course of five to eight years and almost all of them were employed at the Cargill plant. After twelve years there, the parents had returned home to Michoacán three months prior to my visit in 2008 to retire and enjoy the fruits of their labor. With the money they had saved, they had built their house and contributed to the municipality's paving of the road that passed in front. During all these years a neighbor had looked after their house. Now they were able to come back to their home— what they had dreamed of all along. While they remained in Beardstown, each of their children had also managed to buy a piece of land close to them. "This was the dream that kept me going all these years," said Mrs. Garcia. But with their children and grandchildren in Beardstown, Mrs. Garcia and her husband were ambivalent about staying in Tejaro. "We are thinking we might need to go back," she said, referring to the children and grandchildren she had left behind in Beardstown. "You see we left them away from us, from their town . . . now we are here and we are alone. I am telling my husband, what have we done badly? Why we had to take them to a country that is not ours and left them all there?"

While the Garcias were busy working in Beardstown to make their dream come true back home in Tejaro, they were also making a home in Beardstown and developing "roots" there; their grandchildren were in Beardstown. Without the little ones, Tejaro was not the home it used to be or the home they had dreamed of.

The complexity of this imagined "elsewhere" are also illustrated by the case of Magnolia, a former Cargill worker whom I interviewed in Michoacán in 2008. After five years of work in the deboning section of the plant, Magnolia went back to Mexico in 2006 with a ten-thousand-dollar settlement for an on-the-job shoulder injury. I sat with her in the empty beauty salon she had started with her father-in-law. Business was slow, so we were able to spend a couple of hours talking. At least twice, she got tears in her eyes: "I kind of don't believe that this was my life" she said. She talked about the harsh experience of arriving with her children and the search for housing. After several months of sharing a house with an unsavory character and living in rentals in terrible condition, they found a better house to rent. After a year, the owner, a white man, offered it to them at a discounted price, and they bought it. Every year after that, the man would send them a Christmas card telling them how happy he was to have sold his family house to them because they took such good care of it. In these reminiscences, she was recalling the good and bad of the early days in Beardstown. Then, she mentioned her injury and talked about how things turned out differently from what she had imagined.

After the settlement, she had imagined she would move back home to Mexico and have a comfortable life with her settlement payment. She was not alone in imagining "elsewhere" where the impact of an injury on life could be minimized. "Other fellow workers were 'envious' of me," she explained. Some told her, " 'Oh I wish I was injured,' or 'oh don't you wish you were injured in both shoulders then you could return with double the amount.' " In hindsight she laughed at the envy of her coworkers and perhaps at her younger self. She used the settlement money to help finance buying a truck, which was stolen a month after she arrived in town. The rest of the money she invested in a hair styling business with her father-in-law. But that money was also wasted. With the town being economically distressed, business was slow and not paying them a livelihood—so much for her imagined comfortable future.

I had a similar conversation with a young man in his twenties who served me as a waiter in a nearby three-star hotel in Numaran. As I was one of the few guests at the hotel, he had time to tell me his story of migration and of the power of imagination and hope. "We'll take the risk to cross. It is simple, I earn one dollar an hour; that is eight dollars a day. If I cross the border I'll get that [$8] for every hour. So I'll take the risk and if I make it, I work dangerous and difficult jobs. I don't care, I know [if I make it] I'll come back and will be set for the rest of my life." The fact that youth like this waiter imagined a bright future following emigration north does not necessarily mean it will be realized. When he found I was interested in what he had to tell me about his life, the very same young man confided that he had worked in the United States for almost five years, had saved money, and had come back to open a seafood restaurant, cooking having been a skill he had learned through his work in the United States. But the business did not go well, and he closed the restaurant, having basically lost all his savings, and was once again waiting on tables at a dollar an hour.

The promise of the "elsewhere" is fraught with risks. While sometimes dreams and an imagined "good life after migration" come true, more often than not that vision vanishes into a cloud of disappointment. The trigger could be the theft of a truck as in Magnolia's case, a bad investment, or simply an economic downturn that depresses the viability of all business ventures. The Garcias might end up staying in Tejaro through their old age, like the men at the plaza, or return to Beardstown; the waiter may have to sneak across the border to chase his elsewhere again. Nevertheless, there is much to be said for the real or imagined elsewhere as retirement haven—a place to be cared for if things go badly or in the event of good fortune a site where a migrant can "be set for life." The imagination can be a powerful force in making a wage untenable for one worker but acceptable for another.

WAGES THAT STRETCH JUST A BIT FARTHER

The stories above show how transnational families of migrant workers in effect subsidized Cargill wages by off-shoring care work, respatializing their life-cycle stages, and imagining a promising elsewhere. Workers assess the worth of their wages not only in monetary terms but also through a complex set of real or perceived pressures and pleasures—familial obligation, debt, shame, pride, honor, and cultural identity. How do these forces and considerations play out in discerning the viability of wages for workers without transnational families, imaginations and aspirations, be it white locals like Dave, whom we met in chapter 1, or the displaced African Americans from Detroit, like Aaron, Carol, and Alex, whom we met in chapter 5?

To workers without real or imagined transnational resources, the wages of Cargill shrink considerably. Those who are native born are not able to rely on Mexican or Togolese workers' "internationalization strategies" (Fudge 2010, 5). They are not able to leave their child behind or send their sick relative to a place with a huge cost differential for cheap care. Nor do they enjoy the imagination of the elsewhere where their savings can set them up for life or earn them social respect and honor for their ability to contribute to marriages, funerals, or other important rituals. For white native-born workers like Dave, the former

Oscar Mayer and Cargill meatpacker, there is no transnational family and no imagined elsewhere. But, in comparison to minorities and immigrants, he had a greater chance to move to a better job—which he did—or change his line of work. Labor statistics in table 1.1 that shows higher (almost double) concentration of minorities in slaughtering jobs compared to all manufacturing jobs, may attest to this.[12] Dave reflected on his circumstances after Cargill bought the plant and he was being pushed out by younger laborers. He recognized that he had options when things got tough, explaining that "I left Excel [both because I was] unhappy and because there was an opportunity. [They] demoted me to a supervisor and took part or a lot of my pay away, I'm talking ten thousand dollars' worth of pay, and had me train this guy. It was pretty unsettling. Especially what I thought I'd given to the company. . . . I tried to make the best of it but a different opportunity came up [and I took it]."

For African Americans or even Latinos born in the U.S. who do not have transnational families and imaginations, things could be yet different from white natives and international migrants like Mexicans and Togolese. They do not enjoy many of employment opportunities and job mobility of white American workers, yet they do not have the resources of international immigrants. The African Americans I interviewed in Beardstown were also displaced migrant workers dispossessed of work, through previous economic cycles of accumulation in places like Detroit,[13] and relocated to Beardstown in the hopes of a full-time job. But they could not rely on the strategies that Togolese or Mexican workers employed. Transgenerational care and extended family participation in child rearing and family upbringing might be common among African Americans, due to historical reasons and also the contemporary situation in which African American men experience a high incarceration rate. But they do not form translocal families as a cost-cutting strategy or as means of coping with exclusions and criminalization that is enforced through national borders. As Carol said, "I cannot leave my child to be raised by my mother in Detroit, it will cost her as much as it will cost me here." "Plus," Aaron further expanded, "we can't really compare [with African and Mexican immigrants], because . . . if they all could bring their whole family here they would. But they can't, so that's a whole different decision. I hate that they have to live like that."

While migrant workers from Detroit and Togo and Mexico are similar in that they are all displaced and they are all considered foreign in the imagination of the white locals, they are distinct in how they can respond to the crisis of social reproduction. Inequality, as explained by an uneven development thesis,[14] is central to workers' strategies in restructuring social reproduction. The vast inequalities across the United States and Mexico or Togo, in terms of employment opportunities and remunerations determine workers' strategies in restructuring of their care work. Workers with transnational families might be able to stretch their wages a bit farther by benefiting from their families' invisible subsidies and by their performance of obligations and imagination of their future and dreams across two wage zones. The huge gaps in life opportunities across the world are key to capital's ability to accumulate in the face of its crisis of social reproduction. Global inequalities are not an incidental or unfortunate consequence of globalization and global capitalism, as popular discourse asserts—it is a necessary condition for global labor mobility and hence globalization and immigration. In a tragically unequal world,[15] there is a more fruitful ground not only for displacing the labor force but also transferring away or contracting out the cost and risks of social reproduction—to others, to a distant elsewhere.

EMIGRATION: PEOPLE'S PUBLIC POLICY

In an increasingly unequal world of neoliberal globalization, transnational practices of care function as risk absorbers—for those left behind and for those who have moved; for communities of origin and for communities of destination.

Should an immigrant worker be injured, tired, or old and should he or she need to stop working, this immigrant may look to the safety net of families, friends, and neighbors back home. For example, when Sena's husband, Dodji, lost his job in Beardstown, Emefa and Djidonou in Togo raised Sena's two boys for over a year without receiving help. Whatever Sena could send was for payment on her debt to the lender not for maintenance of her sons. In the case of the Garcias, their neighbor cared for the gradual construction of their house and pavement of the road in front so that they could come back to the secure home they dreamed of all along. And Magnolia, the injured Michoacán worker whose investment failed, ended up relying on and living with in-laws.

Transnational families and bonds of care also weave safety nets that reduce risks and absorb shocks for those left behind in immigrants' communities of origin. The complexities of these ties are further illustrated by what Mr. Kofi called a "people's policy for social safety." Mr. Kofi, whom we met in chapter 4, said he was sad that he could not pass on the role of mentoring village youth coming to Lomé to Kossi, given his emigration. But he also added, "Deep inside I am also feeling safer that my nephew is gone. I know should worse come to worse there is a possibility of drawing on his help." He explained that his nephew in Beardstown did more than cover school fees for several relatives. Having an emigrant in the family also improved their social rank. The extended networks of the emigrant share the promise, the potential, the possibility of a real or imagined assurance that one day if all roads are closed, "I have someone to help and you [the person without an emigrant] do not!"

Kossi's emigration in this account worked as a replacement for the social and public services the Togolese government no longer offered. It was a safety net for the relatives he left behind. Whether he would be able to provide for the whole extended family and their extensive needs at home was a different question. What Mr. Kofi indicated was that the very perception of this resource in itself translated to a sense of security and a higher social status.

This is the social security system that the post–Cold War Togo enjoys through transnational, translocal practices that connect the daily bread of Beardstown to Togo, and furnish means for education, health care, and social security for the relations of Togolese emigrants. If for Mexican residents of Tejaro the most effective strategy for gaining access to housing and basic service provision is the export of young men and women, rather than corn, in Togo, the most reliable guarantee for access to now privatized education and health care or some sort of old age social security is not the state, but sending a family member out of the country. Here emigration is *people's public policy.*

OFF-SHORING SOCIAL REPRODUCTION
TO (NON)GOVERNMENTAL ORGANIZATIONS

As corporations shift risk away from themselves, not only families and individuals, but also nonprofit and faith-based organizations in the global South and the global North shoulder those risks and subsidize the cost of labor recruitment and reproduction.[16] As we saw in chapter 2, when Cargill recruits from Puerto Rico arrived in flipflops in the middle of an Illinois winter, a local nonprofit group provided blankets, warm clothes, and shoes for the newcomers. Similarly, we saw the key role that churches and nuns played in assisting Mexican recruits to settle into Beardstown and work effectively in their Cargill jobs. In the case of West Africans, capital shifted risks of international labor onto the state through the Diversity Visa process in the sense that the state became the means for screening potential workers for employers—keeping out the unhealthy, the uneducated, the untested, those who will be of no value. In the absence of the DV, employers would have to do their own screening.

That the public and nonprofit sector social service programs subsidize the private firms and low-waged jobs they offer is no news.[17] Many low-waged, part-time workers employed in the fast-food sector, for example, have to rely on food stamps, public health services, or reduced price meals at public schools as well as faith-based charities, soup kitchens, and shelters to make ends meet. In the United States the post-1990 rollback of already modest state welfare supports has made nonprofit and faith-based organizations crucial to the livelihood of the working poor.[18]

But the subsidies to the low wages corporations like Cargill pay their workers do not occur only through organizations and programs here in the United States. For Mexican or Togolese workers to remain in these high-risk, low-paying jobs, costs also have to be transferred to institutions and organizations in their communities of origin—schools, churches, NGOs, and a whole industry of so called "development programs." As dysfunctional, corrupt, or autocratic as they might be, public hospitals, free and low-cost clinics and care providers in Michoacán supply health services to youth like the Fernández children until they reach the productive time of their life cycle and head for el Norte. We must keep in mind that these workers have no access to social security or health care in the United States. Working with false social security numbers means workers make contribution to a fund that they cannot access. Hence, at the end of their productive working cycle, they have little choice but to rely on the limited Mexican social security and public health care systems. As fragile as these public support systems might be, Mexican immigrants can access them when they return home with their injured or simply worn-out and aged bodies.[19]

An initiative of Mexican government that started in 1990 and expanded over the last decade illuminates the transnational transfer of social reproduction costs to the immigrants' home institutions especially well. Under this initiative, Mexican immigrants in the United States can have health care entitlements for their families back home in Mexico and for themselves when in Mexico. To support immigrants, the Mexican Social Security Institute (Instituto Mexicano del Seguro Social, IMSS), has nine offices in the United States, and by making an annual contribution as low as one hundred to two hundred dollars per year, immigrants and their families can now benefit from government social services.[20]

Simply put, a capitalist system demands productive workers, infrastructure, and collective goods for its operations, but the capitalists do not want to bear their full costs. For a period of history, the welfare state in the global North and developmental state in the global South sought to address this contradiction through public policies.[21] However, in the present era of the neoliberal restructuring of the state we see an exacerbated tension between capital accumulation and social reproduction. To enjoy greater surplus, capital transfers the cost and risks of labor to institutions, individuals, and communities locally and translocally.

—

BEYOND THE GLOBAL CARE CHAIN: COLD CHAINS OF MEAT, WARM CHAINS OF LABOR

In less than thirty days after a hog is killed at the Beardstown plant, pork from that hog, which is "fresh," as in "not frozen," but vacuum sealed, is put on a shelf in a store in Tokyo for Japanese consumers (Griffis and Ross 2014). A series of refrigerated trucks and containers called "reefers" constitute the "cold chain" that connects Beardstown to consumers around the world, including those in Japan. In "Between the Bottomland and the World," Ryan Griffis and Sarah Ross (2014) remind us of another chain that makes the consumption of U.S. pork in Japan and elsewhere around the world and the country possible: the trucks that bring in the pigs from farms in the Midwest and across the country to Beardstown, which they call a "warm chain." These trucks, approximately one hundred of them, each carrying an average of 180 hogs equipped to spray animals with water and keep them cool, arrive daily in Beardstown.

But there is yet another "warm chain"—the warm chain of transnational and translocal workers who feed and raise the piglets in huge farms, who slaughter the pigs, and who cut, process, pack, and ship the pork to destinations around the world. These workers and their families and friends in communities of origin try their best to smooth over their interrupted lives and families to make the warm chain of animal transport and the cold chain of product distribution that reaches the consumers' tables viable and profitable for the industry. While the cold chain is talked about as an industrial reality, the warm chains of labor and care that are necessary to any cold chain of product distribution are often made invisible.

In developing the concept of a "global care chain," feminist scholarship captured a "series of personal links between people across the globe based on the paid and unpaid work of caring" (Hochschild 2000, 131). For instance, relatively well-resourced families and women transfer costs down the chain of care to women in the Philippines, who leave their own families behind to care for affluent families in Manhattan or San Francisco.[22] This concept helped to demonstrate that the cost of social reproduction was not merely moved to the private sphere but was moved from the global North to the private sphere of the domestic unit in the global South. Care work, in other words, was being transferred to global "elsewheres"—to locations abroad where women were recruited to bear the privatized cost of care work for domestic units in the United States.

The stories chronicled above deepen our understanding of the crisis of social reproduction in the era of neoliberal capitalism and the complex translocal and transnational practices through which immigrant industrial workers at Cargill's Beardstown plant make their lives—in a material and nonmaterial sense. Amidst growing insecurities that capital imposes, workers like Sena, Magnolia, and the men at the plaza personify the way global corporations transfer the costs and risks of mobilizing a workforce to other locations. This transfer is sometimes to individuals, groups, and organizations where the jobs are, other times to groups and organizations elsewhere within or across national borders. An army of people and myriad organizations in immigrant workers' communities of origin are involved in making their social reproduction—biophysically, culturally, and emotionally—viable on

Cargill wages. Family members nursing children and caring for the family and elderly whom immigrants leave behind, neighbors who keep a dream of a home alive by caring for the property immigrants leave behind; the hope, honor, and pride that these communities maintain for their migrants as they embark on risky journeys and perform hazardous jobs out of a sense of obligation, or tolerate the disillusionment to meet cultural expectations.

The concept of "global restructuring of social reproduction" developed through these stories broadens and thickens the idea of the "global care chain" by uncovering how this transfer of cost down the chain to the elsewhere occurs not only in the domestic realm with care workers and not merely through the work of care performed at household levels. Workers in all economic sectors (industrial, domestic, formal, informal) take part in this global restructuring of social reproduction—a process of key significance to the survival of capitalism in this era. A range of organizations along with individuals and families locally and translocally contribute through their "cushioning practices" to social reproduction not only at the individual level of workers and their households but also at collective levels of their communities and the places with which they identify.

Through market and nonmarket domains of care and at multiple scales from households to local, national, and global levels, Beardstown immigrant workers with transnational families and imaginations socially and spatially restructure their lives to stretch Cargill wages. Their transnational practices intimately connect Beardstown to seemingly far away locations in Mexico and Togo and contribute to social reproduction of people and place. Their contributions construct homes, pave roads, provide public works and schools and keep businesses alive not only in places of origin,[23] but also at their destinations—a topic more fully explored in the following chapters.

PART IV
WE WANTED WORKERS,
WE GOT PEOPLE

Figure 7.1: Cargill's pig-head planters in Beardstown plant. Artwork courtesy of Sarah Ross.

7 — WE WANTED WORKERS

AT THE ENTRANCE TO THE CARGILL PLANT IN BEARDSTOWN, TWO smiling pig-head planters welcome visitors to the slaughterhouse (see figure 7.1). How is one slaughtered with a smiling face? And why of all images and objects that a planter at this slaughter house could represent, the choice of a pig head?

Unlike the company towns of the early twentieth century, contemporary company towns in the meat and food industry move to sites that had already been developed with private investments and, most importantly, with public tax money. The corporations no longer build houses, schools, or daycare facilities for their workforce, yet they operate what are de facto company towns. The power of the company in these towns does not involve brick and mortar but institutional and financial arrangements justified through certain discursive and bureaucratic means. Furthermore, unlike company towns of the previous era, contemporary meatpacking towns like Beardstown rely on public and private funds to house a diverse cohort drawn from various ethnic, racial, linguistic and national backgrounds. Cargill's Beardstown operation represents this new company town model in many ways.

CARGILL AS GLOBAL CITIZEN

The company's websites and annual reports declare Cargill to be the global leader in nourishing people, stating that their mission is "to create distinctive value," that their approach is "to be trustworthy, creative, and enterprising" and that their performance measures focus on "engaged employees; satisfied customers; enriched communities; profitable growth."[1]

In Cargill's lexicon, the discourses of "global citizenship" and "corporate responsibility" loom large. According to the company website, Cargill celebrates and prides itself on promotion of diversity, improvement of workplace safety, and community giving. "Corporate responsibility is part of everything we do. It is a company-wide commitment to apply our global knowledge and experience to help meet complex economic, environmental and social challenges wherever we do business."[2]

The website also proudly announces that as part of the firm's social responsibility, it has been able to substantially improve workers' occupational health and safety. Under the subheading of "Safety is our greatest responsibility," Cargill stresses the corporation's commitment to improve workplace safety by "enhancing work activity interventions, reducing human errors, strengthening its incident investigations, and improving how it measures safety incidents."[3] It reports on the company's progress by reducing the Recordable Injury Frequency Rate, measured by total recordable injuries per 200,000 hours worked. For Cargill workers, the company claims, this rate has been consistently going down, from 3.1 in 2009 to 2.0 in 2013.[4]

In addition to profiling their health and safety performance, Cargill writes of the deep caring the company has for the communities where it operates. "Cargill helps build vibrant and stable communities where we live and work by supporting programs that provide long-term solutions to community issues, engage our employees and leverage their expertise, and offer opportunities to collaborate with others."[5] Under the heading "Strength through Diversity," their website states, "We embrace the variety of back-grounds and life experiences our employees bring to work. As colleagues, we offer the perspectives of different genders, languages, local customs, physical abilities, races, religions, sexual orientations, gender identities, life experiences and socioeconomic statuses, and we vary in our personal styles of thinking, expressing ourselves and problem-solving."[6]

In 2012, for example, Cargill contributed 2 percent of its global consolidated pre-tax earnings to programs that improve nutrition and health, education, and environmental stewardship. The company's charitable giving reached $69.9 million across fifty-seven countries. It established a five-year, ten-million-dollar partnership with CARE, a leading humanitarian organization, to help people in targeted countries raise their standards of living through better education, training, and job opportunities. The goal was "helping 100,000 people lift themselves out of poverty by 2013 in Brazil, Côte d'Ivoire, Egypt, Ghana, Guatemala, Honduras, India and Nicaragua."[7] In addition to CARE, among Cargill's key "Global Corporate Responsibility Partners" are Feeding America, the Global Food Banking Network (GFN); the Nature Conservancy; World Food Programme (WFP), and World Wildlife Fund (WWF).[8] At the local level, the company claimed that the Beardstown plant contributed more than $160,000 to area schools, organizations, charities, events, and occasions to the benefit of residents in more than five counties.[9]

"GOD, GIVE ME COURAGE TO DO THIS"

While the company's web profiles and publicity have aimed to put a new, caring spin on the meatpacking industry's image, which has long been an icon of workplace brutality and cruelty, the realities of the Beardstown factory floor as well as the experiences of workers tell a different story—a tale closer to a neoliberal-era version of Upton Sinclair's *The Jungle* than the image the company promotes.

In 2008, an officer of the University of Illinois Extension invited me to join a guided three-hour group tour through the Beardstown plant of Cargill Meat Solutions. Although the tour was for local entrepreneurs, the officer, whom I had interviewed the prior week and who knew about my book project, asked if I wanted to come along. I could not have been more delighted to accept the invitation.

At the plant, I learned that before workers kill the hogs, they knock them out by guiding them into a pen that descends into a pit filled with carbon dioxide gas. This stun technology makes the hogs dazed and less resistant.

After the pen rises from the pit, workers shackle each hog by a hind leg to a moving overhead rail—no easy task, with hogs averaging 265 pounds. Hanging upside down, the hogs pass workers through different sections of the plant to be slaughtered, cut, processed, packed, and shipped. Once unconscious, the carcasses' journey down the assembly line starts while hanging by ankles, ready to be drained of their blood. Along the fast-moving conveyor belts, the workers' white butcher coats and white helmets seemed to highlight the blood that dominated the environment.

The day when I was there, a girl in her twenties was in charge of cutting the jugular veins and carotid arteries of the hogs at the outset of their journey. I recall her because of her stoic yet angelic face. She stood facing the moving line of the pigs positioned just at the right height for her to use a sharp knife to stab the carcasses, which gushed blood all over her. She repeated this move at least nine thousand times each day, or once every three seconds. As the upside-down hogs continued their journey along the assembly line, with their blood draining out of them, they passed open flame furnaces, water jets, and paddles that helped to rinse and de-hair the animals. The hogs were then dressed out: the hide and hooves were removed, the guts were dropped from the body cavities, the heads taken off, and the carcasses each split in half. In this first half of the process on the "kill floor," workers did a lot of heavy lifting, pulling, gripping, and ripping with knives, with blood and fat flying. Hogs sometimes fell from the line and had to be reattached.

Jobs on the kill floor are the hardest and also highest paid, one senior worker explained. Once the animal has been through the kill floor, and before it enters the cut floor to be sliced up and processed for different consumption products, the carcass passes into a freezing chamber for a "quick chill" to give it a longer shelf life while it is being handled. Processing the carcasses into various pork cuts takes place in a section of the plant on the cut floor which is kept just above freezing temperatures. Packages to be shipped to distant locations like China, Russia, and Japan go through an additional stage of blast freeze to preserve them for their long journeys.

I visited the plant during the morning shift, which almost all interviewees agreed has a greater concentration of the white workers. Africans and Mexicans were more likely to work the less desirable afternoon shift often with overtime lasting until one in the morning. As the tour proceeded through various sections of the plant, I noticed a visible difference among workers in addition to the color of skin and gender: the color-coded helmets indicating the position they held. For example, a white helmet was for regular workers on the production line, dark blue meant line supervisor or manager, light blue a trainer, light brown indicated a union representative, dark brown a safety representative, green stood for outside company or hearing-impaired workers, orange was quality assurance and technical employees, purple was for ergonomics monitor. To cope with the cold, many wore layers of sweaters under their white butcher coats with hoodies and caps under their helmets. Working in the refrigerated air with cold objects on cold surfaces places heavy stress on workers' joints. Some I interviewed talked about the stress of going from the freezing temperatures inside to those outside, which in Illinois also often involve extremes (hot and humid summers and ice cold winters). "Your body goes through a shock," said one interviewee. "I feel almost sick all the time," another one said.

The plant is an intense and, by many accounts, an overwhelming space. The machinery and conveyor belts move quickly, the foul smell is pervasive, and on the kill floor the noise from squealing pigs, apparently sensing their imminent death, is constant. It was only after that visit to the plant that I truly understood the moving testimonial that a West African man had made in April 2008 during the town hall meeting that Africans had organized in Rushville, to promote greater intercultural understanding in the town. Held at the Presbyterian Church and advertised in the local newspaper, the meeting was attended by only a few white locals, among them the pro-immigrant mayor of Rushville, his wife, and a few church affiliates. The rest included about thirty Africans, most of them young men, with about three or four women and two old men. In that meeting a young Togolese man stood up and introduced himself as a mechanical engineer who arrived in Rushville in March of 2004. He described what he felt on the first day at work. "The first day I passed through the Cargill gates I inspected the area; I told myself it is going to be horrible; so I talked to God. 'God, help me. Give me courage to do this,' because I had my family back home and their lives were in my hands." That day at the plant I thought of this man. I thought of the courage and the determination of all the men and women I interviewed, who stepped into this space, fought their fears and pains, and kept working.

KILLING ME SOFTLY

In 2004, a Human Rights Watch report declared meatpacking to be the most dangerous factory job in the United States (Human Rights Watch 2004, 14). The risk of health and work-related illness and injury among meat packers is two and a half times that of the average for manufacturing workers. In 2001, for example, while on average 8.1 out of one hundred manufacturing workers were injured or ill due to their work, for meatpackers the figure was twenty out of one hundred (ibid., 55–56). While there has been some improvement in occupational health standards for the meat industry, slaughtering and processing jobs remain more dangerous and hazardous overall than other manufacturing jobs. As of 2010, the U.S. Bureau of Labor Statistics reported that in comparison to other industrial and manufacturing sectors, animal slaughtering and processing jobs (excluding poultry) were twice as likely to record cases of nonfatal injuries and illness (8.8 versus 4.4 per hundred workers) and three times more likely to record cases of job transfer and restrictions (6.0 versus 2.4 per hundred workers).[10]

What makes the risk of injury higher in meatpacking than it is in most other industries is not only handling hogs weighing up to 260 or 270 pounds per animal, but also working with sharp knives and saws on animals on a fast moving conveyor belt. An additional health risk for workers in the meatpacking industry is injury due to repetitive motion, higher than that in many other manufacturing jobs—often in the form of tendinitis.

At the Beardstown plant, more than six hundred cases have been filed against Cargill since 2000, according to the Illinois Workers' Compensation Commission. In response, the company has paid out about $6 million. More than half of the cases were for "repetitive-stress trauma." An *Illinois Times* interview with Springfield attorney William Lamarca, who has been handling worker-compensation cases for employees of the Beardstown plant since 1980, indicates repetitive-stress injuries are inevitable if an employee continues working on a meatpacking line. Most of the fifty to one hundred cases against the Beardstown plant that Lamarca's firm has handled were settled when a worker lost use of a hand or an arm as a result of carpal-tunnel syndrome or other repetitive-stress injury. The affliction starts with inflammation and swelling in joints, which compresses nerves and causes pain or numbness. "From what I've been told by doctors, the body is just not designed to perform that type of activity for any duration," he said. "It just wears out" (Fitzgerald 2006).

With the technological innovations that lowered the skill level needed for performance of these jobs has come a greater level of repetition. Each worker is required to perform fewer tasks but perform those tasks with far more frequency. Meat packers make the same knife cut ten thousand times a day or lift the same weight every few seconds, and these repetitive motions cause serious injuries to their backs, shoulders, or hands. Swollen hands, fingers that cannot bend, or nails that peel off are common among the meatpackers whom I interviewed. In the case of fingernails, it is the process of detaching skin from the hog that puts too much pressure on the tips of fingers and cause nails not to get blood circulation. One Beardstown meatpacker I spoke with in 2008 who had lost nails this way said, "Imagine hammering your fingers and nails three thousand times a day. Your nails come off." These repetitive motions increase each time the line speeds up to meet higher production rates or when a worker is missing on the line. Several interviewees indicated that the line was occasionally made to move faster to meet a contract deadline or during a greater demand time.[11] Others noted how they have to work faster routinely when a coworker took a break and line speed is not adjusted down. Saturday work is not uncommon. For example, in December 2007 workers participating in my first focus group had worked six days a week since early September.

During an eight-hour shift, workers get a fifteen-minute break after two hours and a thirty-minute lunch period after another three hours. To leave the moving belt for use of the bathroom in between these breaks, workers need to get approval from the supervisor, or blue helmet. The supervisor then needs to adjust the belt speed accordingly to compensate for the missing worker—in theory. In practice, according to interviewees, this adjustment is not always made, and this in turn creates friction among workers who feel they have to pay with their sweat and risk when another worker takes a bathroom break. "Nasty comments fly off once you need to step away" one interviewee commented.

Several others mentioned how their requests for a bathroom break were ignored or simply pushed back. Indeed I learned about two occasions where the worker had to "go while working on the belt." One occasion that my interview, a male white worker in his thirties, witnessed the worker was a young female

African immigrant. He heard the supervisor tell the worker "you better not leave that line. You leave that line, you're getting fired." But he went on to explain that this happens mostly to workers who do not know their rights: "They can't do this to workers who know the regulations." For example he told me of an older African American on the line, who had been a blue helmet on his previous factory job. This worker, he explained, asked for a bathroom break but was ignored, so he just walked away and left for the bathroom. When he came back, the supervisor wanted to write him up. So he told the supervisor, "Look here man . . . when I have to go to the bathroom, I'm going. I'm going to look for you one time, if I can't find you, I'm gone. When I need to go, I need to go." Then he went to the front office and said to them "I wonder what the USDA, how they would feel if they knew that somebody used the bathroom on themselves on the line and they were still handling this meat? And I wonder . . . how OSHA would feel about it?' . . . So he had it out with them." In admiration of this worker, my interviewee said, he is one of the few who speaks up around there: "The rest of them don't speak up. . . . [They] are all scared. . . . So you know what they do? [The blue helmets] don't bother him, but they bother them [the immigrants]."

Despite the company's celebration of its success in reducing the rate of injuries, I found work-related health problems to be common among the meatpackers whom I interviewed. One of the earliest cases I came across was a Togolese woman I call Ami. Tall and strong, she wore a black hand-knitted hair net and a tight blue top and had a kind smile on her tired face. Ami had a bachelor's degree in management and used to work as secretarial staff for an international NGO back in Lomé. Her husband was a veterinarian. Here in Illinois, they both "cut meat." I spoke to her in Rushville in 2007. When they won the lottery to move to the United States five years before that, they left behind two of their children. To avoid paying for child care for their two-year-old, U.S.-born daughter, Ami works the evening shift, her husband the morning one. Their neighbor helps them for an hour or so with child care during transition between Ami's and her husband's shifts.

I interviewed her around eleven on a Friday morning. She had worked the night before. I usually offered a weekend option to interviewees and left the place and time up to them, and Ami had chosen to meet that morning at her place because, as she said, "I have to get up and get things ready anyway. My daughter never sleeps in." I asked her when she got to bed the previous night.

She explained that when she got home it was one in the morning but she did not sleep till three. She went on to explain that it was not easy to come home and go to bed. She had to allow time for her body to adjust. Standing eight to ten hours in a space cooled to forty degrees, her fingers would swell and her whole body would ache. "You know, in Cargill, we Africans, we're not used to that weather of cold. Yes, it's cold [inside the plant]. . . . It's because of the air condition that sometimes you feel bad, you feel pain all over the body and you work at a speed, a rhythm that you've never done before." She then went on to explain that her way of dealing with this was to take pain killers. But she also realized that was problematic. "If I begin taking it, every four hours take two pills. Because sometimes you feel that [much pain] and I am scared, I'm scared."

Earlier that day when I had asked her to sign my Institutional Review Board form, I had noticed her fingers were so swollen that she could not bend them and had difficulty holding the pen. Seeing my surprise, she put the pen away and showed me that her fist could not close. "No problem, many of us have the same problem," she said. She went on to explain that the stiffness in her fingers was due to working in the cold air and to the repetitive motions she had to make at work. Her pain had crept in slowly but several workers advised her to not report the issue for fear of dismissal. "They tell me, if you have pain last thing you do is to show it to them [the supervisor, the management, the clinic at the plant]. They find a reason to dismiss you before it becomes their [the company's] problem."

Several interviewees also indicated a reluctance to report work-related health problems for fear of job loss. Apparently their fears were not unfounded. As recently as 1999, thirty-one disabled workers succeeded in lawsuits filed in 1994 against Cargill's Beardstown plant for exactly the same reason. These injured workers had been granted medical leave, then terminated after twelve months when they could not perform the duties of any vacant jobs at the plant.[12] A recent report by the United Food and Commercial Workers union (UFCW) also confirmed a range of reasons for underreporting of occupational illness and injuries, including worker fears surrounding immigration status and resultant retaliation by employers, employers' motivation to undercount injuries in order to win safety awards, and managers incentivized by low-injury bonuses; in addition, some employers have instituted programs requiring workers who report injuries or accidents to undergo drug testing—adding additional risk to reporting.[13] According to this UFCW report, studies conducted by the National Institute of Occupational Safety and Health (NIOSH) raised doubt about the accuracy of the recorded cases of occupation and health risk by the Bureau of Labor Statistics (BLS) and suggested that the BLS and the Occupational Safety and Health Administration (OSHA) missed 20 to 50 percent of the nation's workplace injuries.

My interviewees' stories revealed the underlying reasons for this underreporting. Several workers talked about how they did not see the plant's medical crew or the union as being on their side and feared that reporting any health problem might lead to their job loss. One West African worker, Fredrick, mentioned that he broke an arm seven hours into his work shift at the plant but the company's clinic challenged his claim and the union did not help. "I was seven hours into work on my line! Yet they said I brought my broken arm to the plant before the shift started!"

Multiple interviewees mentioned that they did not see the existing union (UFCW local 431), to which all workers of the Beardstown Cargill plant are automatically signed up, as an advocate for workers. In cases of medical or performance-related disputes, several workers maintained that the union serves as "an arm of the management." For example, when a supervisor writes up an employee for breaking a rule (three or four write-ups can lead to a suspension and ultimately a dismissal), even if the write-up is unjustified, the union representative invariably signs off on it. Robert, a 36-year-old white native of Illinois I talked with in 2012, explained,

> "They [the supervisors] are required to inform you that you've been written up, . . . and they are required to have you sign, but if you [the worker] refuse to sign the write-up, the union representative will have to sign saying that you have refused to sign. And then you write on the back why you refused to sign it. [But] a lot of immigrants think that the union is signing for them . . . [while] the union is saying you refuse to sign . . . [and] if you don't write why you're refusing, it is seen as a consent, as an agreement."

The language used and the interpretation of how injuries are reported have also become issues. In cases where workers cannot suppress the pain with pills or aspirin creams, many face difficulty in getting accurate translations of the papers they must sign upon injury. In one case, a young Togolese woman in her twenties, only a few months after starting work at the plant, slipped and fell on the wet floor, shattering her ankle, but she did not receive any settlement or compensation from Cargill. She spoke limited English and did not understand the implications of what she was signing. Hence, she signed papers that stated that the company had offered her an easier job to perform at the plant in light of her injury but that she refused to accept that job—hence by implication clearing the company from responsibility and reducing the viability of a case, if it were to be filed against the company— or so the legal aid she sought out told her subsequently. "I cannot fight the legal battle with the plant," she said. "All law firms in Beardstown work for Cargill, not one will dare to take my case. They all take side with each other." She had sought a lawyer in Springfield, but the trip back and forth was costly and lengthy, plus at the time her spouse still worked at the plant so she had to tread lightly. Showing me the scars from an operation at the Jacksonville Hospital, and a large bottle of pain killers, she said she still suffered pain and could still not use that foot properly. She basically gave her ankle to Cargill, "with no compensation not even a sick leave for one week."

For many of the undocumented workers with false papers, workers' compensation was also out of the picture. Indeed, some of them talked about how child support was deducted from their paychecks even though they had no child—but then, they had purchased a false document of a person who the courts had ruled had to pay child support. Others, documented or undocumented, often did not know their rights or did not want to engage in a legal challenge that could mean the loss of the deal they were offered by the company. But my conversation with Magnolia, whom I interviewed in Michoacán in 2008 after her work-related shoulder surgery, suggested that there was a rule of thumb for the price tag attached to each injured body part. For example, she told me, "For a cortisone shot on each finger that gets locked, you get about five thousand dollars; for laser surgery on shoulder, you get ten thousand dollars; if they cut your flesh, the most invasive kind, you get fifteen thousand dollars."[14] But how much you get, as I learned from another immigrant, also depended on who you were and what you knew. "If you are undocumented, they know you will not complain so they get you less. My husband early on after three months got locked fingers and got three shots, he could have received money for those shots, but he did not know and no one told him. There is really no advocate, but word of mouth is the best ally," a Mexican interviewee said to me in Beardstown.

Magnolia also told me about a curious postsurgery practice that three other interviewees had reported: "I was released from my shoulder injury this day, I had to go back for some complication that took another several hours before I got home late night. Yet I had to go to report to the plant for my morning shift. I don't understand. They did not make me work. They had me punch-in my time card, then gave me a chair and had me put my feet up and sit down. It was hard, and it did not make sense, why could I not go home and rest? I was not doing any work anyway!" Several other injured or hospitalized workers talked about the same routine, where they had to show up at work and sign in even though they were unable to perform work—a bureaucratic practice that did not make sense to them.

Once I told her how OSHA records are calculated—namely, in terms of number of days lost to work-related illness or injury—Magnolia made a long sigh, followed by, "I see. Now I see!" The point of the routine was simply to keep the company's work-related statistics low.

POLITICS OF PATRONAGE: CORPORATE COMMUNITY GIVING

As explained in chapter 2, when Cargill purchased the Oscar Mayer plant in 1987, Beardstown had already lost several other employers, and anxiety over yet another employer was running high not only among residents, but also among city and state authorities. To attract a corporation to purchase Oscar Mayer and hire the pool of labor available in Beardstown, the state of Illinois offered a $215,000 labor retraining grant to the local community college consortium under the Jobs Training Partnership Act (JTPA) to retrain the Oscar Mayer workers. Under that program, former Oscar Mayer workers could receive training to find new employment.[15] In addition, the municipality included the plant in its newly established Enterprise Zone (EZ), which was created in 1986–1987 to cope with Oscar Mayer's departure. This froze Cargill's real estate tax payment at the 1987 level of $750,000 for the following twenty years.[16] These were not exceptional advantages offered to Cargill. Many companies setting up plants in depressed rural areas are offered such packages to make the municipalities that otherwise do not have employers for their young (or old) populations attractive. These areas need the companies to keep people and other businesses in place.[17]

In 2007, when the tax haven the company had enjoyed since 1987 came to an end, a curious set of negotiations took place. In 2006, in anticipation of the end to the tax haven, the County Assessment Board had assessed the property value for the Cargill plant in Beardstown at $27 million. Cargill challenged this as excessive (Ursch 2006). The company brought in a brand new team of accountants and argued for a reduced assessed value of $7 million. They wanted to file an appeal with the Property Tax Appeal Board (PTAB) and threatened to leave Beardstown—the ultimate threat for the town, the county, and the state. The County Review Board, which did not want Cargill to take the case to the state-level PTAB, had an incentive to reach an agreement with Cargill and "settle complaints before the challenge is sent to the state for a decision, as state usually sides with business" an official interviewed in Beardstown told me in 2008. To seek a solution to the conflict, an ad hoc negotiating team, consisting of the chair of the County Board Assessment committee (Mr. Parish), the mayor of Beardstown (Mr. Walters), and the superintendent of the school district (Mr. Bagby) met with the Cargill plant manager, Mark Klein.

It is not known exactly what happened behind the doors of this closed session, but the outcome of the meeting was a deal struck among the attendees: the review board would settle on reducing Cargill's assessed property value from $27 million to $13 million, which saved Cargill $485,000 in tax payment. In a small town a cut of this magnitude in tax revenues is devastating—especially to tax-dependent entities like schools that had expected a larger budget in anticipation of the reassessed plant's property value. "The agreement means that the Beardstown school district likely will lose about $200,000 or less in annual revenue and the city will lose about $50,000," the mayor of Beardstown said. "Both the city and the schools will start feeling the full brunt of losses in 2011."[18] "To cushion the blow to taxpayers," as the mayor put it, Cargill agreed to making payment in lieu of taxes, which would allow the tax bodies to adjust to the reduction of revenues from taxes over three years and find other employers to make up for the losses. The taxing bodies decided to opt for the maximum amount of payment per year, which charted as three annual payments of $400,000 and one payment of $100,000 on the fourth and last year, bringing the total payment to $1.3 million. Although the idea was to give the taxing bodies some time to adapt, in practice, this reduction of Cargill's tax obligations increased the tax burden on residential properties and cut revenues from tax-funded entities in Beardstown—the school district, the library, the park district.

This scheme did not merely offer a financial advantage to Cargill; it also offered the company a myriad of political opportunities for developing relationships with private and public agencies in town. As one interviewee in charge of one of the units funded through local taxes stated, "I would much rather receive the money as part of my budget and in tax payment, than having to be cap in hand dependent on company donations." The old saying "Taking with one hand and giving with the other" applies here, except in this instance, Cargill took large sums from the local community in tax savings with one hand and gave the community a fraction of what was taken with the other hand.[19]

The political patronage and power that this financial arrangement offered Cargill magnified the already enormous economic power it has in town. In 2008, when a Chicago-based nonprofit organization approached me to help them find a host in Beardstown for their multilingual workers' rights workshop, I got a firsthand glimpse of this political reality. The library, the school, and even the churches turned down the requests for hosting a workshop on such a topic. Several of these entities had previously agreed to host a nonprofit that offered immigration rights workshops right after the ICE raid in Beardstown, but when it came to labor rights, none wanted to risk an unhappy patron. In one incident the potential host I had approached for such a workshop was not receiving donations from Cargill, yet the person in charge turned down the request explaining, "I don't work for the company, but my son or daughter might reach out to the plant for a summer job, my niece or nephew might need a job." He went on to point out that everyone in Beardstown would be careful about upsetting the plant management, even "if they didn't work there and they didn't depend on the company for income. Still, they might have a spouse who works there and might want to have her or his bid [for a change of work position within the plant] accepted." In short, in a place like Beardstown, everyone was tied to the company. "Hey you won't do anything that they don't like. That's just not on. . . . There is a nine-hundred pound gorilla in this room," a city official told me. When a Mexican described Beardstown to me, she likened it to "a *pueblo* [village] with a powerful *cacique* [boss, henchman]."

CORPORATE MULTICULTURALISM

One interviewee in Rushville told me, "When people were afraid to go to the world, the world came to them." In her experience, this world was brought to Rushville by Cargill. If it was not for companies like Cargill, places like Beardstown and Rushville would have stayed as before, keeping the world out with hatred and violence. Meatpacking and agricultural industries have become the main agents of social diversification of previously predominantly white communities in rural areas of the Midwest and the South.[20] Mostly focused on Latinos' migration to the rural Midwest, studies have documented the dynamics of change by looking at minority-majority interactions— Latino versus white populations. The absence of preexisting social institutions to mediate this transition and to offer social services and interpreters are frequently stated as the main difficulty for Latinos settling in new destinations and creating tension.[21]

Some of these emerging meatpacking towns have had more difficulty than others in coping with rapid demographic change. One infamous case in Postville, Iowa, which made national media headlines, involved Agriprocessors, a family-owned company and the largest producer of kosher meat in the United States, which brought in Orthodox Jews followed by Guatemalans and later Somali laborers. The town's rapid demographic changes led to serious tensions exacerbated by workers' ethnic, racial, linguistic, and religious differences. "Out of bounds" company practices that included child labor were also part of the scandal. The Postville case gained media attention both for the large scale ICE raid in which more than three hundred workers were arrested (at that point the largest single ICE raid ever) and for the complex dynamics of labor and immigration in town and at the plant wherein the company had been able to take advantage of the precarious status of the immigrant labor force and the physical, social, and institutional isolation of Postville as a town. Ultimately, the company's practices led to the shutdown of the plant in 2008 and the imprisonment of its owner.[22]

Unlike Postville's Agriprocessors, Beardstown's Cargill has been much more successful in governing the diverse populations it has brought to a once all-white town. A turbulent demographic change, with potential for provoking violence, as in the 1996 Ku Klux Klan march and cross burning in Beardstown, or racial tensions like those in Postville, is not in the interest of corporations. As Cargill states in its website, "Building . . . stable communities" is important to its interests.

Celebration of its diverse workers through cultural events is one step toward securing a stable enough community in Beardstown for the company's smooth operation of its plant and economic gain. Cargill therefore makes financial donations to annual celebrations of Cinco de Mayo, Mexican Independence Day (see figure 7.2), and Africa Day, as well as other occasional ethnic celebrations held in Beardstown and Rushville. At all such events, Cargill is effusively thanked for its sponsorship.[23]

But there is a limit to corporate multiculturalism. Indeed corporate multiculturalism reduces promotion of diversity to mere song and dance events. For example, reflecting on a Cargill-funded and -organized International Day celebration held at the local school in April 2008, one interviewee succinctly pointed out how the event, predominantly run by paid staff for various service organizations, reduced multiculturalism to entertainment, and to an event where glossy brochures with images of happy people of color were handed out. "Chinese acrobats were hired to perform, when there is no Chinese in the community or school district." He then went on to point out "[here] instead of making cultural celebration a way of understanding, you make it a spectacle."

To illustrate the hypocrisy involved in corporate multiculturalism, the fate of the Committee for Intercultural Understanding is a case in point. In 2007, a group of Beardstown residents initiated a multilingual, multiracial gathering to discuss the shared problems of residents across the linguistic, ethnic, and racial divides. Among them were West African, white, and Latino workers from the plant as well as clergy and affiliates. Together, they identified racial profiling by the monolingual police force as a critical problem for minorities in Beardstown. Before they were able to organize their plan of action, one of the plant managers showed up at a Sunday meeting of the group, where he heard one of the Mexicans referred to by a different name than the one he used at the plant. On Monday morning he confronted the Mexican, suggesting that he might be working under a false name at the plant.[24] After that, no Mexican worker showed up at any meetings. The Intercultural Understanding Committee was no more.[25]

Labor studies have documented how corporations use ethnic and racial differences to weaken labor solidarity and to manage labor more effectively

Figure 7.2: Full-page Cargill-sponsored *Cinco de Mayo* celebration announcement in the local newspaper, *La Estrella de Beardstown*.

on the production floor.[26] Cargill is no exception. As we will see in discussion of the production line's linguistic choreography, language and ethnic differences can become points of contention setting workers apart; similarly, the vulnerability of diverse workers based on legal status can be exploited to suppress the possibility of intercultural understanding. Through so-called "corporate multiculturalism," Cargill celebrates diversity in order to silence it, that is, to suppress the commonalities among diverse racial and ethnic groups as a potential for solidarity.

Cargill is, however, not unique in its discursive use of multiculturalism. A growing number of institutions have come to speak a language of "diversity," using rubrics of "multiculturalism." Looking at educational institutions and the entertainment industry, scholars have critiqued the usage of multiculturalism as a highly capitalized and market-driven enterprise that celebrates diversity as passive, unproblematic, and in ways often limited to glossy images and exotic cultural performances.[27] Corporate multiculturalism tends to be "viewed as a travesty of multiculturalist ideals. . . . [It] is motivated, not by notions of dignity or worth, but by a set of economic concerns" (Hjort 2005, 137). These economic concerns mean managing diversity in a way that keeps the workforce divided and more vulnerable to exploitative practices. Hence, while corporate multiculturalism claims to celebrate diversity and cultural differences, it capitalizes on ethnic and racial difference and prejudice to maximize profit and its own political control.[28]

COCONUTS AND OREOS

As the narratives of several English-, Spanish-, and French-speaking workers revealed, not only are interracial tensions and the enacting of stereotypes rife in the production line, but management also exploits those tensions and differences to set workers further apart. Because of the hazardous tools and equipment workers use, my interviewees made clear, Cargill does not tolerate any physical altercations among workers at the plant. Such confrontations call for immediate dismissal from the company. But the verbal abuse among coworkers based on socially and historically constituted prejudice is commonplace and taken advantage of by the management to keep the labor "in line," press wages down, and speed up production. Referring to how Cargill took advantage of undocumented workers and immigrants, one worker said, "Don't ever [let] them tell you that Cargill is an equal opportunity employer, that's a damn lie. . . . they scare them to death about [revoking] visas and sending them back."

My interviewees also talked about the emerging tensions among coworkers when the linguistic composition of their line was based on alternate positioning of Spanish-, French-, and English-speaking workers. I call this "linguistic choreography of the production line," whereby diverse workers are placed in the line in ways deliberately designed to frustrate communication and development of workers' solidarity. A West African worker told me how he felt betrayed by the Mexican coworkers on his line, who reporting him to the supervisor instead of directly talking with him. "We can forget to use our safety gloves or something like this. . . . Sometimes if it's a Mexican, he won't tell wear your gloves, he will wait and see when there is supervisor. . . . He . . . you know, and that can cause you a warning because you can't work without your safety gloves. . . . [They tell] the supervisor [not you]."

In the choreography of the production line, workers also mentioned the choice of line supervisor as another stratifying and contentious issue that management exploits. Some Latinos resented the fact that a West African (who joined the plant later than they did) "bossed them around," and certain white workers resented any person of color in a position of authority over them. The interviews also revealed resentment over having a woman supervise the line. Racism and sexism combined were the two prevalent obstacles in Carol's mind when she considered applying for a supervising role. "I never applied for production supervisor position, because that's just not my personality, and I know how they are over there. And I've seen how they treat women, it doesn't even have to be your nationality, it's just being a woman period, and I don't like that."

The frustrations workers experienced in being unable to communicate on an increasingly speeding production line often turned horizontally toward an ethnicized, racialized coworker, as opposed to vertically against the line supervisor and corporate management. I frequently heard interviewees blame other racial, ethnic, or language groups for their trouble with the supervisor at the line: "The delay by the lazy XXX worker [who could be Mexican, African, Puerto Rican, American, and so on] up the line cost me a write-up by the supervisor" went the usual complaint.

Bidding is yet another effective means of disciplining workers at the Cargill's Beardstown plant, several workers said. To change their job, the specific tasks they perform, or the time of their shift, workers can place a bid to the management for new openings in the plant and hope to be selected for that new job. Through this bidding system, workers believe management can reward or reprimand them, as it is at their discretion which bidder they select for the opening. For example, for West African or white or black native-born Americans, for whom legality does not function as the Sword of Damocles, the bidding might be a means of discipline. Many interviewees from all groups mention bidding as the means of management control and a threat to their ability to move to better-paying or easier jobs. Most workers, unless they need to coordinate with a spouse for care of children or have other educational or family commitments, prefer the morning shift (five or six a.m. to two or three p.m.). Certain jobs are also easier or less hazardous than the others. Those jobs are also frequently the subjects of workers' bids. "If you have a big mouth, if you do or say anything that the company doesn't like, forget about bidding or ever being moved up to the better shift or a better task," stated one interviewed worker. Most workers told me that the work shifts were ethnicized and racialized, with the whites having greater concentration in the morning shift, West African workers having a larger presence in the second shift, and Latinos spanning across the two shifts but more in the afternoon than morning. Of course the allocation of jobs and shifts are also complicated by the seniority of a worker, which, as explained in chapter 1, closely aligns with race and ethnicity.

The treatment of workers described thus far might lead one to conclude that the union should be taking more concrete action to address such problems. But when I asked people about the union, they showed little faith in its capacity for intervention. Aaron, one of the Detroiters, had this to say:

> "[Cargill] is the biggest union breaker in the world . . . and they know how to do it. And they got a lot of money, and they doing it all over the world. They just union breakers. . . . As soon as they [workers] said we was getting new representation, they [the company] get rid of those people [the outspoken workers]. . . . Cause see, they appointed these two guys, these guys are their puppets, and nobody ever voted them in. I been there eight years, and I ain't never give up one vote, for no union representation."

Referring to abuse of workers' rights that might happen on the line, like the story of the bathroom break one worker had shared with me, Aaron said "On each line, there's an employee with a union rep hat on and I never heard them discuss anything." He went on to say the situation of union at the Beardstown plant was "pitiful." "Do you know why it's pitiful? They take twenty dollars a week out of your check for this representation that you don't have." Aaron was not alone in resenting union dues and having no respect or faith in the union representatives with brown helmets on the line. Other workers, including the white Americans, as well as West African and Mexicans, expressed the same sentiment. Most importantly, those who discussed their injuries with me confirmed this assessment of the local union.

Carol, Aaron's partner, however, did see a more optimistic development when reflecting on the most recent contract negotiations. She noted that some things might be changing with more immigrants sorting out their papers and learning to read and speak in English. She referred to the recent contract negotiations (July 2012) at the big gym in Beardstown, where workers rejected the new contract proposed by the UFCW Local 423 representatives and sent them back to the drawing board to come up with a new contract with higher wage increases and a better insurance package. She went on to say that "80 percent said that they don't want this, it was amazing for that to happen, . . . to turn down the Union. . . . They got enough Africans in there that speak English, and enough Mexicans in there that speak English, with us Americans, that they turned down the union contract this year for the first time." Carol added, "Now they can . . . read everything [on the contract] and we can talk to each other." Aaron observed, "Yes, we can talk to each other for the first time."

As these two workers highlight once again, language is important in labor relations. To manage a diverse labor force ethnic and linguistic interpreters are therefore key mediators. Being able to negotiate in English and Spanish or English and French gives interpreters a significant role in recruitment, training, and maintenance of the non-English speaking workforce. Acting as intermediaries between non-English speakers and management, these intermediaries are particularly important when it comes to cases of injury and contestations, when workers need to know their rights and understand the implications of the documents they sign. The critical role these ethnic intermediaries play in settling disputes between labor and management prompts many interviewees to refer to them as "oreos" or "coconuts": "white inside, black outside." That is, while they look and speak like workers of color, many interviewees who had been involved in cases of labor conflict with management indicated that these intermediaries sided with and acted in the interest of the predominantly white plant management.

Beyond ethnic interpreters, the colloquial analogy to "coconuts" and "oreos" may also describe the public representation versus actual practices of Cargill's claims to corporate responsibility. Cargill projects its public image as a company committed to "promotion of diversity, improvement of workplace safety, and community giving." But looking more closely into its corporate practices at the workplace and in town reveals a different perspective. We see the limits of corporate multiculturalism, which promotes diversity in song and dance but not in understanding. We see how under a veneer of community giving lie financial arrangements that rob the community and its public institutions of their rightful budget allocation through taxation but create back doors of dependency and political patronage through donations as community giving. The narratives of injured workers also reveal the bureaucratic means involved in underreporting work-related injury and illness. Contrary to the company's desired public image as "good neighbors," we see the discursive, financial, and institutional means through which the company governs the town, effectively as its company town. Unlike in company towns of an earlier era, Cargill did not provide infrastructure, houses, and amenities for workers and their families, but moved into a preexisting infrastructure developed by the contributions of previous generations. But as in traditional company towns, the company wields enormous political power in the single-employer-dependent towns to which the food and meat industry relocates.

From Beardstown to Alaska: Where Do Cargill Rejects Go?

In the winter of 2009, I attended a funeral celebration for a Congolese man who had passed away in Congo, but her daughter and her family living in Rushville were honoring him by holding a traditional celebration with lavish food, music, and dance. I was invited to the occasion by Madam Marie, whom I have had the pleasure of interviewing and befriending over time. Several years before, I had recorded the story of her husband, Fredrick, who had broken his arm at work, but the plant's medical crew claimed he had come to work with a broken arm. Though he wanted to fight back, he did not have the means for a battle with the company's lawyers. In the process, he was fired, with no prospect of being hired by others. "Once you are kicked out by Cargill," said Madam Marie, "you are out of them all [referring to large local employers in the area]. . . . You can forget about getting a job with Super Walmart or even Dot Foods, Inc. . . . It's like they tell each other or they check with each other." The idea of losing her job at Cargill was therefore, a doomsday scenario. I had seen Madam Marie several times since our interview, but had refrained from asking her each time about her husband as I knew his unemployment was a sore issue for the family. However, when I did not see him at the funeral his absence was a cause of concern and I felt my inquiry would be acceptable. When I asked Madam Marie about her husband, she said he was in Alaska. He had gone with a group from Beardstown to work on big fishing boats and would be back in March.

When Fredrick came back I met with him and two other West Africans, Koku and Atoma, both Togolese, who had worked with him on the boats in Alaska. Atoma, in his late twenties, had asked for a leave of absence at Cargill to go try the fishing job. Koku, in his thirties, had also worked at Cargill for two years, but had been discharged for "running in with the supervisor." I probed them further. They explained there were about fifteen to thirty African men who regularly went to Alaska from the Beardstown-Rushville area. This had become more common than it had been a few years ago, and while some Mexicans went to Alaska, too, more West Africans tended to make the trip.

From Beardstown to Alaska continued

Fredrick, who had been there three times, said that the first time he went he was with four men from the Rushville-Beardstown area; the second time there were nine. From this conversation I gathered that those who embark on the Alaskan journey are sometimes folks who got in trouble at the plant, sometimes people who hope they can save a lot and pay back their debt faster. "Here the good thing is you know how much lump sum you can have at the end of the season," Atoma said. "You can pay your debt, you are not stuck for being discharged by the plant, you have a way out," Koku said. To make sense of this all I asked Koku, whose English was the best among the three, to tell me his story:

> I worked at the plant three years but then I lost my job. I got into trouble with the supervisor and I was dismissed. I stayed home for one year. I heard about the fishing boats and called and got an interview in Ohio; it was December of 2007. There are two working seasons. Season A: January to March, and season B: June to December. I passed the medical test, bought a ticket to Seattle. I signed a contract for three months' work. From Seattle to Anchorage the company paid for the flight but if I did not finish the terms of my work I had to pay for the flight—twelve hundred dollars each way. The boats were in Dutch Harbor. The flight from Anchorage was in a small plane with thirty people; everyone on that flight was going for work on the fishing boats. Some work is on Akatun, another small island. I took that flight with six other people going to Akatun. It was brutally cold, cold, cold! When I got to Akatun, I worked on land. I worked for packaging and I slept in a room with six men on a bunk. We paid five dollars every day for everything: room, board, and laundry. The pay was $7.50 per hour, and after eight hours each extra hour was paid at $10.70. We worked sixteen hours a day and received about sixteen hundred dollars for two weeks of work. The good thing is that you have no expense and all [the money] was savings. I stayed for three months and brought home eight or nine thousand dollars.

From Beardstown to Alaska continued

They paid me for my ticket to Seattle but for coming back I had to pay for myself. In season B, we work eight to twelve hours getting salmon."

Many of the West African narratives are around repayment of debt. The pressures they feel are enormous: on one hand, to pay for their family left behind and for debt they created to get to the United States and, on the other, for being in "a one man show" in Beardstown. They depend on a single employer with tentacles in almost all other employing organizations in the area. Going to Alaska may have been like going "out of the frying pan and into the fire," but for some, it was a way out.

Figure 8.1: Celebration of Africa Day, Rushville. Photo by the author, 2009.

8 – WE GOT PEOPLE

GIVEN THE DOMINANT PRESENCE OF CARGILL IN THE CITY'S economic and political life, when I started this research project, I expected to find the new immigrants in this small company town living in despair and isolation. I saw Beardstown as a colony of displaced workers who sold their labor to the corporation and in the best-case scenario remitted money to their families and perhaps made a home, to retire to one day in their places of origin. Instead, I saw that despite their experiences of prejudice and racism they had achieved certain spaces of inclusion in public institutions and public spaces, and that they were making a home not only in communities of origin but also in the Midwest in their new place. Spanish-speaking and English-speaking teachers and parents had established a dual language program in schools, where all students received half of their education in Spanish and half in English; West African and Mexican immigrants had overcome an earlier racialized residential geography that separated the two groups between Rushville and Beardstown by engaging in inter-racial renting practices; and they were developing a growing intercultural understanding and appreciation through interracial home-based child care and soccer leagues. Not to be exaggerated, but for a town that had only a short time ago kept itself all-white, a degree of openness found expression among teens who elected a West African as their homecoming king and a Latina as their homecoming queen. When residents spoke to me about their day-to-day life, a certain degree of cross-racial understanding and interaction was apparent—features that did not emerge in discussions about their workplace experiences. I therefore shift the vantage point in this chapter to locations outside the workplace and examine the mediating spaces of interracial and intercultural interaction as they unfold in the realm of social reproduction—that is, home, schools, sports, and child care. The dynamics discussed in this chapter predominantly reflect the experiences of the Mexicans and West Africans as the two main groups of displaced workers that lived in Beardstown and Rushville during the bulk of my fieldwork in Illinois.[1]

INTERRACIAL RENTAL PRACTICES, RESIDENTIAL INTEGRATION

In chapter 2 we discussed how, in the aftermath of the violence that erupted in 1996, the company gently helped with placing West African newcomers in Rushville and separating them residentially from Mexicans and whites in Beardstown to avoid further destabilization of ethno-racial relations. By 2008, following a sharp increase in gas prices, West Africans started looking for housing in Beardstown and relocating to Beardstown. Their move was subsequently made possible by a burgeoning market in rental houses owned by Mexican immigrants.[2] Many Mexican immigrants had bought and fixed up houses, first to live in and later to rent, having taken advantage of a national trend in housing finance that offered low interest mortgages to immigrant applicants with no down payment and no need for legal residency documentation.[3] The high rate of Latinos living in owner-occupied units, however, was not matched among African immigrants,[4] who arrived in Beardstown at least a decade later and in a different housing market.[5]

The differences between the two groups, however, made a good match in the housing market. The new Latino landlords in Beardstown had rental units available while African immigrants were moving into Beardstown. These landlords also offered their units to culturally, linguistically, and racially diverse groups. As a Latino owner of three units, including a mobile home, in Beardstown, explained, "I put my ad up in Spanish. If I don't find anyone, I put the ad in French. Last, I would put it in English." She explained that immigrants were more punctual in their payments and more concerned about getting in trouble with the landlord and law.

Basically, the first wave of immigrants had become able to serve the housing needs of the second wave, and today a large proportion of the West and Central Africans working at the plant have moved to Beardstown. The diverse groups that were recruited for work to the plant, relying on the complementarities of their housing needs and rental practices, challenged the racialized residential geography created for them earlier.

The interracial renting practices assumed further importance in the context of a town that was already residentially integrated in terms of Latinos and whites. Its history as a sundown town meant that the Beardstown had no designated residential area or neighborhood for so-called people of color. In essence, anyone who was not white had been completely zoned out of the town.[6] Thus, when immigrants arrived, there were no preexisting neighborhoods, spatial structures, or zoning ordinances to formally racialize their residential location. Once Cargill recruited workers to its plant, the location of their housing within Beardstown followed availabilities of vacant units, rather than a predrafted racialized zones—hence a significant characteristic of Beardstown: its residential integration. In effect, its dark history contributed to its contemporary development as a space residentially more integrated than many highly diverse cities such as New York City, Los Angeles, and Chicago.[7]

TWO-WAY LANGUAGE IMMERSION

Immigrants in Beardstown have also achieved a notable inclusion in public educational institutions as well as at the library. Schools were perhaps the town's first public institution to feel the impact of immigration: enrollment within the Beardstown school district increased by almost 13 percent from 1990 to 2000 and another 19 percent from 2000 to 2010.[8] These new students changed the racial and ethnic blend within the district. For example, the number of culturally and linguistically diverse (CLD) students in prekindergarten through twelfth grade, who in the 1990s were predominantly Hispanic, increased from 5 in 1994 to 85 in 1997 and to 290 in 2000, or approximately one fourth of the total number of 1,376 students (Cottle et al. 2007). By 2010, those who were not identified as all-white constituted almost 47.5 percent of students. Hispanics constituted nearly 38.5 percent, while students who State Board of Education recorded as black or multiracial increased respectively to over 2.4 percent and 6.6 percent.[9] This trend in the district has continued, with Hispanics constituting 46.1 percent of the student population in 2013, and those identified as black increasing to 6.4 percent.[10]

Such a rapid shift in the district's student demographics had significant implications for the school. To comply with an Illinois mandate,[11] the school administrators felt the pressure of having to offer Spanish language for English learners in the classroom, while they still did not have the appropriate staff to address the school's growing Spanish-speaking student body. Following an extensive ethnographic study, Carla Paciotto and Gloria Delany-Barmann (2011) detail the kinds of dilemmas that the predominantly white teachers and staff faced in this initial phase. They report an incident in which a school administrator who, while watching a grandchild at the playground of a local park, overheard a man speaking Spanish to his children while making a comment to her in English. There and then, she said, "I asked him do you have a job? And he said, 'No, we just moved here from the Chicago area'.... I said, Monday you have a job. Come to our school" (ibid., 229). In that initial period, school officials had to improvise and make use of newcomers' parents.

Together with their student body, the teachers also went through a slow metamorphosis that involved changing not only their skill set but also the way they understood language as a medium of communication and the school as site of cultural mediation. Responding to the state mandate, Beardstown schools first delivered the English Language Learners program, which met the state's minimum transitional requirement and reflected what education scholars refer to as "the perspective of language as a problem" (Paciotto and Delany-Barmann 2011, 226). Beardstown schools also followed an ESL model called "ESL pull-out," whereby Spanish-speaking students were removed from the regular classroom for a certain period of time to be instructed in Spanish. This approach was followed by a Transition and Bilingual Education model (TBE), in which English- and Spanish-speaking students were instructed in separate classrooms with the idea that over two or three years, the Spanish-speaking students would transition to an English only class. But this segregationist approach was not helpful in terms of decreasing the polarization of students in the two language groups. "Seeing the schoolyard tensions among students reflecting the classroom segregation between linguistically different student bodies," one teacher told me, "[we knew] something had to be done." By way of example a TBE classroom teacher shared the following story:

> Before the DLP [Dual Language Program] was established, students from first grade and up would come in from the playground, where the TBE self-contained classes and general education all-English classes would integrate and play, and divulge clear segregation and division based upon language, race or ethnicity. Students would come in and [say,] . . . "Ganamos contra de los blancos" [We won against the whites] in soccer. Replace the game with tag, kickball, cops and robbers, and it would reflect this pattern of division. This would set the TBE teachers on edge. We were not sure if conversations in the gen ed [general education] rooms were the same, but this really disturbed us and gave the social reason for starting to gravitate to the more inclusional dual language model.

Thus, in the 2004–2005 academic year, the school moved to a Dual Language Program (DLP), a bold program that aimed for integration of different linguistic groups in a school by requiring both language groups to receive half of their instruction in the language not spoken at home, in what is also referred to as two-way language immersion (or TWI). For example, every student from an English-speaking family who participates in this program has to do half of his or her curriculum and homework in Spanish, and vice versa.[12]

The school district agreed to adopt DLP, provided that there was parental consent for every participating child. Beardstown teachers then launched what they called "the teachers' movement"—a door-to-door campaign to achieve 100 percent consent among both English- and Spanish-speaking parents. The teachers—some long-standing, native-born locals, and others new, Spanish-speaking classroom aides—along with a Central American school-community liaison paid a visit to every household that had an elementary school child in Beardstown for one-to-one conversation about the value of multicultural education and DLP. "Sometimes we spent hours or a whole evening with one family. . . . The conversation often moved from kids and school to town, change and future," said one teacher who took part in the teachers' movement that summer.

As of November 2008, eighteen schools in Illinois and 335 schools nationwide had DL programs. Of the eighteen Illinois DLP schools, Beardstown was the only one that was rural. Beardstown's public library, more than half of whose clientele are Spanish- and French-speaking immigrants, has also applied a multilingual approach to its services. It offers books and staff services in the three main languages spoken in town and by its young school-age clientele: English, Spanish, and French.

Beardstown's DLP was unique in that it was motivated from below—from a movement among school teachers who organized like members of an army of cultural understanding. Rather than making demands, marching, and rallying, as might be the practice in big cities, English- and Spanish-speaking teachers prevailed through a patient campaign that went door to door. The manageable size of the town and its isolation from other school districts also contributed to their success. Unlike New York or Philadelphia, Beardstown was small enough to make it possible for teachers to spend an hour or an entire evening with each parent of a school-aged child. Moreover, ambivalent or opposing parents did not have an alternative in this situation; they could not move their children to a school in an adjacent residential block—a practice that often increases public-school segregation in large cities.

CLAIMING PUBLIC SPACE: SOCCER
AND CULTURAL CELEBRATIONS

A critical means for claiming public space for the diverse groups of people living in Beardstown has been soccer. On a Sunday afternoon, visitors traveling to Beardstown on Highway 125, where signs of racial hatred had once been displayed, encounter scenes that are unusual in the social landscape of the rural Midwest. At the very entrance to the town, large soccer fields are filled (weather permitting) with racially and linguistically diverse players in colorful uniforms—Latino, African, and white American players all mixed together (figure 8.2). As one white resident humorously observed, "I heard on radio 'soccer is commie' and we'll never have it in Illinois. One day I was driving home and I saw youth playing soccer [at the outdoor fields]. I said 'Holy cow! We must have gone commie!'"

This particular bold public presence of the town's diverse groups is the outcome of a long spatial struggle. Interviewing the founders and the players of the soccer league and its eleven multiracial teams, I learned of a struggle in which minorities asserted their right to play their sport of choice in appropriate public places. One of the league's founders, whom I call "Roberto," explained that "in 1995 immigrants who were in Beardstown and playing soccer

Figure 8.2: Soccer fields at the entry to Beardstown. Photo by Sarah Ross
and Ryan Griffis.

were almost all Spanish-speaking. At the time there were twenty-five of us
from Mexico who played soccer. We would play somewhere out of sight," in
private spaces like the players' backyards. But even though they tried to be
invisible, "the police cars drive back and forth on the street to check on us, . . .
as if we were up to no good." Then for several years they played soccer on
abandoned lots around the town and behind the local school, both of which
were often covered with broken glass and trash. Once, when they had been
kicked out of the field behind the school because of construction, they moved
their games to the park district fields, which at the time hosted only baseball.
But the regular presence of enthusiastic soccer players and their families oc-
cupying the benches and the public park facilities did not go down well. The
white residents complained, so the Latinos could not use the district fields
for soccer. "We had to leave. For two years we had nowhere to go. We used to
drive up to Iowa, two and a half hours away, or to Jacksonville [half an hour
away] to play soccer." Traveling to and from these other towns to play soccer
was not free of anxiety for the Mexican players, who were well aware of the

racist attitudes of people in the region. "My dad was worried about me driving around outside town. He said a lot of KKK lives around here. I said, 'No, they can't do anything to us, we are many.'" Another Mexican "old timer" also noted how they used to carpool and move in numbers.

"But we did not give up," explained Roberto. "We kept talking to the district. And kept playing and making our teams." In 2003, after tireless efforts by the league presidents in negotiating with the park district officials, they at last gained the soccer fields they enjoy today. Ultimately, the park district acquired a piece of land for soccer, and this allowed the Latino players a legitimate presence in the town's public space. "Once we had the land, we worked on making it a functional soccer field. Each player paid five dollars per year, and with that we funded the construction of the wooden shed and benches at the field. . . . Cargill donated trees; the league put in the labor to plant those. The district cares for the grass and mows the field; we the league members clean the fields and pick up trash."

The first team formed was Tejaro. Other teams were also named after the hometowns of players—for example, Morelia, Toluca, Puebla. But today the teams are no longer exclusively made up of players from the towns or regions after which the teams are named. "Each team," explained Roberto, "has more or less three or four African players and perhaps one or two white American players. . . . We get along quite well."[13]

My interview with Diego and Jorge at an all-day soccer tournament on a sunny Sunday in April of 2008 brought further insights. The day before, Roberto had told me about this tournament, so I went to the field to see it for myself. At the sideline, I met Diego and Jorge, who were both from Guanajuato and worked at Cargill. Diego had lived in the United States for twenty years and had been married to a white American woman for five years. This was his third wife, and he had two children with her in Beardstown. But he spoke in broken English. Jorge was also an old timer. He had lived in Beardstown since 1994. While I spoke to them in Spanish, my accent must have been the giveaway that English is my better language, so they moved between English and Spanish when speaking to me. "Things have changed," Jorge said. "*Nos dan mas spacio ahora* [they give us more space now]." When I probed further, he said, "For example, before if we went to the store they look at us like what a strange thing, but now they don't care anymore. *Poco a poco han mejorado* [Little by little things have improved]." "The reality is," he said, "*este pueblo levanto por los Latinos* [this town revitalized because of Latinos]."

When I asked about relations between African and Latino players, Diego said, "*Entre nosotros no hay racismo* [there is no racism among us]." Jorge followed up: "*Fútbol nos unido* [soccer united us] because Africans tell us '*desde chiquito* they played *sin zapatos* and *nosotros egual*' [since they were little they played soccer without shoes and same with us]—we are like each other. We like football and play, and through football we have become more friends. They invite us to their parties, they rent a hall in Rushville for party and invite us; and we invite them to ours. We speak a little of English and they too. It is no problem."

On that beautiful Sunday on my way to and from the soccer field, I drove by the town's park where baseball leagues play and where Roberto said the Mexicans used to play soccer but were kicked off. That day while the soccer field was packed with more than fifty or sixty people—picnicking, cheering families, players getting ready, volunteers selling tacos at a concession stand—I could count no more than a dozen people on the town's baseball fields or tennis courts.

The creation of soccer teams and the acquisition of a soccer field are indeed significant achievements in asserting immigrants' right to this town. These public fields today are new inclusive spaces of interracial, intercultural interaction among the Francophone West Africans and the Latin American immigrants—with increasing numbers of English-speaking white residents joining the teams.

A young Togolese Cargill worker with whom I spoke through an interpreter in Beardstown one spring day in 2007 told me about how through soccer he made friends among Mexicans. "The first day I was shy like, you know, but now is fine." He went on to explain that in Beardstown, one does not have time to do much outside work. Such socializing with other workers as he was able to do was basically only through soccer. Fortuitously, several of his team members were also from his line at the plant. He said that he liked Mexicans, but that they did not socialize outside work: "There is no other thing that links us apart from the soccer."

Housing, schools, and soccer have not been the only means of transforming this former sundown town. The celebration of Mexican Independence

Day in Beardstown (since 1998) and the annual celebration of Africa Day in Rushville (since 2008)[14] are public events that boldly declare the new immigrants' right to the towns and their public spaces. While the first Africa Day was celebrated indoors, subsequent commemorations and other celebrations have been held in the town's public park, starting with a soccer match among Africans and followed by West and Central African music, dance, and food. The celebration of Mexican Independence Day, despite some resentment by white locals, has been growing every year with small but increasing participation by diverse local residents. The first celebration I attended in 2006 was marked by a twenty-one-float parade through the town's streets to the main plaza, where they were greeted by live Mexican music in the gazebo, while Mexican food stalls encircled the plaza. This was the same plaza that in 1996 hosted a six-foot-tall burning cross and a Ku Klux Klan parade!

A leading member of Amigos Unidos, the group that annually organizes the Mexican Independence Day and Cinco de Mayo celebrations, explained succinctly how these celebrations were not mere recreational events. Unlike the International Day event discussed in the last chapter as an example of corporate multiculturalism, these are not spectacles of song and dance introduced from above by paid entertainers and staff. They are rather community events where children and adults participate year-round and put energy into making them meaningful. They stood for something more; something that he suggested meant taking pride in one's cultural identity, a sense of pride at public display.

> "Here is the problem: . . . what are Mexicans known for [in the eyes of average white Americans]? They are known as people that are drunken, uneducated, and illegal . . . Mexicans *trabajan de todo, y comen de todo* [do any kind of work and eat any kind of food]: that is the Mexican identity here. And that is what Mexicans want to do with the celebration of cultural identity in this town . . . [to demonstrate] that they are workers, who are marginalized by everyone and everywhere, they are workers at the bottom of the bottom. But they take pride in their cultural heritage."

The celebrations of Mexican Independence Day and Africa Day have meanings beyond the group that identifies with the event. While in a different context this might not mean much, in the context of this former sundown town the sheer presence of the so called non-white bodies and non-English speech in public spaces—from the plaza to the streets to the sports field to the churches, schools, and libraries—are political and social gains. For

Figure 8.3: Celebration of Mexican Independence Day, Beardstown. Photo by the author, 2007.

Beardstown, simply the presence of immigrants and "others" in public spaces counts as an achievement. Being everywhere, not only in every block of the town, but also in every classroom of the school, in the library and grocery stores, and at the barbeque stands in the public park, immigrants and people of color have appropriated local spaces and created forms of resistance to being criminalized or made invisible.

While referring to the performative politics of the "Occupy" movements, Judith Butler and Athena Athanasiou (2013) highlight the political charge of plural presences in public spaces in ways that resonate with public performance of identity celebrations in the public spaces of Beardstown. They write about assemblage of bodies in public space and certain performative force that results from it. Such collective presence, they argue, does not need to be highly organized or a collective action with a single message. "The 'we are here' that translates that collective bodily presence might be re-read as 'we are *still* here,' meaning: 'we have not yet been disposed of.' We have not

Figure 8.4: Celebration of Mexican Independence Day, Beardstown. Photo by the author, 2007.

Figure 8.5: Celebration of Africa Day, Rushville. Photo by the author, 2009.

Figure 8.6: Mayor of Rushville offered African garments and welcomed to Africa Day in customary West African practice. Photo by the author, 2011.

slipped quietly into shadows of public life" (196). By their collective assembling of bodies and by asserting their plural presences, Latinos and West Africans do more than engage in a cultural celebration; they make a profound political statement.

CHILDCARE AND INTERCULTURAL UNDERSTANDING

While soccer has provided a space for interracial and intercultural relations among men, childcare has served a similar role for women. Mexicans, because of their distinct local and translocal resources and immigration history, are more likely to have their extended families with them than the Africans. Latinos are also more likely to be able to bring in a family member from elsewhere in the United States or from across the border to help with childcare. Often within a larger extended family, there is one young or old woman who stays home to provide childcare for other family members, almost all of whom work at Cargill. West African newcomers have a different history of immigration and different translocal resources and transnational family structures, such that they seldom have their extended families with them. But those West Africans who do have children converge with Mexicans around childcare, as they find the Mexicans' expression of affection and care toward children more akin to Africans'. "They are like us," was how a West African mother put it when speaking about her Mexican caregiver. Another West African interviewee stated, "I go to their house every day to pick up and drop off my child. We talk, I have learned a few words of Spanish, they sometimes invite us to their parties. We are too busy but one time we went. It was fun. . . . In the beginning I used to think differently about them."

On several occasions, I have been surprised by Spanish words and expressions coming from French-speaking Africans. During an International Day celebration at Gard Elementary School in Beardstown, I was sitting next to one of the first West Africans to arrive in Beardstown, a Senegalese woman who worked at the plant and mothered a set of twins. Since I am a mother of twins myself, we shared notes, having what is called "twin mothers' chats." As a young Latina girl passed by, the Senegalese woman said to her, "*Oye, y tu mama? Donde esta?*" [Hey and your mom? Where is she?]. Then, she and the girl continued speaking in Spanish about what was going on with her mother and at her school. Once their conversation was over, I asked my Senegalese acquaintance whether she had had a Spanish education back home. She shrugged and said no. Her twin children were raised by the girl's Mexican family, and so over the years she had picked up the Spanish from daily contact. It seemed like she had picked up more than language but also a rapport with the family. This was not an exception. I heard similar stories from other workers. The growing intercultural interaction and understanding seems to be everywhere: a French-speaking West African yells from the back of the room at a community event "*ándale pues*" (Mexican Spanish slang for "come on now"); a Mexican student in an ESL class makes a pact with a fellow French-speaking student to teach others in the class one French word a day. Not surprisingly, a growing number of interracial romances have also been blossoming in Beardstown.

The increasing numbers of multiracial children enrolled in the district might be a good indication of the latter. While a decade ago, the Illinois Interactive Report Card did not make any report on the number of interracial children registered, by 2007 it indicated that multiracial students made up

4.9 percent of registered students in the district,[15] and by 2010 this figure had risen to 6.6 percent.[16]

My interview with a resident in her nineties revealed broader effects of interracial intimacies. She had a Latino neighbor on one side and an African on the other side. While she did not leave home much, she mentioned, "They are nice people, very nice people, very helpful. . . . If they see me carrying something they offer help. They always say hello." But these were infrequent interactions. What was most puzzling for her was how her feelings about blacks had changed since her granddaughter started dating a young black man. She asked me to follow her to her kitchen so she could show me a picture of the couple she had posted with a magnet on her refrigerator. With her finger crooked and deformed by arthritis, she dislodged the picture and offered it to me to take a good look. It was of a nice smiling couple embracing, one dark and one blond. The girl was in the front and the boy in the back with his arms wrapped around her. They both had big smiles. The grandmother said, "Now that my granddaughter has a black boyfriend . . . I get a funny feeling, some kind of a connection with the black people. . . . It's weird I think, it's kind of scary. Perhaps it is blood, because she is with him so I feel different. It's a feeling I can't explain."

Opportunities for interaction and developing relationships among residents in spaces outside the workplace open possibilities to overcome the competitive and zero-sum relationships that have dominated in the realm of production. As neighbors, tenants, childcare providers, teammates, lovers, and parents, individuals and groups have opportunities to interact and experience dynamics different from those at the plant.

BEYOND FORMAL POLITICS

The formal structures of representation in Beardstown remain largely unaffected by its dramatic demographic and social changes. Most of the immigrants do not have legal citizenship and so cannot vote or take part in the formal politics of this town. The same bigoted mayor, Robert Walters, has been elected into office for four terms, and the city council remains all white and all English speaking and includes only one woman.[17] There is no formal planning agency or entity, nor are professionally trained planning staff involved in development decisions in this town.[18] The council meets twice a month, typically for less than half an hour, and members of the public rarely attend. The mayor is the obvious kingpin in this structure. According to one local authority, "There has never been a time when the council voted down one of the mayor's proposals in council." Indeed, voting at meetings is not even critical to decision-making within the local authority. The real decisions are made elsewhere, an interviewee suggested. Mr. Roberts, a member of the sixth generation of a local farming family, pointed to a nearby table in a local diner, saying that is where the "old boys' club" meets and makes the real decisions. "This is the 'city council,' here. Right here is where all the town decisions are made every morning sometime between seven-thirty and eight-thirty. First comes Jim and gets his coffee, then comes John and gets his coffee, after them usually come Robert and Tom. By eight o'clock we have a full council where they discuss what is what and what needs to be done."[19]

In a town that depends on a single employer, any form of collective community organizing outside the company's ambit is likely to appear threatening. But despite the enormous constraints, and absence of formal structures for intercultural dialogue and integration, Mexican and West African immigrants have achieved a certain inclusion in public institutions and public spaces to make a home in Beardstown. These spaces of inclusion were not mandated from above by any formal institution, nor were they achieved through confrontational politics or large-scale protests. In Beardstown, immigrants and their allies have built sites of intercultural and interracial interaction beyond the workplace and asserted their right to have a public presence in this town. They have done so not through metropolitan-style large-scale marches, or through formal processes of so-called community development planning and citizen participation, but through unassuming practices and everyday undertakings, the kind of noncollective, nonconfrontational practices that Asef Bayat (2010) describes as the "quiet encroachments" occurring in some authoritarian countries.

More significantly, the story of immigrants' inclusion in Beardstown does not follow the stereotypical "melting pot" model. In certain respects they have moved beyond this model. For example, they have pushed the educational system beyond ESL or programs in which where Spanish-speaking children have to transition to English-only classrooms. In Beardstown, English-speaking children, and indeed increasingly French-speaking children, all have to learn another language. It is a mode of inclusion where two linguistic groups take a step to meet each other. Similarly, in sports, Beardstown immigrants have not sought inclusion of their children in popular American sports such as baseball or football, although some do. At schools and in little league baseball in district parks, the priority for the immigrant community has been to make space in the public realm for the sport of their choice—soccer.

Shifting our vantage point beyond the formal politics and relations of production at the workplace is key to recognizing agency among Beardstown immigrants, making people and their placemaking practices visible as they build a community and recreate this place as their new home. While institutional hierarchies of school and park districts remain dominated by white and English-speaking members, both native-born and immigrant residents have used local schools, soccer fields, family-based childcare, and residential neighborhoods as significant sites to renegotiate interracial relations, through which they make place.

The vantage point from which we look is important in what we see or do not see in the story of Beardstown. "Looking from above," searching for large-scale formal organization, be it of planning or politics, and collective action within or outside formal structures, one is bound to see Beardstown as a place where immigrants are passive subjects. "Looking from below," however, paying attention to the range of informal arrangements and activities that mediate the relationships among diverse groups in Beardstown, reveals a very different picture.

The kinds of interrelations that develop in communities among diverse groups are not only shaped by race, ethnicity, or immigration status but, as Lamphere and colleagues argue, also influenced by the specificities of mediating institutions and sites through which they interact (1992, 2).[20] In the particular case of Beardstown, mediation sites outside the plant and beyond the formal politics have offered important opportunities for interaction and emerging interracial, intercultural dynamics—opportunities that we would have missed if we focused solely on the realm of production or on formal political processes and structures.

When we focus on the plant and on the formal politics as the mediating sites for interracial dynamics among a diverse recruited workforce, the logic of corporations dominates what we detect—namely, displaced minority labor forces who are pitted against each other at the plant and governed outside the plant by formal institutions that remain all-white and unaffected by the demographic shifts in a town ruled and governed by the company's interest. Isolated and dependent on a single employer, the new arrivals are bound to be passive victims of global capitalism, trapped in the heartland, in "the middle of nowhere."

But if we shift the vantage point and consider the emerging interactions mediated through spaces and relationships outside the workplace and outside the formal structures of politics and so-called community participation, in the realm of social reproduction—places like schools, homes, parks, libraries, and childcare centers—we see a range of other possibilities and relationships. When looking from below and through the microworlds and everyday practices of people, we come to grips with the intense everyday negotiation of experiential and aspirational difference among people who share a given local place.[21] Ash Amin (2004, 39) calls this relational politics at the local level a "politics of propinquity," a "politics of negotiating the immanent effects of geographical juxtaposition between physical spaces, overlapping communities, contrasting cultural practices." Relational politics of place pays attention to physical space and the role it plays in negotiation of issues thrown up by living with difference on the same proximate turf, and "sharing a common territorial space" (ibid. 39). This is relational politics at the local level.

The immigrant labor force recruited to the Beardstown plant arrived in a town without public and social service agencies experienced in dealing with the needs of diverse groups. Moreover, the preexisting formal institutions such as the town council, the park district, or the School District Boards never opened up to include the racially diverse new residents. To renegotiate their interracial relations and assert their right to be present in this former sundown town, immigrants and their local, native-born allies took advantage of mediating sites outside formal structures, within the realm of social reproduction. They took advantage of absences and constraints and opened up a space within the existing institutional cracks. For example, in the absence of preexisting rental housing complexes to receive immigrants, like those an old-style company town might have offered to its workers, residential neighborhoods became an alternative mediating site in the emerging interactions of diverse groups. Through interracial rentals of refurbished housing units, these groups promoted residential integration. Similarly, in the absence of private, public, or nonprofit affordable child-care services or company-provided daycare at the plant, immigrant women established informal home-based childcare and made this a site that mediates their relationships.

For planning,[22] the discipline in which I teach and train students, a discipline to which placemaking is of core interest, these observations are instructive in several ways. Studying transnationalism and placemaking from below highlights the importance of vantage points in the kind of politics and processes we can detect or suppress. They also bring to light the important practices by people on the ground as citizen planners. As we decenter the metro in the analytical structure of globalization, we also decenter professional planning in the vast scope of actors and practices involved in placemaking. Most importantly—what I consider as the key contribution of this story—these observations help us to take seriously the significance of local place for the dynamics of people in placemaking.

—

PLACE MATTERS

The story of Beardstown helps us to reflect on the role that local place plays in the kinds of transnational and social relationships that emerge in communities of destination. The varied resources, networks, and racialized histories of local actors situated within a specific place constituted by certain social and spatial relationships make a difference in the experience of interethnic dynamics—that is, of transnational immigrants vis-à-vis native born people of European descent and among immigrant groups alike. In Beardstown, it is through marginalized spaces that these groups renegotiate their relationships within the realm of social reproduction. Through a multifocal and interscalar analysis, we can see how specificities of spatial proximity matter in emergent relational politics in a local place and how these relational politics differ from those of metropolitan areas or global cities.

Paying attention to the interactions among and between immigrants and native-born residents not only at the plant but also in the realm of social reproduction at schools, neighborhoods, parks, and sport fields, we note nascent cultural understandings as immigrants make their homes in the heartland. Without rendering one reality less important than the other, I simply stress the need to consider processes and practices involved in spheres of both economic production and social reproduction. Looking beyond the work-place and through the everyday practices of these workers and their families, the vitality of this community, seemingly against all odds, is evident. While within the plant workers might be set against each other, within the town they live side by side, their children go to the same school, their little ones are cared for by the same providers, and they play on the same soccer teams. They create budding solidarities and forge new cultural understandings. They re-negotiate the ethnoracial divisions and tensions that local racism and global capitalism impose among them.

Far from engaging in a naïve celebration of multiculturalism and diver-sity, I understand how these networks of trust and reciprocity also work for technologies of neoliberal governance. Indeed, transnational immigrants are often upheld as ideal neoliberal citizens: self-reliant and able to do much with little. Workers health, for example, is in Cargill's interest, and thus so is their having an active sports life. But I see difficulty in labeling immigrants as either victims or contributors to a neoliberal mode of capitalism. It is these binaries and closures that an interscalar, multifocal perspective will over-come. The social and spatial changes in this town are neither consistent, nor stable. We heard of the Mexicans' experiences of racist violence when they first arrived in an all-white Beardstown; we also heard about the African Americans' experiences of racism and prejudice with Latino youth, and how white locals constructed West Africans as "better black," comparing them to the Detroiters.

Differences among the diverse groups in Beardstown are relational; and shape relational politics that are complex, tentative, and open to future rene-gotiation. "Always temporary and fragile, always the product of negotiation and changing intersectional dynamics" (Amin 2004, 39), a relational politics of place overcomes binaries of victimhood and heroism.

To understand the inter-ethnoracial relations and their relational politics, the local context matters. It is not merely as the site of enactment of those social dynamics; it also forms them. The spatial juxtaposition of difference and the proximity of specific physical and social attributes are vital to the emergent cul-tural, economic, and political dynamics among diverse groups in a particular place. These relations evolve quite differently in a place like Beardstown than a metropolis like Chicago—a so-called global city. In the latter, immigrants might be better able to build and sustain distinct ethnic institutions and cultures, which, in turn, might minimize the sort of interethnic relations I document in here.

In contrast to metropolitan areas, the possibility for anonymity in a company town like Beardstown is limited. Combined with dependence on a single employer, the town's size imposes an enormous constraint on the kind of political or collective action that can emerge. Here, no collective action takes place outside the watchful eyes of the corporation. But then, the small-town status of Beardstown has also made certain opportunities possible. Ownership of homes and rental properties, for example, is more affordable for immigrants. Unlike metropolitan areas with racially and ethnically segregated neighborhoods that channel new arrivals to certain areas based on their ethnic and racialized affiliation, previously homogenous sundown towns like Beardstown had no internal zoning regulations. This meant that newcomers found houses wherever there was a landlord willing to rent or sell a unit to them. The fact that immigrants in a short time were able to become homeowners and landlords further strengthened the possibilities for diverse people to live side by side and engage in interracial interactions.

Similarly, in terms of the education system, the spatial attributes of Beardstown played a role in the emergence of the DLP. What facilitated the teachers' ability to achieve this was their determination as well as the manageable size of the town in which they could conduct a door-to-door campaign. The fact that ambivalent or opposing parents did not have the easy option of moving their children to a school in the adjacent residential block—a process that often facilitates segregated public school enrollments—was also helpful in this regard.

What also contributes to the emergent dynamics of Beardstown are its material characteristics—taking materiality to mean "the physical world that surrounds us: nature, human-made objects, our bodies, and even more broadly, the way space is organized around us, and the concrete practices and technologies we employ in our everyday life" (Gille 2013, 157).[23] Size is only one aspect of the material characteristics of a local place. Size alone does not determine the unfolding social dynamics. In a small homogenous and physically isolated but affluent town, the arrival of immigrants would lead to reactions and development different from those in Beardstown. A global sense of place, as Doreen Massey (1991) writes, is "the accumulated history of a place, with that history itself imagined as the product of layer upon layer of different sets of linkages, both local and to the wider world" (29). In the case of Beardstown, its being historically a sundown town, a heavily industrial blue-collar town, a small and affordable town all matters, along with the composition and the complementarities of diverse incoming groups. This is not to argue that Beardstown is unique, although everyplace is unique in the sense that specificities continually change (Massey 1991). However, I wish to highlight that the social and the spatial character of the place, what I call the materiality of the place, matters.

Many aspects of social and spatial relationships that shape transnational processes in Beardstown are different from those documented by the vast literature on global cities. This company town that is the local site of intense global capital accumulation is also a locus of alternative spatial formations and transnational processes that may facilitate distinct social dynamics and politics. We can, however, recognize the means by which local actors achieve a dignified life if we pay attention to the unassuming forms of their humanity and their everyday practices in a range of mediating spaces, including those in the realm of social reproduction. Measured against metropolitan areas or collective actions that occur in realms of production, the emerging transnational spaces of the heartland may appear simply as spaces of despair for victimized newcomers. But by studying nonmetropolitan areas and towns in their own right, we can register the ways in which immigrants and their local allies can renegotiate the relationships that global capital imposes on them, and we can see the humanity and agency of people making place and a new home in this global heartland.

CONCLUSION

The Global in My Backyard

The world is like a Mask dancing. If you want to see it well you do not stand
in one place.

—Chinua Achebe, *Arrow of God*

THAT SUNDAY IN MAY 2005, WHEN I TOOK MY FIRST DRIVE TO BEARD-
stown, I gained a new glimpse of the global, this one virtually in my Illinois
backyard. As a scholar of globalization, I had in previous decades studied the
relationship between global policies and local development of communities
in cities of Latin America and Africa. From Guadalajara, Mexico, to Cape
Town, South Africa, I had examined how those stripped of their substantive rights as citizens fought back and made homes for themselves and their
families not because of but *despite* formal urban politics and policies. What
I found in my Illinois backyard was not wholly different from my observations in Latin American and African cities—but now, in Beardstown, I saw
similar struggles from a different vantage point.

Achebe's reference to the dancing Mask in the African proverb cited in the epigraph applied directly to me as I struggled to understand the transformation of that midwestern town. In the course of my research for this book, I traveled around the world to hear the stories that wove together the complex lives of people who were making a place for themselves in Beardstown. I combined ethnography and political economy—the worm's-eye view and the bird's-eye view—to see Beardstown from inside and outside and to discover "the dancing Mask" of this small town in the heartland—a global heartland.

What we see through the stories of Beardstown are not exceptions, and my arguments here are not only about Beardstown. These stories offer insights that make generalizable, interconnected contributions methodologically, conceptually, and politically—insights that help us theorize place and placemaking relationally and expose the global cost of migrant labor. The methodology of this project, that of studying its subject from the vantage points of different actors and distinct macro- and micro-analytic scales, recovers the interconnected stories and the unequal stakes involved in them. These stories go virtually unacknowledged in contemporary accounts of migration and global labor mobility, yet they are essential in explaining the transformation of Beardstown *in relational terms*. They demonstrate Beardstown's transformation through its constituent relationships within and outside its territorial bounds. These are relations of race and labor, of production and social reproduction; they include inter-immigrant relations as well, at the workplace and beyond. All of these are central to placemaking in Beardstown as well as in Michoacán and Togo.

A relational conceptualization of place, as Doreen Massey, Gillian Hart, and other human geographers remind us, sees local place as porous, not as a bounded, discrete territory. Place shapes and is shaped by its histories, practices, and processes that are not confined to the territorial bounds of its locality. Social relations that shape Beardstown stretch across the globe. A relational approach seeks to recognize people, processes, and practices inside and outside its territorial boundaries, here and elsewhere, today and in the past, all of which make a place and give it meaning and politics.

Through such an approach, I recover voices and stories often hidden, made invisible, or left out of the picture, to theorize place and placemaking relationally. Voices we hear in this book help us see Beardstown as an open entity, which has been able to combat its depopulation not independent of, but through, histories, forces, imaginations, and actors inside and outside its territorial bounds. Recovery of suppressed voices and stories helps us to see how the economic revitalization of Beardstown is shaped through and beyond work performed at its manufacturing plant and workplaces and to see the dynamics of care and cultural reproduction invested from afar by families, individuals, and institutions across national boundaries. These voices also allow us to see beyond the formal politics of large-scale collective action (or lack thereof) to explore the informal politics and intergroup dynamics beyond the white–non-white binary. This relational theorization contests the closures that dominate the analytics of migration and global labor mobility.

A relational understanding of place and placemaking overcomes many binaries and closures by looking at the interrelationships among people, places, processes, and practices. It pays attention not only to the extraterritorial relationships but also to nuanced interrelationships within the territorial bounds of a place; not only to the macro-worlds of structural forces and processes but also to the refined micro-worlds of everyday practices; and not only to the dynamics of labor at the workplace but also to the dynamics of people outside the workplace in neighborhoods, schools, sport fields, streets, and public spaces. It interrogates ethnic and racial dynamics not only through relationships between whites and people of color or between native-born and foreign-born groups, but also through interethnic, interracial and inter-immigrant group interactions. It considers not only everyday practices within Beardstown but also everyday transnational practices that connect Beardstown to the world outside. It examines not only the economic logic of staying in dangerous, dirty, and difficult meatpacking jobs but also the imagination and the cultural and emotional motivations for staying or leaving, for making a place here in Beardstown and/or there in Mexico or Togo. This perspective focuses not so much on formal urban and labor politics (unions and city halls) as on the tiny little interactions that move in the direction of sort of alternative politics—perhaps of solidarity or compassion.

When place is understood relationally, with its translocal and transnational interconnections exposed, it is hard to picture place as stable or coherent—or as a "settled community" (Massey 1995, 46). It is true that the increasing globalization and time-space compression of the present era give rise to an exclusionist localism, regionalism, and nationalism, and to a heightened "need" for "a blessed haven of retreat from an uncomfortable world" (ibid., 48)—a kind of stable, bounded, coherent community. But that is precisely what this book shows to be realistically impossible. To make a home in the heartland is not at all to seek some such retreat—not when there is nothing bounded, stable, or coherent about Beardstown.

In the absence of understanding gained through this kind of interrelational conceptualization, the story of Beardstown could be misconstrued either as a success story—a rosy tale of "multiculturalism" and the "American Dream" come true, with immigrants making a home in a small midwestern town and revitalizing it as well—or as a dark tale of racism, exploitation, and inter-group competition. Recovering the complexities of the story of Beardstown without falling for either of the two narratives, however, is possible through the patient work of ethnography and difficult work of weaving it with politi-cal economic analytics. It is by recovery of these less acknowledged and at times contradictory interrelationships that we can understand places like Beardstown beyond generalizations of a planetary magnitude, capture the differences that particularities of place make, and challenge the notion of local place as a bounded, coherent, and stable community.

In its relational theorization *Global Heartland* overcomes analytic closures by allowing us to see (1) interconnected production and social reproduction of migrant labor; (2) materiality of place and politics of in-placement; and (3) unsettling categories of belonging.

INTERCONNECTED PRODUCTION AND SOCIAL REPRODUCTION OF MIGRANT LABOR

A common story told about places like Beardstown is that immigrants come to these towns because of jobs that are available; they stay at those jobs be-cause places like Beardstown are affordable and safe to live in; and because from there, they can remit the surplus of their earnings to their families back home to help them out and ultimately to make a place and house there for themselves. On the contrary, the stories of Sena, Kossi, and the Fernández family reveal that immigrants did not simply follow jobs to Beardstown; nor was the money they sent home a surplus, intended to "give a hand." Such views are simply an outcome of focusing on communities of destination or origin without accounting for a series of interrelationships between production and social reproduction of labor force, between remittance and out-sourced care work, and between production and social reproduction of place in one community and another. A relational theorization seeks to correct these analytic shortcomings.

The immigrant labor force we met in Beardstown did not simply arrive there in search of jobs. They were systematically produced through processes of dis-possession and dislodged to places like Beardstown to take low-paid, high-risk jobs. For example, for Mr. Fernández, who lost his rural livelihood to NAFTA because he could not compete with the low prices of imported dried milk, the relocation of his sons to Beardstown was an induced migra-tion, as were the "migrations" of educated Togolese who were displaced to Beardstown following West Africa's post–Cold War restructuring policies. Detroiters were also produced as a mobile surplus workforce for corpora-tions like Cargill. But their production was through processes of deindus-trialization that took place decades earlier in the rust belt. Uncovering the stories of Fernández, Kossi, Sena, Aaron, and Carol helps us overcome an analytic closure by revealing the relationship between dispossession and displacement—processes that systematically produce a surplus workforce fueling global labor mobility. Referring to such processes as "emigration to the Midwest" obscures the processes that produce the movement of labor from one location to another.

Relational theorization does not separate processes of dispossession and the crisis of social reproduction. Global labor mobility might be induced through dispossession and the "expulsions" Saskia Sassen (2014) describes, but it is the social reproduction of this displaced labor force that sustains this process. Transnational workers fragment their lives spatially and tem-porally and outsource aspects of social, cultural, and biological care work to communities, individuals, and institutions in other places. Sena leaves her children and her elderly mother behind with Emefa and Djidonou and sends them twenty-five dollars a month. The Mexican workers I met at the Numaran plaza took their old, slow, and injured bodies to Michoacán to be cared for by the Mexican Institute of Social Security and other public health institutions and nonprofit organizations in Mexico. Madam Marie with pride paid to perform her father's funeral cultural rituals. Tejarans in Beardstown were able to fund longer processional ceremonies for their local saints' days in Michoacán. The performances of biological and cultural care needed for social reproduction in these cases are fragmented to take place at different moments in different places—places that are physically distanced but relationally intimate. To understand global labor mobility, hope, pride, guilt, and imaginations that are attached to an "elsewhere" are also important. Laborers with transnational connections might be able to bear a lower cost of social reproduction and a greater promise of future reward when they have an "imagined elsewhere." Transnational families, through complex means of social and cultural reproduction and their free or underpaid social and cultural care work, subsidize the low wage that workers receive in places of destination. Migrant workers with transnational ties and imaginations are forced to break their lives into pieces to be outsourced at low cost and performed by their families, institutions, and support networks elsewhere. Outsourced lives subsidize the cost of social reproduction for the workers and their families—a strategy less likely to be available to native-born workers who do not have transnational connections, be they African Americans or white U.S.-born workers.

A relational theorization challenges an important analytic misconception in migration studies about remittances. Remittance is not an outcome of global labor mobility; it is an integral aspect of it. Remittances are not a surplus workers "siphon out of Beardstown" to their families in communities of origin; nor are their families and friends in communities of origin recipients of a "freebie," as one might call it.

Let us be clear: far from being a "freebie" or assistance, the remittances Cargill workers send home to their transnational families and networks are undervalued payments they make for work and the in-kind resources offered by their communities. These in-kind resources are not limited to care work and the like. As the stories of unemployed youth in Tejaro or lottery visa aspirants in Lomé reveal, these resources also take the form of recognition, pride, respect, cultural reaffirmation, and the hope that keeps workers in Beardstown. A relational theorization recognizes the multidirectional flows of resources, accounting not only for resource contributions by immigrants (as in remittances) but also for their support network at home. Remittances sent home for social and cultural reproduction of migrant workers and their families are integral to the production of a migrant labor force.

MATERIALITY OF PLACE AND POLITICS
OF IN-PLACEMENT

Seeing interrelations between remittance and the social reproduction of the labor force also has significant implications for relational theorization of place and placemaking. Places such as Tejaro or Lomé, we are often told, are developed through resources immigrants send home. Immigrants' money earned abroad funds roads, infrastructure, houses, and even sports fields. In these stories immigrants are cast as villains who siphon out resources to their places of origin or heroes who sacrifice their own leisure and work hard to send remittances home. Neither scenario makes visible how people in such places as Tejaro and Lomé provide for development of places like Beardstown.

Moving across vantage points and seeing lives connected gives us an alternative perspective on resource flows and the range of actors contributing to the revitalization of Beardstown. We see how social reproduction of places such as Beardstown in the global North relies on the unpaid or underpaid work performed by people in communities in the global South, whose practices subsidize immigrants' wages and hence allow them to stay in low-wage jobs in communities of destination and make a home in communities of destination—a process I call "in-placement." The displaced workers' placemaking in communities of destination (in-placement) and the devastating and cruel processes of *displacement* to which they have been subjected, cannot be separated and seen in isolation from each other. Following dispossession and displacement, immigrants invest in houses and public works in their communities of origin, but they also invest in placemaking in their destination—in the case of Beardstown, making a global heartland.

Corporations are not alone in benefiting from these global processes of dispossession and displacement that ultimately bring them low-waged workers subsidized by their families, friends, and institutions back home. We in the global North—as consumers, shopkeepers, homeowners, and residents—also benefit directly from such induced processes of global labor mobility. We can enjoy consumer goods, in this case food and meat products, at affordable prices at our dinner table, and we can enjoy public resources where immigrants live and work. For example, from the collection and use of the tax revenues that these workers pay, we in places of destination can enjoy the maintenance and even improvement of our schools and public libraries, as we saw in Beardstown. We as shopkeepers can count on a steady clientele. As homeowners, we can enjoy a healthy housing market for buying or renting houses. We need to recognize how immigrants' processes of home-making, or in-placement, in destinations directly benefit us as individuals and as communities; and how they, the immigrant workers and their transnational families, pay the price through their embodied suffering (Holmes 2013).

Conceptually, these insights make an important contribution to globalization scholarship, particularly in respect to global labor mobility and local development. The benefits of migration to social reproduction in communities of origin are often discussed in concrete terms, whereas the benefits of immigration captured by the global North are represented in indirect concepts such as "accumulation of capital." Uncovering a relational production of place and processes of in-placement in destination, this book overcomes the false binary construction of the global as abstract and the local as concrete—a conceptualization that stems from imperial convictions that the North *produces* globalization and the South *experiences* it; that the experiences of the North are generalizable to be theorized but those of the South are case studies. Studying ethnographically the global social reproduction of Beardstown shows how people of the North gain in concrete terms. They gain schools, fixed-up houses, and revitalized local economies through resources invested by immigrants and their families in their processes of in-placement.

In the opening chapter of this book, I asked, if we look outside the spotlight of the global cities, away from the gaze of large metropolitan areas and the large-scale political activism that formal immigrant coalitions shape, what would we see in terms of the urban dynamics of migration? What would we see if we focus on the dark shaded areas, the blind spots created by the intense conceptual light that dominant urban scholarship of globalization shines on its usual subjects? Would we see similar spatial dynamics in splintered and polarized places? We know that today, no space escapes capitalism. Places like Beardstown cannot be conceptualized as rural towns in some traditional sense that assumes that the "rural" exists outside capitalist relationships. Rural places have *always* been places of flows, of in- and out-migration, of displacement (of Native Americans, for example), and of in-placement. But if all spaces are urban in the sense that they are an integral part of capitalism as Beardstown is, then in this age of global capitalism and in the "global village" where we live, does place make a difference in dynamics of the globally mobile labor at the local level? Clearly, the politics we see in Beardstown are different from those played out in Chicago, for example, where diverse migrant workers organize collectively in solidarity and heroically to renegotiate their right to the city and participate in movements such as Occupy Chicago. But in the absence of those forms of migrant activism and politics, I asked, are we to see places like Beardstown as spaces of despair and exploitation? Moreover, would the intergroup dynamics in Beardstown be similar to those in another nonmetropolitan meatpacking town? Does the local context matter in how diverse populations negotiate their interrelationships and therefore the kinds of interracial, inter-immigrant, intercultural politics that emerge?

The nuanced recovery of processes of in-placement helps us bring to light the significance of local context—that is, local context not only in its social but also in its material sense. Materiality of place, as discussed in chapter 8, involves a range of characteristics in the physical world that surrounds us, characteristics that are socially and historically constituted and materially expressed. Sociality of place produces and inhabits a particular solid form. The solidity of this built form, as unstable as it might be, has not only a social but also a material existence that makes a difference in the emergent conjunctional politics of the place. The politics of place emerge not only through a place's sociohistorical positioning in capitalist relationships, as the scalar positioning argument proposes,[1] but also by virtue of certain material features of that place. We know that sociality and materiality of place are not separate but they are also not the same. Combined, sociality and materiality of place produce specific place-based politics that need to be recovered and acknowledged.

Emergent urban scholarship, which rightly critiqued the physical determinism that dominated urban scholarship in the early twentieth century, seems to have swung the analytic pendulum to the opposite end in the early twenty-first century. In stressing the social construction of space and the formation of cities in relation to the broader structures of capitalism, that emergent urban scholarship has paid little attention to the materiality of its subject matter and hence what I call assuming a "post-material" position in urban scholarship. It is precisely by seeing through such a post-material analytic optic that the emergent urban scholarship ends up with its metrocentric theorization—a metrocentrism that silences a range of places and place-based politics, as in Beardstown.

A brief detour will help to explain my positon in critique of post-material and metrocentric theorization. This century, which by some is declared as century of the city and the Urban Age,[2] has already seen energized debates among scholars who seek to theorize the urban anew and offer new ways of understanding and analyzing the urban—analytically, methodologically, and ontologically. One strong camp, at the center of which are Euro-American scholars, has engaged with the hypothesis Henry Lefebvre put forward forty years ago and coined the term "planetary urbanization."[3] Advocating for an integrated theorization of urbanization and capitalism, they stress that just as no corner of the planet escapes relations of capitalism, so no space escapes being urban. They call for an analytic shift from city, which is often understood as bounded territory or physical object, to a planetary urban society.[4]

This theorization of capitalism and production of space, in challenging the binaries of city/non-city, urban/rural, town/country, and society/nature, makes a significant ontological contribution to the study of places like Beardstown—places that in a binary construction are described as rural, as in outside the intense relations of industrial and global capitalism. While the notion of planetary urbanization helps to overcome this shortcoming, it fails to account for specifics of place and the difference the particular materiality of place makes in the kinds of politics and global-local relationships it fosters. In absence of such, the analytical framework for understanding processes of globalization, migration, and local development defaults to a perspective of urban scholarship predominantly shaped through experience of metropolitan areas and global cities—a metrocentric perspective.

As I advocate in this book, we need a relational theorization of place and placemaking to advance urban scholarship beyond generalizations of a planetary scale, which overlook the microworlds of people and the provisional politics they engage in a range of places. In this book, while I stress and embrace the relational openness of the place, I also make a case for paying attention to the difference the solidity of place makes. In other words, we must pay attention not only to how difference is produced but also to how difference is produced differently in different places—places differentiated by not only their social but also their material characteristics.

The diverse groups that live in Beardstown negotiate their existence in this place differently than those living elsewhere, whether that be a place that does not have a similar history of race and labor, or a place that is not a company town run by one single giant multinational, or a place without the brutal history of sundown towns which does away with any need for spatial segregation within a town. The facts that Beardstown is a company town and a sundown town, small in size and population play a role in the emergent politics of this place and dynamics of migration. For example, when teachers tried to implement two-way language immersion in the school, the fact that there was only one school helped with preventing the usual segregation process we observe in other cities with multiple school choices. The fact that it was a sundown town with no preexisting ethnic neighborhoods made it possible to have a complete mix of neighbors. The affordability of the housing market and the relative ease with which new immigrants become homeowners in the 1990s also played a role in creating a new generation of Mexican homeowners who could rent to newcomers, who happened to be by and large West Africans. The absence of preexisting ethnic-based services made for more interethnic services, such as childcare. Space, based on a distinct institutional structure as well as specific social histories and physical characteristics, mediates particular relationships among diverse groups that negotiate their relationships of power. Place—a social and material place—might facilitate and/or frustrate certain relations of power among actors and agents. It might frustrate interaction, and promote further competition by segregation within the dominant and entrenched racialized hierarchies of society. It might also facilitate in small ways the possibilities of interactions that bring about understanding and solidarity.

Relational theorization, however, encourages us to see beyond formal versus informal politics or politics at work versus politics in neighborhoods. It encourages us to see the opportunities that lie in between these false binaries by breaking the separation that is assumed between them. By seeing the potentiality of emerging informal politics of a place among diverse immigrant groups, be it through playing soccer, caring for children, neighboring, or learning each other's language, we expand the realm of politics and possibilities of organizing in such places as Beardstown, where a multinational giant rules with an iron hand and makes possibilities of solidarity through workplace politics more difficult.

In short, context creates opportunities and imposes constraints in a locally created transnational space. The transformations achieved in Beardstown were not the result of organizing, which metrocentric literature on global cities and immigrants' large metropolitan destinations highlights. Rather, they were shaped through possibilities and constraints of their specific context, with a materiality distinct from that of global cities, for us to observe through the prism of a global heartland.

Paying attention to the specific possibilities and limitations of the local place and its politics may also reveal opportunities for activism otherwise missed. In single-employer company towns such as Beardstown, where mobilizing in the workplace is extremely difficult, especially considering the existence of pro-management unions, the insights we gain through ethnographic study of workers' micro-worlds outside the workplace show that there are alternative means of promoting labor solidarity. Through children and neighbors and grocers and nannies and teammates, workers might get to know each other in different terms and form compassions that structures and institutions of labor do not facilitate. We need to explore the alternative spaces outside the production site that could have potential for creating solidarity among diverse populations within the community at large.

In the global South, where a large portion of labor is unemployed or is involved in informal sector work, residential neighborhoods and living quarters, as opposed to workplaces, are indeed a realm for effective organizing and activism and have served as the epicenter of a politics of solidarity among poor and marginalized groups (Salo 2015). The debates on labor solidarity have hence shifted to see social movement unionism or community-labor organizing as a strategy to organize and mobilize outside the sites of production, within residential neighborhoods—townships as they are called in South Africa, or *campamentos* and *colonias* as they might be labeled in many parts of Latin America. In the more recent labor histories of the United States, this alternative form of labor organizing is reflected in the relatively newer Community-Labor Collaborations (CLCs) where, for example, around pressing issues of low-waged and precarious work CBOs and unions collaborate and form coalitions to advance their cause (see Krinsky and Reese 2006; Kim 1997). While traditionally labor and community solidarities might be initiated by labor organizations, we should pay attention to how such relationships and strengthening of labor solidarities could also be initiated through informal politics that workers and their families engage in outside the workplace as people and not necessarily as workers.

But as place is open and unsettled, so are the politics of place that may embrace both dynamics of competition and solidarity among diverse groups.

Politics of place are not fixed; they are contested and constantly changing. In the stories of placemaking in Beardstown, there is no guarantee that the place itself, the social and material assemblages that make this place, will not shift or that the dynamics of its politics will not change. The dynamics of the diverse social groups in this town are fragile, and the contested struggle of labor and capital mediated through sites of production and social reproduction in Illinois, as well as in other places across the country, can swiftly alter the place and its politics. This book has not been devoted to predicting a future, but to understanding the social, historical, and spatial contingencies of the present.

PRODUCTION OF DIFFERENCE—UNSETTLING CATEGORIES OF BELONGING

The social dynamics we observe in Beardstown are the outcome of the specific social groups that have come together at a particular moment in history in a particular set of social and institutional relations and a particular place. Fixed categories of citizenship, immigration status, or even race cannot explain the dynamics of these groups relative to each other and the dominant white local population. Togolese, Mexicans, and Detroiters are produced through distinct sociohistorical processes and are marked by distinct socioeconomic, cultural, linguistic, class aspiration, and legal characteristics. Moreover, their differences are also relationally produced in the specific context of a former sundown town. To reduce such complexities to fixed categories of belonging in terms of immigration status, formal national citizenship, or visible race as in skin color would be a grave mistake.

We discussed restructuring processes of capital, labor, and state that have dispossessed and displaced not only the transnational migrant groups, the Togolese and the Mexicans, but also the translocal domestic migrant group, the Detroiters. Though all are displaced workers, they are produced through different sociohistorical processes. Togolese immigrants in Beardstown are part of a more recent wave of African immigration to the United States and have legal status with a path to citizenship. Mexicans, many of whom are undocumented, have a long and broad history of migration in this country and a sense of entitlement to being and working in the United States, regardless of their immigration status. "We did not cross the border illegally, the U.S. border crossed us," immigrants' rights activists often proclaim, referring to the nineteenth-century war through which the United States appropriated

Mexican territories. The Detroiters have national citizenship and hence are supposed to have the same rights as local whites in civil, political, and social protection. Accordingly, one might think that Detroiters would have been more accepted in Beardstown than the other groups who are not citizens. But as we saw in the narratives of white locals, black Detroiters were not only treated as being equally "out of place" as the West Africans but also constructed as "the other black immigrants," "the bad ones." Census data and plant statistics also collapse African Americans and West Africans into one generic category of "Blacks." But despite their visible similarities, these groups have distinct migration and diasporic histories—histories that, as shown in this book, racialize them differently and position them hierarchically differently vis-à-vis the dominant white population. Alex's remark that whites in Beardstown "lynched us not them [the West African new arrivals]" reminds us that this differentiation must be understood as historically constituted. In Beardstown, Detroiters are racialized differently from the other immigrant groups and situated at the bottom of the social hierarchy by many among the white European-American locals as well as by African and Mexican immigrants.

These observations challenge the idea of social stratification based on fixed categories of belonging such as citizenship, immigration, or race. Stories of Beardstown reveal the complexities of producing difference in relational terms and the instability of these categories. Just as aggregating distinct groups of Togolese and Mexicans grossly obscures who they are, so is differentiating social status on the basis of citizenship or color of skin alone. Detroiters' American citizenship and historical roots in the United States offer no escape from stereotyping and marginalization by the dominant culture.

Unsettling the categories does not mean that we need to do without them. For instance, legal status is a critical factor in stratification among the labor force. The creation of national borders that then create "illegal" workers is key to the processes of production that fuel and subsidize the accumulation of capital by global corporations such as Cargill. What we observe here is not that legal status, formal national membership as a citizen, or visible characteristics of racialized groups are insignificant. Rather, they are complex and conjunctional. Categories of race, immigration status, or citizenship are not wooden but relationally constituted; they produce difference differently in different places and give rise to distinct politics that are open to renegotiation.

These realities also confirm new conceptualizations of citizenship that are not tied to the territorial and political bounds of the national state or limited to a set of formalized recognitions. Rather than a bundle of rights granted from above by the state, citizenship is understood as processes constructed from below by citizens' local, translocal, and increasingly transnational practices, which secure tangible gains independent of their formal status vis-à-vis a national state. In this alternative conceptualization, the terrain of citizenship is unsettled (Smith and Guarnizo 2009). It is not the nation but the city, the town, the neighborhood, and the concrete places where inhabitants make their dignified living and livelihood that constitute the heart of the citizenship's contestations. In this context, the expectation of social well-being has shifted from formal, top-down, and national to informal, bottom-up, and transnational processes and practices. To fulfill their expectations of a dignified, humane livelihood, people take their interests in their own hands. Whether they be from minority populations of the global North or marginalized residents of the global South, they employ direct practices whereby citizens do not relegate the defense of their interests to others—be they politicians, bureaucrats, or planners. Furthermore, they do not confine their claims-making actions to "invited spaces of citizenship" such as the senate, the municipal councils, the planning commission's community hearings, citizen review boards, and NGOs. Such citizenship practices occur in self-determined "invented spaces of citizenship" where people participate through direct action to respond to specific contexts and issues.[5]

Although Beardstown might be a unique place, the relationships it entails are not. The story of Beardstown might or might not be similar to other emerging multicultural packing towns in Midwest, but the relational methodologies and analytical frameworks offered in the study of a unique place like Beardstown are generalizable and far from unique. What stories are told or silenced, what agencies are noted or neglected, depends on ways of looking and framing. Through the story of Beardstown, I hope to offer a way of looking, seeing, investigating, opening, and making visible for socially responsible research undertaken anywhere and on any topic.

Beyond the conceptual and theoretical contributions of this book, my hope above all in telling the stories of Beardstown is that they can help us think globally and *expose the human cost of our local privileges*. Through a lens that allows us to see relationships across different, seemingly isolated local communities and at various scales, I hope this book helps in constructing a world more conscious of global inequalities. By making a case for relational thinking about the movement of people from one place to another and the development of place and placemaking, this book attempts to make visible how lives here are connected to those out there through unequal power relations—and in doing to so expand the "geographies of responsibility," as Doreen Massey (2004) calls them.

Let there be no doubt that this book is not about an American Dream or the making of a global heartland where home is an insulated, stable space to settle and make one's own. The relationships are shifting; so are the meanings of the place and its politics. If there is a dream-come-true story to be told in Beardstown, voices we have heard in this book should also remind us of the global nightmare the American Dream entails. It will reveal how the dream and privilege of one world relies on the destitution of the other; the cheap price of meat and food in one place is at the expense of not only the workers working here in the heartland, but also all of their families and neighbors back home—an army of people providing support and making the workers' lives in Beardstown viable.

Like the neighbor's baby whom Mrs. Sanchez nursed to life less than a century ago, an army of families and people in distinct communities are responsible for revitalizing and nursing towns like Beardstown back to life. It is not only Sena, but her daughter in Lomé, not only the Fernández brothers at the Cargill plant but their father in Tejaro, and not only Ami and Kossi but their children growing apart from their parents, who have vested their lives in the cheap meat offered to consumers. These are the bacon and ham served at our breakfast table.

APPENDIX

Demographic and Labor Tables,
Profile of Interviewees

DEMOGRAPHIC TABLES

Table A1. Summary of population census data for Beardstown and Rushville, Illinois, 1890–2010

1890	1900	1920	1930	1940	1950
Beardstown (Cass County, Il)					
Total = 4,226	Total = 4,827	Total = 7,111	Total = 6,344	Total = 6,505	Total = 6,080
W = 4,226	W = 4,826	W = 7,111	W = 6,326	W = 6,505	W = 6,079
B* = 0	B = 1	B = 0	B = 0	B = 0	B = 1
Whites as % of total population in Beardstown					
100%	99.98%	100%	100%	100%	99.98%
Rushville (Schuyler County, Il)					
Schuyler County*	Schuyler County*	Schuyler County*			Total = 2,682
total population =	total population =	total population =			W = 2,680
16,013	16,129	13,285			Negroes =
Coloreds = 10	Negroes = 7	All-white county			1 male
(7 male and	(5 male and				Other races =
3 female)	2 female)				1 female
Whites as % of total population in Rushville					
					99.92%

Sources: All the population and race data reported here are obtained from the decennial census reports of U.S. Census Bureau (available at: http://www.census.gov/prod/www/decennial.html). The following tables for different time periods were used to obtain these values: Year 1890: Table 19: Population by sex, general nativity, and color, of places having 2,500 inhabitants or more, 1890, Table 22: Native and foreign-born and white and colored population, classified by sex and by counties, 1890. Year 1900: Table 22: Native and foreign-born and white and colored population, classified by sex and by counties, 1900, Table 23: Population by Sex, General Nativity, and Color, for places having 2,500 inhabitants or more, 1900. Year 1920: Table 9: Composition and characteristics of the population for counties, 1920, Table 11: Composition and characteristics of the population, for places of 2,500 to 10,000, 1920. Year 1930: Table 13: Composition of the population, by counties, 1930, Table 16: Composition of the population, for incorporated places of 2,500 to 10,000, 1930. Year 1940: Table 29: Race and age, by sex, with rural-farm population, for incorporated places of 1,000 to 2,500, 1940, Table 30: Composition of population for incorporated places of 2,500 to 10,000, 1940. Year 1950: Table 38: General characteristics of the population, for urban places of 2,500 to 10,000, 1950. Year 1960: Table 22: Characteristics of the population, for urban places of 2,500 to 10,000,

1960	1970	1980	1990	2000	2010
Total = 6,294 W = 6,290 B = 1	Total = 6,222 W = 6,210 B = 1	Total = 6,338 W = 6,312 B = 1 Spanish origin = 50	Total = 5,270 NHW = 5,221 B = 1 H = 31	Total = 5,766 NHW = 4,650 B** = 28 H = 1,032	Total = 6,123 NHW = 3,741 B** = 322 H = 1,994
99.93%	99.8%	99.58%	99%	80.6%	61%

Total = 2,819
All White
	Total = 3,300
	W = 3,298
	Other races = 2
		Total = 3,348
		W = 3,343
		No Blacks
		Spanish
		  origin = 16
		American
		  Indian = 3
			Total = 3,229
			W = 3,218
			H = 2
			B = 2
			American
			  Indian = 4
			Other = 5
				Total = 3,212
				W = 3,184
				H = 5
				B = 2
					Total = 3,192
					W = 3,016
					H − 48
					B** = 99

100%	100%	99.8%	99.65%	98.63%	94.49%

1960. Year 1970: Table 31: General Characteristics of places of 2,500 to 10,000, 1970. Year 1980: Table 16: Total persons and Spanish-origin persons by type of Spanish origin and race, 1980. Year 1990: Table 6: Race and Hispanic origin, 1990. Year 2000: Table 3. Race and Hispanic or Latino, 2000. Year 2010: Table 3: Race and Hispanic or Latino origin, 2010.

Note: All categories are derived from the census documents for their respective years. Definitions used to construct and describe racial categories in the census are as follows: colored = persons of Negro descent, Chinese, Japanese, and civilized Indians; B* = all persons of Negro descent; B** = not Hispanic black or African American alone; H = Hispanic or Latino; NHW = not Hispanic White alone; and Spanish-origin = persons of Spanish origin may be of any race. In order to create the graphs included in chapter 1 as figures 1.8 and 1.9, we considered "white" to be census defined "non-Hispanic white." Also, older census years (1980 and before) specified "Spanish-origin" population instead of Hispanic population; in such cases they are considered to be Hispanic population. Where city or township data were not reported for Rushville between 1890 and 1920, county data are used.

Table A2. Number and percentage of Hispanic and non-Hispanic population: Illinois, Cass County, Beardstown, and Rushville

	1990		2000		2010	
	Hispanic	Non-Hispanic	Hispanic	Non-Hispanic	Hispanic	Non-Hispanic
Illinois	904,446	10,526,156	1,530,262	10,889,031	2,027,578	10,803,054
	7.91%	92.09%	12.32%	87.68%	15.80%	84.20%
Cass County	56	13,381	1,162	12,533	2,291	11,351
	0.42%	99.58%	8.48%	91.52%	16.79%	83.21%
Beardstown	31	5,239	1,032	4,734	1,994	4,129
	0.59%	99.41%	17.90%	82.10%	32.57%	67.43%
Rushville	2	3,227	15	3,197	48	3,144
	0.06%	99.94%	0.47%	99.53%	1.50%	98.50%

Sources: U.S. Bureau of the Census 1990, Summary File 1, Table P010, Hispanic Origin by Race, data collected from www.socialexplorer.com (accessed December 2014).

U.S. Bureau of the Census 2000, Summary File 1, Table P008, Hispanic or Latino by Race, data collected from http://factfinder2.census.gov (accessed December 2014).

U.S. Bureau of the Census 2010, Summary File 1, Table P5 Hispanic or Latino Origin by Race, data collected from http://factfinder2.census.gov (accessed December 2014).

Table A3. Racial distributions of population in Beardstown 1990–2010: percentage and (numbers)

Race	1990	2000	2010
White	99.07	80.65	61.10
	(5,221)	(4,650)	(3,741)
Black or African American	0.02	0.49	5.26
	(1)	(28)	(322)
Hispanic or Latino	0.59	17.90	32.57
	(31)	(1,032)	(1,994)
American Indian, Eskimo, or Aleut	0.09	0.23	0.11
	(5)	(13)	(7)
Asian or Pacific Islander	0.23	0.36	0.34
	(12)	(21)	(21)
Other race	0.00	0.38	0.62
	(0)	(22)	(38)

Sources: U.S. Bureau of the Census 1990, Summary File 1, Table P010, Hispanic Origin by Race, data collected from www.socialexplorer.com (accessed December 2014).

U.S. Bureau of the Census 2000, Summary File 1, Table P008, Hispanic or Latino by Race, data collected from http://factfinder2.census.gov (accessed December 2014).

U.S. Bureau of the Census 2010, Summary File 1, Table P5, Hispanic or Latino Origin by Race, data collected from http://factfinder2.census.gov (accessed December 2014).

Note: Here non-Hispanic white, non-Hispanic black or African American, and other non-Hispanic races are reported in their respective races (i.e., white, black, others, etc.); Hispanic or Latino populations, irrespective of their subgroups (white, black or others), are reported as Hispanic population.

LABOR TABLES

Table A4. Employment dynamics in animal slaughtering and processing, Cass County, 1994–2013

	Employment	Variation (±)	New Hires	Separations	Turnover %
1994	1,743	N/A	1593	1410	80.9
1995	1,879	137	1902	1851	98.5
1996	2030	151	1571	1633	80.4
1997	1960	−70	1559	1584	80.8
1998	1831	−129	1694	1632	89.1
1999	1934	103	1274	1259	65.1
2000	1951	17	979	961	49.3
2001	N/A	N/A	N/A	N/A	N/A
2002	2060	22	1176	1028	49.9
2003	2139	79	956	875	40.9
2004	2321	182	1012	965	41.6
2005	2276	−45	1017	**1021**	44.9
2006	2249	−27	930	977	43.5
2007	N/A	N/A	N/A	N/A	N/A
2008	N/A	N/A	N/A	N/A	N/A
2009	N/A	N/A	N/A	N/A	N/A
2010	2340	N/A	470	977	41.8
2011	2340	0	380	457	19.5
2012	2274	−66	1020	1060	46.6
2013	2254	−20	527	**560**	24.8

Source: U.S. Census Bureau. 2014. Quarterly Workforce Indicators Data. Longitudinal-Employer Household Dynamics Program http://lehd.ces.census.gov/data/#qwi. The bold figures indicate data availability for three quarters only (accessed June 2015).

Note: To calculate the data for Cargill plant in Beardstown we explored the U.S. Census Bureau, Quarterly Workforce indicators by county and type of manufacturing as NAICS (3116). This data points at the Cargill's plant in Beardstown, because it is the only major animal slaughtering and processing firm in the county. The annual number of separations is calculated according to the formula of the Bureau of Labor Statics, based on the average of the four quarterly reports. Similarly, the annual employment is calculated based on the average of the four quarterly reports. View http://www.bls.gov/bls/glossary .htm. The percentage of average annual separation is the number of full separations for the year divided by average monthly employment for the year or full quarter employment stable, http://qwiexplorer.ces.census.gov/static/explore.html?s=f433f&v=line&t =ac0&fc=true&st=IL#x=0&g=0.

Table A5. Labor force ethnic and racial composition in animal slaughtering and processing in Cass County, fourth quarter 2013

	Latino or Hispanic	White not Latino	Black or African American alone	American Indian or Alaskan Native alone	Asian alone	Native Hawaiian or Pacific Islander	Two or more race groups
Total employment	578	1312	235	27	62	9	35
% employment	25.6	58.1	10.4	1.2	2.7	0.4	1.6

Sources: U.S. Census Bureau. 2014. Quarterly Workforce Indicators Data. Longitudinal-Employer Household Dynamics Program http://lehd.ces.census.gov/data/#qwi (accessed June 2015).

Data calculated by race and ethnicity tables for Cass County, animal slaughtering and processing, fourth quarter 2013, http://qwiexplorer.ces.census.gov/static/explore.html?s=f433f&v=line&t=ac0 &fc=true&st=IL#x=0&g=0 and http://qwiexplorer.ces.census.gov/static/explore.html?s=f4340&v =line&t=ac0&fc=true&st=IL#x=0&g=0.

PROFILE OF INTERVIEWEES

Table A6. Profile of interviewees in Beardstown and Rushville

Interviewee #	Gender	African	Latino, Latina	American of European Descent	African American	Cargill Worker	NGOs/ Civic Associations	Authorities	Private and Other Organizations	Date of Interview
1	F		X			X		X		6/7/06, 4/5/08
2	M			X				X		6/7/06, 11/29/07, 5/27/08, 2010
3	F			X				X		6/7/2006
4	M			X			X			6/7/2006
5	F		X					X		6/7/2006
6	M			X			X			2006
7	M			X				X		2006
8	F			X					X	6/7/06, 7/11/07
9	M			X				X		11/2/07, 4/2/08
10	F			X				X		11/2/07, 4/1/08
11	F			X						11/2/2007
12	M			X					X	11/2/2007
13	M			X				X		10/18/2007
14	M			X					X	10/18/2007
15	M			X					X	11/2/2007
16	M			X				X		11/2/07, 4/2/08
17	M			X					X	10/18/07, 2008
18	F			X					X	5/28/2008
19	M			X					X	10/18/2007
20	M			X				X		11/29/2007
21	F			X				X		4/1/2008
22	M			X				X		4/26/2008
23	F			X			X			4/1/2008
24	M			X						4/1/2008
25	M			X				X		4/26/2008
26	F			X			X			11/7/2008
27	F			X			X			4/6/2008
28	F			X						4/1/2008

Table A6. Profile of interviewees in Beardstown and Rushville

Interviewee #	Gender	African	Latino	American of European Descent	African American	Cargill Worker	NGOs/Civic Associations	Authorities	Private and Other Organizations	Date of Interview
29	M			X						4/26/2008
30	M			X						4/1/2008
31	M		X					X		4/6/08, 5/27/08
32	M		X			X				4/6/2008
33	F		X					X		4/26/2008
34	F		X							4/26/2008
35	M		X						X	4/1/2008
36	F		X							3/31/2008
37	F		X			X				2/14/2009
38	M		X			X			X	4/1/2009
39	M		X			X				5/3/2009
40	M		X			X				5/3/2009
41	M		X			X				5/3/2009
42	M		X				X			2/14/09, 2008
43	M		X			X				4/26/2009
44	F		X							2009
45	F		X							2009
46	F		X							2009
47	F			X						5/27/2008
48	F		X			X				4/27/2008
49	M			X				X		4/27/2008
50	M		X			X				4/19/2008
50a	M		X			X				4/20/2008
50b	M		X			X				4/20/2008
51	M	X								2006
52	M	X				X				5/28/2007
53	M	X				X				5/28/2007
54	M	X				X				5/28/2007
55	M	X				X				7/10/2007
56	M	X				X				10/15/2008
57	F	X				X				7/10/07

(*continued*)

Table A6. Profile of interviewees in Beardstown and Rushville

Interviewee #	Gender	African	Latino	American of European Descent	African American	Cargill Worker	NGOs/ Civic Associations	Authorities	Private and Other Organizations	Date of Interview
58	F	X				X				7/10/2007
59	M	X				X				3/31/2008
60	M	X				X				4/29/2009
61	F	X				X				4/27/2008
62	M	X								8/15/2009
63	M	X					X			3/29/2008
64	F	X				X				3/30/2008
65	M	X				X				3/30/2008
66	F	X								4/24/2009
67	F	X								4/24/2009
68	F	X								4/24/2009
69	M			X		X				9/20/2010
70	M	X								7/2010
71	M			X		X				3/2010
72	M			X						4/2011
73	F			X						4/2011
74	F			X						4/2011
75	F			X						4/2011
76	F			X						4/2011
77	M			X		X				4//2011
78	M			X		X				4/2011
79	M			X		X				4/2011
80	F				X	X				7/2012
81	M				X	X				7/2012
82	F				X					7/2012
83	M				X					7/2012
84	F			X						2008
85	F	X				X				7/2010, 6/2012
86	M		X Nr							11/1/2009
87	M			X Nr						2009
88	M		X			X				4/20/2008
89	M		X			X				4/20/2008

NOTES

1. There is a long and charged debate on how the groups of Americans with the most difficult histories should be referred to. In this book I do not capitalize black or white when referring to Americans of African or European descent, nor do I capitalize "black American" or "white American." I use the terms "black," "African American," and "black American" interchangeably. When I use the term "whites," my reference is to Americans of European descent; considering the sundown town history of Beardstown, I sometimes I use "local residents" as short hand for "whites," who unless otherwise specified, can assumed to be native-born of white European descent. Moreover, I use the terms "Latino," "Latina," and "Latinos/as" to refer to people whose roots are in Mexico and Central America. However, when official documents like the census use the term "Hispanic," I adopt it when reporting on such data. While I try to avoid the term "non-white" and instead use "people of color," when engaging with census documents or quoting words of others I have had to make reference to "non-whites."

2. James Loewen (2005) coined the term "sundown towns" to describe towns in the North that wanted to have a black labor force after the Civil War but did not want blacks living there. In these towns, blacks had to leave by sunset—hence the name "sundown towns."

3. See appendix, table A1.

4. In 2000, the white-Hispanic index of dissimilarity for Beardstown was 57.6 compared to 62.1 for Chicago, 63.2 for Los Angeles–Long Beach, and 66.7 for New York (see McConnell and Miraftab 2009).

5. U.S. 2010 census data indicate that in Beardstown 43.3 percent of Hispanic households and 71.1 percent of non-Hispanic white households lived in owner-occupied housing units (table H15 and H17I, U.S. Bureau of Census 2010). For comparison, the data for the country showed respective percentages to be 47.3 percent for Hispanic household and 72.2 percent for non-Hispanic white households (table H15 and H17I, U.S. Bureau of Census 2010). Considering the recent arrival of Latinos to Beardstown this comparative data is quite impressive.

6. The two-way language immersion program is also referred to as the Dual Language Program (DLP). Beardstown is the only rural school in Illinois with such a program. As of November 2008, eighteen schools in Illinois adopted the program; 335 did so nationwide (Delany-Barmann and Paciotto 2009).

7. On July 1, 2015, as I reviewed the last round of proofs for this book, Cargill announced the sale of its pork division including the Beardstown plant to the U.S. subsidiary

of a Brazilian-based international meat processor—JBS USA. The $1.45 billion deal included a Cargill processing plant in Ottumwa, Iowa, as well as feed mills in Arkansas, Iowa, Missouri, and Texas and hog farms in Arkansas, Oklahoma, and Texas. The newspaper announcement reported that JBS entered the U.S. pork market in 2007, when it bought Swift & Co. It sells products under the Swift and Swift Premium brand names. *My Journal Courier*, July 1, 2015. http://myjournalcourier.com/news/1202/cargill-beardstown-plant-sold-in-1-45-billion-deal.

8. "Cargill Beardstown," http://www.cargill.com/wcm/groups/public/@ccom /documents/image/na31720660.pdf (accessed October 2014). This workforce includes: females 701 (32 percent); males 1,480 (68 percent); Asian/Indian 28 (1 percent); African/ African American 176 (8 percent); Caucasian 1,380 (63 percent); Hispanic 597 (27 percent). Age distribution: twenties (33 percent); thirties (25 percent); forties (23 percent); fifties (14 percent); sixties (6 percent). (Cargill Fact Sheet, 2007, "Cargill Meat Solutions: 20 Years in Beardstown"; fact sheet prepared and handed out by Cargill staff at the tour of the plant on July 10, 2007.)

9. The Beardstown plant receives hogs from Illinois, Missouri, Iowa, Indiana, Michigan, and Arkansas. Cargill, "Cargill Beardstown," http://www.cargill.com/wcm/groups/public /@ccom/documents/image/na31720660.pdf (accessed October 2014).

10. The Beardstown plant produces for the top five global markets: Mexico, Japan, Canada, Russia, and Korea (ibid.).

11. For the history of Cargill, see Kneen (2002). For a chronological account, see Cargill Timeline 1865-present at https://www.cargill.com/wcm/groups/public/@ccom/documents /document/doc-cargill-history-timeline.pdf (accessed December 2014).

12. Cargill is a giant multinational corporation involved in the production of many vastly different but deeply connected goods such as Always Tender® (meats), Sunny Fresh Foods® (eggs), Diamond Crystal® Salt, Gerkens® Cacao, ClearLane® De-icer, North Star Steel, CarVal Investors. For more, see also Griffis and Ross (2014).

13. In fiscal year 2013, Cargill had net earnings of $2.31 billion, roughly a 30 percent total increase since 2009. Total sales for 2013 came to $136.7 billion. (See Cargill, "Five-Year Financial Summary," http://www.cargill.com/company/financial/five-year/index.jsp, accessed December 2014). According to *Fortune* magazine, if Cargill were publicly held, it would be ranked tenth on the list of largest U.S. companies (Cargill 2013a).

14. See Walker 2003a and Hebron 1987b. The new hourly wage dropped the starting wage from $8.75 to $6.50 an hour (Walker 2003a). In 2014, Cargill wages for production workers ranged from $13.30 to $18.05 per hour. See "Cargill Beardstown."

15. In Beardstown and Rushville, I conducted three focus groups with immigrants and more than eighty-nine semi-structured and in-depth interviews (see the appendix table A6 for interviewees' profile). I expected my being an immigrant—and clearly identifiable as one by my looks and my accent—to make it hard for the white residents who had negative sentiments about the immigration to their town to speak their mind. For this reason several of the interviews with white residents were conducted by my white research assistant. With Spanish-speaking respondents, I conducted the interviews in Spanish. With West Africans, four of the interviews were conducted with the assistance of a French interpreter; otherwise I conducted the interviews in English. I also benefited from several community and household surveys that were conducted in Beardstown and Rushville in 2008 and 2009. The Illinois Institute for Rural Affairs conducted a trilingual mail-in household survey in Beardstown. This survey, which brought in results mainly for the English-speaking households (N=468), was

complemented by random surveys that were conducted among the immigrant households. The Spanish-speaking University of Illinois Extension staff conducted these among the Latinos immigrants in Beardstown (N=45), and an AmeriCorps volunteer conducted similar surveys among French-speaking immigrants in both Beardstown and Rushville (N=59). While these surveys do not offer a representative sample, they were helpful in offering a numeric representation for much of my qualitative observations.

16. At each of these sites, I conducted fifteen semistructured and in-depth interviews. In Mexico I conducted all interviews in Spanish; in Togo all interviews were conducted in Ewe with the help of an interpreter.

17. According to federal regulations, all research involving human subjects requires approval from an Institutional Review Board (IRB). To obtain approval, the research must not pose any risk of harm to its subject. In 2006, at an early stage of my project involving interviews with trainers of immigrant workers, I approached the company's public relations department. A staff member there reviewed my IRB, approved it, and provided me with contact information for two employees who train new French- and Spanish-speaking recruits. But the night before those interviews were to take place, the public relations staff member left me an upsetting voice message with a false accusation that in my forthcoming interviews, I would somehow be departing from the agreed-upon terms of the contract. I canceled those interviews as I did not want to put the interviewees at risk, nor did I wish to jeopardize my research. But I did file "an adverse event form" with the IRB office at my university on June 8, 2006.

18. In the online version of the article, the following statement appeared instead at the end of that report: "UPDATED 2012-02-06 15:49:19 to remove references to transnational recruitment teams, which Cargill said it does not utilize, and to paying a bonus to employees who bring on new hires, which is not company practice" (Rhodes 2012; text no longer online).

19. I have observed the plant on one occasion, but I have not conducted research inside the plant. On the few occasions that I tried to interview plant public relations staff, there was no response to my request. Nevertheless, many interviewees inside and outside of Beardstown spoke about their workplace experiences when discussing their immigration experience in Beardstown.

20. Human Rights Watch 2014, 14 and 30.

21. "Heartland" is roughly the area in the middle of the United States that is linked by the Mississippi River from New Orleans in the south up to Minneapolis in the north, and from Omaha and Kansas City in the west to Detroit and Cleveland in the east. Mark Twain once called it the "body of the nation." For more see Heartland, http://www.heartlandeindhoven.nl/info_EN.php (accessed June 2015).

22. Longworth (2008, 103).

23. See Hart (2006) and Massey (2004).

24. Burawoy and colleagues (2001, 150). Also see Gille (2001) and Guarnizo and Smith (1998).

25. For a comprehensive documentation and discussion of this shift, see contributions to the following edited volumes: Massey (2008); Zúñiga and Hernández-León (2005); Allegro and Wood (2013); Gozdziak and Martin (2005). Also see Lichter and Johnson (2006, 2009); Kandel and Cromartie (2004); Kandel et al. (2011); Frey (2006); Donato et al., (2007); Durand, Massey, and Charvet (2000).

26. See contributors to Griffith, Broadway, and Stull (1995); Warren (2007); Kandel and Parrado (2005).

27. See Light (2006); Latapi et al. (1998); Durand, Massey, and Charvet (2000); Massey, Durand, and Malone (2002); Donato, Aguilera, and Wakabayashi (2005).

28. See Massey, Durand, and Malone (2002); Hernández-León and Zúñiga (2003); Orrenius (2004).

29. Millard and Chapa (2004); Fennelly (2005); Zúñiga and Hernández-León (2005); Marrow (2011).

30. Mott (2010); Brown, Mott, and Malecki (2007).

31. This work highlights how the sudden surge of immigrants heightens the burden and pressure on public agencies, social services (Erickson 1990), and housing stock (Griffith 1995); increases crime (Gouveia and Stull 1995) and social disorganization (Crowley and Lichter 2009); and multiplies health hazards (Hakenberg and Kokulka 1995).

32. For example see Sandoval (2013); Trabalzi and Sandoval (2010); Miraftab and McConnell (2008).

33. See Sandoval and Maldonado (2012); Fennelly (2005); Grey and Woodrick (2005).

34. For the former point of view see Millard and Chapa (2004); for the latter see Fink (1998, 136), reflecting on almost all studies in volumes edited by Lamphere (1992) and by Stull et al. (1995).

35. Grey (1995); Lay (2012).

36. Among exceptions are Lay (2012); Sandoval (2012); Fennelly (2008).

37. Harvey (1984); Castells (1983); Fainstein and Fainstein (1986).

38. See Harvey (1985).

39. Smith (2002); Katz (2001); Lawson and Klak (1990).

40. See Bakker (2003); Bakker and Gill (2003). Nancy Fraser (2013) argues that second-wave feminism unintentionally helped neoliberalism by critiquing the family wage, focusing on identity politics at the expense of economic justice, and allowing its critique of the patriarchal state to be used to dismantle the welfare state and to privatize and domesticize care.

41. See Beneria (2008); Friedman (1992); Miraftab (2010); Chant (2010); Roberts (2008); Mitchell, Marston, and Katz (2004).

42. The burden of this state restructuring has fallen to a great extent on women, who work for free not only on behalf of their families but also their neighborhoods and towns in the public realm—free labor that feminist critics refer to as "municipal housekeeping." For example, on waste collection, see Miraftab (2004; 2005).

43. Alain de Janvry (1975) extends the theory of unequal exchange between center and periphery to provide an interpretation of rural underdevelopment in Latin America and economic functionality of the subsistence sector and rural poverty. The subsistence sector, he argues, is a purveyor of cheap labor to the commercial sector of the economy.

44. Additional contributions to this analysis have come from scholars of apartheid South Africa who demonstrate how families and support networks in homelands subsidized the social reproduction of mine workers by bearing child-raising responsibilities as well as offering workers a place to take their ailing or aging bodies (Wolpe 1972). Today, some see commonalities in apartheid control of rural-urban connections and subsidies with rapidly urbanizing China under its *hukou* system (Alexander and Chan 2004).

45. See de Janvry (1975); Klooster (2005). See also Binford (2009) with respect to seasonal agricultural workers in Canada. He develops the concept of a "dual frame of reference" through which workers gauge Canadian wages in relationship to Mexican wages and conditions of social reproduction.

46. See Barnes (1999); Hansen (1989).

47. Shellee Colen (1986), reflecting on similar relationships in the contemporary United States, coined the phrase "stratified reproduction" to describe the racial history of policies and programs concerned with women's reproductive rights and how they empower privileged women and stigmatize or control reproductive behavior of less privileged women.

48. For bracero families, see Rosas (2011); for care givers, see Ehrenreich and Hochschild (2003) and Parreñas (2001).

49. See Fudge (2010); Kunz (2010); Iskandar (2010). The use of remittances in Mexico is the best-documented case. As Mexican citizens have increasingly resorted to the formation of transnational families, the government has also turned to a remittance-based model of economic development known as the "Three for One" program (*tres por uno*). This program, which is an initiative of the Mexican state, formally links the resources of immigrants through their voluntary associations (e.g., Home Town Associations) with the resources of the state to deliver on public works projects. For every dollar offered by an immigrant association toward public works projects, the local, state, and federal governments each add one additional dollar—hence its name, "Three for One."

50. See Levitt (2001); Mercer, Page, and Evans (2008); Mohan (2006). Remittances mobilized through organizations like immigrants' Home Town Associations based in the global North are therefore increasingly the source of social reproduction in the global South, both economically through immigrants' financial contributions to collective public works items and culturally through ceremonies that maintain ethnic identities and religious lives.

51. Nonetheless, empirical evidence shows that in the aggregate, countries of immigrants' destination benefit more than their countries of origin (see Sanderson 2013a, 2013b).

52. Portes and Manning (1986); Waldinger, Aldrich, and Ward (1990); Jones-Correa (1998).

53. Represented by the earlier work of John Friedmann and Goetz Wolff (1982), this scholarship shows that what global processes do to the nature of work they also do to cities. For Saskia Sassen (1991), the shift from an industrial to a service-based economy in the global North has created an urban society that is economically and spatially fragmented, as well as highly polarized. For her, this "dual-city" arises from globalization processes that do not foster the expansion of a middle class. Peter Marcuse and Ronald van Kempen (2000) show how globalization fosters "quartered cities," where specific types of neighborhoods (quarters) accommodate specific social groups that are spatially quartered by their income, race, and/or ethnicity. Stephen Graham and Simon Marvin (2001) push this conceptualization further by looking at urban infrastructures and at the hidden forces that contribute to a splintering of urban spaces into many fragments with highly unequal levels of infrastructure. Taking a somewhat different perspective, Manuel Castells (2005) sees the relationship between globalization and city in terms of a double movement: while urban dwellers might have a greater experience of inclusion in terms of having transnational families and networks, they experience greater exclusion in their local communities as a result of spatial residential differentiation. In sum, this literature stresses the formation of a "fragmented metropolis" whereby urban dwellers are increasingly separated and polarized both socially and spatially (ibid., 52).

54. Robinson (2006); Shatkin (2007); McDonald (2008); Roy (2011); Goldman (2011).

55. Burawoy et al. (2000, 2).

56. Guarnizo and Smith (1998, 11).

57. See Guarnizo and Smith (1998); Aguayo (2008).

58. Glick Schiller and Caglar (2011b).

59. Sheppard 2002; Brenner (2011).

60. Glick Schiller and Caglar (2011c, 191).

61. Sandercock (1998, 2003).

62. Davis (2001); Irazabal (2012, 2014); Irazabal and Farhat (2008); Rojas (2010). Also see contributors to Diaz and Torres (2012) and Irazabal (2014).

63. Main and Sandoval (2015); Rios (2015); Sarmiento and Beard (2013); also see contributions to Hou (2013) and to Rios and Vazquez (2012).

64. Friedmann (2010).

1. WELCOME TO PORKOPOLIS

1. The city's official website, http://www.cityofbeardstown.org, welcomes visitors to Beardstown, the watermelon capital of the nation (accessed October 2014).

2. The "Beardstown Ladies" were a group of sixteen middle-aged and older women, mostly housewives, who became international media celebrities because of their success in making high-return stock investments, which were said to be 24 percent. Later, the Beardstown Ladies admitted to miscalculating and exaggerating this return rate, but at the time, in the 1980s and the early 1990s, they were not only media sensations, appearing on *The Donahue Show,* CBS's *Morning Show,* NBC's *The Today Show,* and ABC's *Good Morning America,* but also honored for six straight years by the National Association of Investors, which included them in their "All-Star Investment Clubs." Their first book, *The Beardstown Ladies' Common-Sense Investment Guide* (1994), sold over 800,000 copies by 1998 and was a *New York Times* bestseller (Smith 1995; *New York Times* 1998).

3. In this trial, Lincoln used an almanac for 1857, the year when the defendant was accused of murder, to prove that there was no moonlight at the time of the alleged murder and that the state witness's claim to be able to see the perpetrator from afar was unfounded.

4. In a paper that McConnell and I published (2009), we calculated that the degree of segregation in Beardstown was lower than in Chicago, New York, or Los Angeles. We argued that for a working-class town that kept itself all-white through much of the twentieth century, there was no need to put in place zoning regulation that enforced segregated neighborhoods. All non-whites were "zoned out." Hence, when ethnically and racially diverse residents arrived, they were dispersed all over the town, as there were no preexisting specific quarters for them to join. See McConnell and Miraftab (2009) and Miraftab and McConnell (2008).

5. For index of dissimilarity, I follow the calculation method developed by McConnell in McConnell and Miraftab (2009) using Census Bureau maps to identity census tracks and census blocks that lie within the town's boundaries. Here, using the 2010 census data for the approximately 390 census blocks that lie within Beardstown's boundaries, I calculate, as we did in McConnell and Miraftab (2009), only the white and Latino integration/index of dissimilarity. Formal calculations of the index of Hispanic-white dissimilarity for Beardstown, using block-level data, indicate that the Beardstown index of dissimilarity reduced from 59.4 in 2000 to 54 in 2010, a drop that indicates a greater integration of Latinos and whites across census blocks. Latinos, who constituted more than 32 percent of Beardstown's residents in 2010 as opposed to 18 percent in 2000, appear to be dispersed fairly equally across block groups. Indeed, based on the 2010 census, Latinos constitute between 24.8 and 42.9 percent of Beardstown's seven block groups. In McConnell and Miraftab (2009), we

explain index of dissimilarity above 50 percent to mean that "more than half of rural Latinos would have to move to be evenly distributed with non-Hispanic whites across all census blocks" (page 618). A 50-plus index of dissimilarity, we argued, "is consistent with research about "new rural boomtowns" (ibid.)—nonmetropolitan communities with the fastest-growing Hispanic populations over the decade (Lichter et al. 2008; Parisi and Lichter 2007). On average, nonmetropolitan places with the largest Hispanic increases since 1990 had a mean Hispanic-white index of dissimilarity in 2000 of 63.4 (Lichter et al. 2008). Segregation in 2000 of the top twenty "rural boomtowns" ranged from 41.2 to 76.7, and 70 percent of these places had indexes of dissimilarity over 60 (Parisi and Lichter 2007). At 54, Beardstown's Hispanic-white segregation in 2010 was therefore consistent with that of other rural Hispanic boomtowns.

6. The landscape of the region where Beardstown is located is known as the corn belt and bread basket of the United States. See Ryan Griffis and Sarah Ross (2012; 2014) for drainage of this landscape to transform it from marshland to prime agricultural land.

7. A subsidiary branch of the Illinois tribes called the Mascouten Indians had a large settlement around the later site of Beardstown. When Thomas Beard arrived in 1819 on the site later to be named after him, the northwestern portion of the area was occupied by the Kickapoo Indians. French traders used the Beardstown site as their headquarters in the decades preceding the settlement. In 1832—the year of the Black Hawk War—Beardstown served as a rendezvous for the troops and a depot for supplies (Perrin 1882). Also see the Illinois State Museum's "Harvesting the River," http://www.museum.state.il.us/RiverWeb /harvesting/history/settlement/beardstown.html (accessed October 2014).

8. Since then, the port of Beardstown has continued to function as a distribution hub for cargo boats traveling up and down the Illinois River. On a daily basis, barges can still be seen pushing rows of cargo boats down the river. The boats are filled with Archer Daniels Midland and Cargill agricultural products and grains sent down to the New Orleans port. This connection between Beardstown and New Orleans has become even more significant in light of the Hurricane Katrina's damage to the New Orleans infrastructure.

9. An incident during my visit to New Orleans in 2012 is intriguing and enlightening in understanding Beardstown as a transnational space. In a home converted to a private museum of voodoo and voodoo practices, the collector had a series of maps on display, including one that sketched the slave routes feeding the port of New Orleans. In this map Togo was marked prominently as a supplier of 23 percent of the slaves sold in West Africa and brought down to New Orleans during the period marked as 1719, 1721, and 1723. Just about three centuries later, Togo again feeds the labor needs of this country, albeit this time the Togolese and West African laborers arrive at the other end of the waterways that connect the port of New Orleans to the heartland—at Beardstown.

10. In "Meatpacking in Illinois History," an article published on the Illinois Periodicals Online (IPO) site, Wilson Warren explains how this shift in the scale of meatpacking required the development and implementation of several industrial innovations. In the earlier era, "packers needed to store river and lake ice cut during the winter months to pack during the summer months as well as the winter. To sell their meat products in eastern markets, Chicago's packers invested heavily in railroad livestock cars and holding facilities. The railroads invested large amounts of capital in stockyards and stockcars for the livestock trade. Chicago's Gustavus Swift developed the first successful fleet of refrigerated rail cars designed for the dressed beef trade." See http://www.lib.niu.edu/2006/iht1320636.html (accessed October 2014).

11. Beardstown (IL) *Beardstown Gazette* 1979, 100.

12. Beardstown (IL) *Beardstown Gazette* 1979, 101.

13. The 1922 Burlington railroad strikes were in response to a shift from federal to private operation of railroads. On March 1, 1920, railroads that had been placed under federal rule during World War I were returned to private operation with important consequences for the gains of railroad workers under the federal rule. Unions, by then widespread, demanded a continuation of the existing national agreements and various innovations introduced during federal operations as well as increased wages and changes in rules and working conditions. With railroads unwilling to meet the demands, railroad shopmen went on strike on July 1, 1922, and threatened to bring the nation's railroads to a halt. The strike did turn violent. "By the end of July, 2,200 deputy United States marshals had been appointed and National Guard troops were on duty in seven states amid reports of violence from Fresno, California, to Worcester, Massachusetts. . . . The strike was ended by the Railway Employees' Department on February 1, 1925" (Flynn 1993, 67).

14. Beardstown (IL) *Beardstown Gazette* 1979. "Beardstown Yesterday and Today: 1829 to 1979."

15. In 1857, the General Gas Corporation of Baton Rouge, Louisiana, began construction of a plant in Beardstown for manufacturing liquefied petroleum gas storage tanks. The plant was to occupy seventeen acres and have a production capacity of 25,000 tanks annually (*New York Times* 1953a, L37). In the same year, the Baker Manufacturing Company, maker of snow plows and road building and earth moving equipment (headquartered in Springfield, Illinois) awarded a contract to the Luria Engineering Company to build a 40,000 square foot plant in Beardstown (*New York Times* 1953b, F5). In addition, the flour mill that opened its doors in 1875 merged with the Colorado Milling and Elevator Company. The Bohn's Aluminum Company and the Wells Lamont Glove Company (1936) continued to operate in Beardstown for much of the twentieth century. See Beardstown (IL) *Illinoian-Star* 1946, "Wels Lamont Comes Through," January 14, page 2.

16. This includes the Rich Lumber Company (1964), the Alton Box Board Company (1971), Kent Feeds plant (1969), and Trinity Steel plant (1964).

17. See "Cargill, Beardstown: the Beardstown, Illinois Facility" (no date). http://www .cargill.com/wcm/groups/public/@ccom/documents/image/na31720660.pdf (accessed December 2014). Also, Cargill Fact Sheet 2007. "Cargill Meat Solutions: 20 Years in Beardstown." Fact sheet prepared and handed out by Cargill staff at the tour of the plant, July 10, 2007.

18. For more on the history of flooding in the Illinois Valley and the construction of the levee system, see Daniel Schneider (1996). In this eloquent environmental social history of the Illinois River, Schneider demonstrates that even the levee system was developed in part as a response to fears of transients using the resources of the floodplain. Schneider explains how much of the levee system was built as a way to privatize or enclose floodplain land previously treated as a commons. There were two main groups doing the levee construction: rich landowners with fishing and duck-hunting clubs who could no longer keep poor hunters and fishermen from poaching and so converted their wetlands into corn fields by building levees; and richer, large-scale commercial fishermen who also could not keep transient fishermen (who lived on houseboats rather than owning land) from their fishing grounds and so converted their fishing lakes into agricultural lands through levee construction. Property rights in agricultural land were more readily recognized and less contested than property rights in

wetlands and their fish and wildlife. Many of these transient fishermen were Portuguese, and racial prejudice also played a role in the move to enclose the floodplain, Schneider writes.

19. Springfield (IL) *State Journal-Register* 1989. "Rushville Chamber Backs Prison Work Camp Plan" November 22, page 18.

20. For county level data, see Appendix 1 Table A2. For state level data, see next note.

21. See Appendix Tables A2 and A3.

22. Oral histories referred to here are from McConnell and Miraftab (2009).

23. As mentioned in the introduction, where I use potentially identifying information, as I do here, I have obtained interviewees' consent accordingly.

24. See Williams and Ostendorf (2011); Warren (2007).

25. The black workers were brought into the meat industry as strikebreakers in the late nineteenth century, a period of widespread labor action. Even though strikebreakers came from various racial groupings, blacks were the most noticed. This reinforced existing racism on the part of white strikers.

26. See Horowitz (1997); Warren (2007); Williams and Ostendorf (2011); Barrett (2002); Perry and Kegley (1989); Kandel and Parrado (2005).

27. In the period 1980–1988, the rate of illness for meatpacking, per one hundred workers increased from 2.5 to 9.1 (Horowitz 1997, 278). For a five-year period from 1984 to 1989, the loss of workdays per one hundred workers due to illness spiked from 42.1 to 136 and due to injuries and illness from 232.3 to 358.7 (*Meat Facts 1990* and *Meat Facts 1991*, both published by the American Meat Institute [Washington, DC]). According to 2001 U.S. Bureau of Labor Statistics, the meat industry continues to be have the most dangerous jobs with the highest rate of injury for manufacturing jobs, though the industry's rate of the injury and illness has declined from an estimated 29.5 injuries and illnesses per one hundred full-time workers in 1992 to 14.7 in 2001 (Government Accounting Office 2005).

28. "In 1952 one man hour of labor produced 51.4 pounds of dressed meat. By 1977, output had tripled to 154.6 pounds" (Horowitz 1997, 253).

29. The Big Four were Armour, Cudahy, Swift, and Wilson.

30. For example, District Local UFCW 431, which covers the Beardstown plant, has a diverse membership, representing workers in the following industries: Box Manufacturing; Cafeterias; Canned Soft Drinks; Canned Soups & Foods; City Sewer & Maintenance; Doctors' Clinics; Gelatin Processing; Hospitals; Hotels & Motels; Intermediate Care Facilities; Job Training & Vocational Rehabilitation Services; Meat Packing & Processing; Men's & Boy's Clothing; Nursing Care Facilities; Pet Food Manufacturing; Plastic Manufacturing; Poultry Processing & Products; Refrigerated Warehouse; Industrial Machinery; Retail Foods; Rendering Plants; Barber Shops. See the Local's website at http://www.ufcw431.com (accessed October 2014).

31. See Horowitz (1997), table 15, 276.

32. Ibid.

33. Springfield (IL) *State Journal-Register*, November 29, 1983; see also Perry and Kegley (1989, 157).

34. Anthony Hebron, "Oscar Mayer to Close Beardstown Plant," *State Journal-Register*, October 3, 1986, page 15.

35. Beardstown (IL) *Illinoian Star Daily* 1986a. "Keep cool and align" editorial, October 1.

36. West 1986b.

37. Springfield (IL) *State Journal Register* 1986. "Official Advises Beardstown Leaders on Programs for Oscar Mayer Plant," October 22, page 1.

38. Springfield (IL), *State Journal Register* 1987, "Funds Awarded to Help Ex-Oscar Mayer Workers," November 19, page 1.

39. Beardstown (IL) *Illinoian Star Daily* 1986. "OM Offers Contract Extension to Local 431" October 17, page 1.

40. Walker (2003a, 1).

41. See Beardstown (IL) *Illinoian Star Daily* 1985, 1. The local newspaper's editorial piece (*Illinoian Star Daily* 1986a) titled "Keep Cool and Align," reports that news of the Oscar Mayer (OM) closure brought "waves of disbelief" to "Beardstown, Cass County and the state itself. . . . The OM announcement was unexpected and un-nerving. Just three years ago we successfully fought and reveled in our success when intervention by government and business leaders helped bring about ratification of a new OM contract. Perhaps we rested on our laurels too long." Headlines of Beardstown's *Illinoian Star Daily* for the 1985 and 1986 period reflect this anxiety. Some examples include "Efforts to Solve OM Closing" (West 1986a); "[Mayor's] Main Goal to Find a New Employer" (West 1986b); "Living on 'Borrowed Time'" (Barker 1986); "Officials Optimistic about OM Sale" (West 1986c); "Cooperation Is Key to Easing the Effects of an Oscar Mayer Closing" (West 1986d) and "Mayor Walters: 'Go Forward and Not Stop'" (*Illinoian Star Daily* 1986b).

42. Excel, the nation's second-largest beef firm, markets and processes many agricultural commodities. Cargill bought Excel in 1979. Excel had success with the "boxed beef" concept, which it planned to use with pork. Boxed beef is cut into pieces at the slaughterhouse and sold to beef packers, instead of being sold as whole sides of beef. "We believe we can make Beardstown a leader in the pork processing industry," a company representative said (Hebron 1987a, 1).

43. Walker (2003a, 7).

44. Through the Jobs Training Partnership Act (JTPA), the state offered additional incentives to potential buyers of the OM facility. In July of 1987 the consortium that was to help Cargill in hiring the retrenched workers received a $215,000 grant (Hebron 1987b).

45. For data pointing to the Cargill plant in Beardstown, see appendix, table A4, Employment dynamics in animal slaughtering and processing, Cass County, 1994–2013.

46. See appendix, table A5, Labor force ethnic composition in animal slaughtering and processing in Cass County, fourth quarter 2013.

47. See U.S. Department of Labor, Bureau of Labor Statistics, 2014. Occupational Employment Statistics, May 2014 National Industry-Specific Occupational Employment and Wage Estimates; Animal Slaughtering and Processing—NAICS 311 600, http://www.bls.gov/oes /current/naics4_311600.htm#51-0000 and Manufacturing Sectors 31, 32, and 33—http:// www.bls.gov/oes/current/naics2_31-33.htm#51-0000 (accessed June 2015).

2. IT ALL CHANGED OVERNIGHT

1. See introduction pages 13–15 for literature on migration to nontraditional destinations.

2. See Mark Mather and Kelvin Pollard (2007), "Hispanic Gains Minimize Population Losses in Rural America." Population Reference Bureau. http://www.prb.org/Publications /Articles/2007/HispanicGains.aspx (accessed December 2014).

3. Massey, Durand, and Malone (2002); Hernández-León and Zúñiga (2003); Orrenius (2004).

4. To date, despite the fact that more than 32 percent of Beardstown residents are Hispanics, the local police department has only English-speaking officers.

5. Winick (1995); Moll (1995).

6. "A love triangle that had gone bad," was how Mayor Walters later put it in a town hall meeting. Arambula had reportedly been repeatedly harassed and beaten by Brewer, a friend of the ex-husband of his white girlfriend. Five days after the killing, Arambula was detained at his home in Monterrey, Mexico, but Mexican authorities refused to extradite him to Illinois. This triggered infuriated Beardstown residents to set the bar on fire. A twenty-eight-year-old Rushville resident was later arrested for arson, and the Illinois state police patrolled the town for weeks. A Latino who lived in Beardstown at the time, like several other whites and Latinos I spoke to, saw the incident as self-defense "the Mexican man had been beaten and had reported to the police to no avail."

7. See Massey and Denton (1988) and Charles (2001).

8. Different sections of the plant have different start times. The first shift start times for various sections are as follows: cut floor 5:55 a.m, kill floor 6:55 a.m., belly line 8 a.m., new ham line 8:00 a.m., and old ham line 6:55 a.m. They all work at least eight hours. Winter starting time is two hours early on some Mondays, mostly on the kill floor.

9. Forty-nine employees were taken into custody for alleged immigration violations. "The two managers, who officials said were Mexicans in the United States illegally, and 11 of the workers arrested were charged with aggravated identity theft. Identity theft charges were brought against 14 additional employees of the cleaning service, but they have not yet been arrested, said Gail Montenegro, a spokeswoman for the immigration agency" (Sander 2007).

10. Thornburgh (2007).

11. In December of 2006 alone, immigration agents raided six meat-processing plants operated by Swift and Company in six states, detaining 1,282 immigrants believed to be in the country illegally and charging hundreds with identity theft. Since the Swift raids, smaller raids occurred in many states (Sander, 2007).

12. While the index of dissimilarity in Beardstown, as per our calculation, indicates a low level of segregation among whites and Hispanics (see chapter 1, n. 5), the assessment of segregation/integration with respect to African Americans in particular is not possible. This is due to the small number of African Americans who live in Beardstown. While we are unable to assess segregation of Detroiters versus black immigrants or other immigrant groups in Beardstown, studies in larger localities that allow such measurement, indicate extreme segregation when it comes to African Americans. For example, Parisi et al. (2011), find that blacks remain in spatially segregated neighborhoods with dissimilarity indexes higher than any other ethnic or racial group. They argue that this is a reflection of America's black exceptionalism, the hypothesis that in American society the color line is more porous for Latino and Asian immigrants than for black Americans. American color line primarily encircles African Americans rather than capturing members of other groups called "people of color" (see Sears and Savalei 2006; Gans 1999). Similarly, another study of segregation among African Americans, Hispanics, and Asians in Los Angeles (Charles 2001) shows extreme segregation for African Americans. Despite some improvement, African Americans remain substantially more isolated than other minorities in Los Angeles. The Detroiters account of "for sale signs going up" around them suggests if they were larger in number in Beardstown, similar processes of spatial exceptionalism may have occurred.

13. The U.S. State Department provides a list of professional and vocational skills that are considered for this visa type. In Togo, however, due to the high volume of applications, high school graduation is also included as a requirement for Togolese applicants to the Diversity Visa.

14. Some of West Africans in Beardstown one might say experienced what Erik Wright (1989) calls a "contradictory class position" where they thought of themselves as professional class but they were relegated to working as manual laborers with other less-educated native or foreign-born workers.

15. In 2008, several surveys were conducted in Beardstown and Rushville. The Illinois Institute for Rural Affairs conducted a housing survey in three languages in Beardstown. For this they asked me for input and assistance with formulation of questions on housing and household characteristics, with randomizing their sample, and with translations of surveys to Spanish and Francophone French. This survey, which predominantly brought in results for the English speaking households (N=468), was complemented by surveys that were conducted randomly among the immigrant households. Spanish-speaking University of Illinois Extension staff conducted these among the Spanish-speaking immigrants in Beardstown (N = 45), and an AmeriCorps volunteer conducted similar surveys among French-speaking immigrants spanning across Beardstown and Rushville (N=59). They have made available to me the key findings of the survey, which are reflected in the body of the text in this chapter.

16. The corresponding numbers for Latinos and Africans who had to leave one or more children behind are, respectively, 6 of 38 respondents and 22 of 33.

17. The corresponding numbers for Latinos and Africans with high school education (or more) are, respectively, 6 of 43 respondents and 32 of 59.

18. The corresponding numbers of homeownership for Latinos and Africans are, respectively, 18 of 45 respondents and 1 of 20. For an in-depth explanation for this difference, see chapter 8.

19. For more on this, see Nederveen Pieterse (2007).

20. Africans make up the smallest immigrant groups in the United States. As of 2010, among the nearly 38 million foreign-born persons living the United States, only 3.9 percent were African immigrants (McCabe 2011). Migration by Africans is also a recent trend. The majority came to the United States in the 1980s and 1990s. African migration to places like Beardstown is even more recent. Before the 1970s, a significant share of the African-born U.S. population lived in traditional gateway metropolitan areas (e.g., Los Angeles, Miami, Chicago, New York, and Houston) (Gozdziak and Martin, 2005; Frey, 2006; Portes and Rumbaut, 2006). However, when we analyze Integrated Public Use Microdata Series (IPUMS-USA) data (Ruggles et al. 2010), a shift in settlement patterns of African immigrants can be identified. IPUMS data analysis shows that by 2010 the proportion of African-born population living in gateway metropolitan areas (Los Angeles, Miami, Chicago, New York, and Houston combined) decreased from 43 percent in 1950 to about 23 percent.

21. Herbert Gans (1999) theorizes this racial dynamic among minorities in America as "black exceptionalism": immigrants, as the new racial and ethnic minorities in America, distance themselves socially from blacks to avoid facing "the seemingly permanent inferiority that goes with being black" (375). Joe Feagin (2000) conceptualizes this dynamic in terms of America's white supremacist racial structure whereby the racism that Latinos and other people of color experience is an extension of an "anti-Black orientation" (267). In this discussion, the dynamics of black African immigrants and black Caribbean immigrants with respect to black Americans is further instructive as it reveals how black immigrants cultivate social and cultural distinctions from African Americans in order to gain acceptance among whites. For more on social dynamics of black Americans and black immigrants, including those from Africa and the Caribbean, see contributions to edited volumes by Shaw-Taylor and Tuch (2007)

and by Arthur and Takougang (2012); an excellent review essay by Waters, Kasinitz, and Asad (2014); Denton and Massey (1989); Vickerman (2001); and Benjamin Bailey (2001).

3. MICHOACÁN'S LARGEST EXPORT IS PEOPLE

1. *Fiestas patronales* are celebrations organized by the Catholic Church in honor of the saint of the town (*El santo patrono del pueblo*). Each town has its own *santo patrono*.

2. After Guanajuato and Jalisco; see INEGI (Instituto Nacional de Geografía y Estadística), 2010, "Migración," 27, http://www.inegi.gob.mx/prod_serv/contenidos /espanol/bvinegi/productos/censos/poblacion/2010/princi_result/cpv2010_principales _resultadosIV.pdf (accessed December 2014).

3. Banco de México, (no date) "Ingresos por Remesas Familiares," (data available for 2003–present), http://www.banxico.org.mx/SieInternet/consultarDirectorioInternet Action.do?accion=consultarCuadroAnalitico&idCuadro=CA79&sector=1&locale=es (accessed December 2014). While remaining in first place as a remittance receiving state of the country, Michoacán saw a dramatic drop in the amount of its remittances, decreasing from $4,500 million in 2005 to $2,139 million in 2013. This might help explain the growth of *nacrotraficantes* in the state.

4. According to the National Council for the Evaluation of Social Development Policy (CONEVAL), Michoacán is the sixth poorest state in Mexico and twelfth in child mortality (see Instituto Nacional de Estadística y Geografía (INEGI), "Tasa de mortalidad infantil por entidad federativa," 2014, http://www3.inegi.org.mx/sistemas/sisept/Default.aspx?t =mdemo55&c=23602&s=est (accessed December 2014).

5. CONEVAL, "2012 poverty measurement: 2010–2012 National and Federal Entity poverty measurements results" 2012, http://www.coneval.gob.mx/Medicion/Paginas /Medici%C3%B3n/Pobreza%202012/Pobreza-2012.aspx (accessed October 2014)."The identification and measurement of poverty in Mexico take into account the following indicators: per capita income; household average education (average number of years at school); access to health care services; access to social security; quality and size of housing; access to basic services; access to food; degree of social cohesion" (translated from the Spanish; see above, accessed October 2014).

6. Recognizing the importance of immigration for its people, Michoacán was indeed the first Mexican state that in 1992 created a migrant services office in Morelia, the state capital, to offer legal and administrative services to migrant workers who might have lost important papers in transit or who had suffered a work injury in the United States and were back in Mexico for care (LaFranchi 1995).

7. The *Los Angeles Times* published a report on Tejaro that estimates the town's population at 4,200 (Ellingwood 2008). This is in accordance with my interview with the municipal chief (*jefetura municipal*), who indicated the town's actual population to be around 4,000, despite the census figure of 7,000. This discrepancy is due to the fact that remaining families list emigrant family members as part of their household.

8. See Cohen (2011) and Mitchel (2012), among others, for more recent literature on braceros, revealing that the current export of a Mexican labor force to the United States is a continuity of the earlier wave, but without the legal protections that the Braceros Program offered the workers.

9. The program continued long after the war, terminating only in 1964.

10. Historically, the inadequacy and the problematic nature of land reform in Michoacán have made its agricultural sector less viable as a source of livelihood for *ejidatories* (peasants with communal landownership). In general, because the parcels were very small and had poor quality soil, the state saw high rates of emigration to other regions of Mexico and the United States.

11. See Schwartzman (2013); Yunez-Naude (2003). In 1986, Mexico became a full member of the General Agreement on Tariffs and Trade (GATT). However, the Mexican government undertook no major changes in the structure of protection of agricultural products until the end of the 1980s. Up to that time, all product markets in which CONASUPO intervened were subject to import licenses administered by the Ministry of Commerce (Yunez-Naude 2003, 104). In 1983–1988 CONASUPO accounted for 95 percent of total rice imports but only 25 percent in 1989–1993 and zero in 1994–1996. Its share of total imports of beans fell from 99 percent in 1989–1993 to zero in 1994–1996; of corn from 89 percent in 1983–1988 to 38 percent in 1989–1993 and 16 percent in 1994–1996; and of wheat, from 68 percent in 1983–1985 to 15 percent in 1989–1993 and zero in 1994–1996 (ibid., 103–104).

12. See Yunez-Naude (2003, table 1), "Stages of CONASUPO's Liquidation (1985 to 1999)," 102, and table 5, "Basic Crops: Production and Import (thousands of mt tons) 1980–1999," 116.

13. Before Mexican workers supported American agriculture, 200,000 Chinese workers were contracted to fill the labor hole and cultivate California fields until the Chinese Exclusion Act. Subsequently, the Japanese replaced the Chinese as field hands (Gyory 1998).

14. "The First Immigrant Workers," http://www.farmworkers.org/immigrat.html ("Welcome to the farmworkers' website!" accessed October 2014).

15. Cited in Rodriguez-Scott (2002).

16. See Cornelius (1989); Cohen (2013); Mitchel (2012).

17. By 2005 the number of people deported from the United States because of a criminal record, largely convictions for immigration offenses, had risen from 37,724 in 1996 to 90,426. (Human Rights Watch Report 2008, 33). Overall, removals also rose; in 1997, for the first time in history, they surpassed 100,000 and then soared to nearly a quarter of a million by 2005. In addition, the fortification several hundred miles of the border, along with the assignment of more border patrol officers to the region, has made crossing a more risky venture. For narratives of immigrants, human rights groups, community organizers, and lawyers on the human costs of such border fortification see Fernandes (2007).

18. With encouragement and support from sympathetic pundits, especially in the United States, Salinas turned privatization into a holy crusade. He was praised for having "achieved" one of the fastest and most "successful divestitures of public assets anywhere" in the world (Salinas 2010, 185), selling some of the country's biggest parastatal companies, including public television, the telephone system, airlines, and banks. Over 80 percent were sold or dissolved. The most recent front of this private-sector takeover of public assets is the national petroleum company, Pemex.

19. See Rick Relinger (2010, graph 1).

20. In a *New York Times* Op-Ed piece Joseph Stiglitz (2004) writes that "while the hope was that NAFTA would reduce income disparities between the United States and its southern neighbor, in fact they have grown—by 10.6 percent in the last decade. Meanwhile, there has been disappointing progress in reducing poverty in Mexico, where real wages have been falling at the rate of 0.2 percent a year."

21. At the time of NAFTA negotiations, corn growers constituted 40 percent of all Mexicans working in agriculture.

22. Pramila Jayapal, "Root Causes of Immigration—NAFTA," February 13, 2011, http://www.weareoneamerica.org/root-causes-immigration-nafta (accessed December 2014). See also Binford (2009), as well as Bacon (2008a), who argues that NAFTA essentially annexed Mexico as a low-wage industrial suburb of the United States.

23. Harris (2010). Collin Harris. 2010. "NAFTA and the Political Economy of Mexican Immigration." ZNet, June 8. http://zcomm.org/znetarticle/nafta-and-the-political-economy-of-mexican-immigration-by-collin-harris/ (accessed December 2014).

24. In the 1980s one response to the economic changes was the movement of thousands of young workers, primarily women, to the *maquiladora* factories along the U.S. border. Set up by runaway U.S. firms to take advantage of cheap Mexican labor and deregulated production, the *maquilas* flourished for a time (Fernandez-Kelly 1984). However, as the globalization of production intensified, many of the *maquila* investors relocated to the even cheaper labor zones of Asia and Central America, leaving behind yet another pool of surplus labor in Mexico and another cohort of potential migrants.

25. With the 2007 economic recession, the rising number of undocumented Mexicans arriving in the United States dropped dramatically. However, according to the Pew Center's estimates, by 2013 Mexican-born immigrants still made up about six million or 52 percent of the unauthorized populations in the United States (Preston 2013).

4. WINNING THE LOTTERY IN TOGO

1. As a German colony, Togo was called "Togoland." Using African forced labor to work rubber, palm, cotton, and cocoa plantations under brutal conditions, German colonial administrators and companies turned the colony into an efficient economy. With the weakening of Germany after World War I, the scramble for Africa was renewed, and the Germans' share of Togoland was divided between Britain and France. The portion administered by Britain became part of Ghana; the portion administered by the French became what today we know as Togo. A key feature of the colonial history of the country was the perpetuated tension between the two largest ethnic groups: the majority Ewe in the south and the minority Kabre in the north. German colonizers had favored the Ewe people and groomed them as their interpreters and the educated class.

After Olympio was assassinated, the presidency was taken over by several transitional individuals before it was turned over to his assassin, General Gnassingbe Eyadema. A Kabre who began his career as an ordinary soldier, General Gnassingbe Eyadema ruled the country for thirty-eight years in a dictatorship said to be responsible for thousands of political killings and disappearances. A key to his success in suppressing political opposition was the creation of an all-Kabre military, nicknamed the "army of cousins" by the public. Following his death in 2005, General Eyadema's son Faure Gnassingbe Eyadema was confirmed president, thanks to military-backed, rigged elections.

2. Also see the 1999 Country Reports on Human Rights Practices, released by the Bureau of Democracy, Human Rights, and Labor, U.S. Department of State, February 25, 2000, http://www.state.gov/1997-2001-NOPDFS/global/human_rights/1999_hrp_report/togo.html (accessed December 2014).

3. Among the notable alums of the school is Umar Farouk Abdulmutallab, who was charged with attempting to blow up Northwest Airlines Flight 253 to Detroit on Christmas Day 2009.

4. United Nations Statistics Division, National Accounts Section, available from the National Accounts Main Aggregates Database website, http://unstats.un.org/unsd /demographic/products/socind/inc-eco.htm (accessed November 20, 2010).

5. See Toporowski (1988); Moura (1990); Lee and Astrow (1987).

6. For a complete list of projects and operations that the World Bank has had in Togo, see http://www.worldbank.org/projects/search?lang=en&countrycode_exact=TG (accessed December 2014).

7. See Trading Economics, http://www.tradingeconomics.com/togo/gdp-growth -annual (accessed October 2014 and June 2015).

8. See ibid.

9. See Kohnert (2011), 21–22, table 3.

10. See Kohnert (2011).

11. World Bank staff calculation based on data from IMF Balance of Payments Statistics database and data releases from central banks, national statistical agencies, and World Bank country desks. See World Bank, "Migration and Remittances Data," n.d., http://siteresources .worldbank.org/INTPROSPECTS/Resources/334934-1288990760745/RemittanceData _Inflows_Oct2014.xls (accessed December 2014).

12. See Trading Economics, "Emigration Rate of Tertiary Educated (% of Total Tertiary Educated Population) in Togo," n.d., http://www.tradingeconomics.com/togo/emigration -rate-of-tertiary-educated-percent-of-total-tertiary-educated-population-wb-data.html (accessed December 2014).

13. Calculated based on the U.S. Department of Justice (1997), 24–25, table 2. The 1965 Immigration and Naturalization Act, which repealed earlier race-biased statutes, contributed to the increasing number of African immigrants in the United States since the 1960s and made possible the reunion of families with African immigrant sponsors. The 1980 Refugee Act also contributed by broadening the qualifications for refugee status and allowing more African refugees to enter the United States for resettlement. The Immigration Reform and Control Act of 1986 legalized the immigration status of Africans who entered the United States prior to 1982 (Yeboah 2008).

14. Ibid. Paul Zeleza (2009) summarizes systematic analysis of American census data published by Migration Policy Institute covering the period 1850 to 2000 (Grieco 2004; Dixon 2006) as follows: "The number of African-born migrants in the US population rose from 551 in 1850 to 2,538 in 1900, climbing to 18,326 in 1930, 35,355 in 1960, 199,723 in 1980, 363,819 in 1990, and 881,000 in 2000. In 2005 there were more than a million. As rapid as this rise may seem, Africans accounted for a small proportion of immigrants to the United States: 3 percent of the nearly 33 million foreign-born residents in 2005, up from 0.4 percent in 1960 and 1.9 percent in 1990. The bulk of the African immigrants came in the 1980s and 1990s, during which 192,000 and 383,000 entered the country, respectively. In the years 2000–2004, an additional 229,000 arrived" (37).

15. According to Hiheta (2005), the first wave of Togolese diaspora in the global North falls into what Zeleza described as the diaspora of decolonization. This consisted of Africans who emigrated to the global North and settled there during the independence struggles in their respective African countries. Having lived in a French colony, the early wave of Togolese emigrants went to European French-speaking countries such as France, Switzerland, and Belgium. The second wave of Togolese emigration falls into what Zeleza calls the diaspora of structural adjustment—that is, those who were displaced by the devastating social economic impacts of the structural adjustment policies implemented on the continent.

16. For more on DV see Wasem (2010); Akyemang-Konadu and Takyi (2001).

17. Every year more than five million people submit their information for the DV lottery, and 110,000 are selected randomly by a computer. They are the DV Lottery Winners. However, only 55,000 worldwide will receive the visa. They are the DV Lottery Immigrants (DV Visas). See U.S. Department of Homeland Security, Green Card Through Diversity Visa Program,http://www.uscis.gov/green-card/other-ways-get-green-card/green-card-through -diversity-immigration-visa-program/green-card-through-diversity-immigrant-visa -program.

18. An approximate breakdown of the debt created through DV migration for Aku is as follows: visa fee at the embassy, $410 (nonrefundable even if your application is denied); postage and transport, $100; medical exams, $307; acquisition of a passport, $62; translation of documents to English (like high school diploma and others), $103; airfare, between $1,400 and $2,000 (depending on season or date of the year). In addition, the cost for the first few weeks before finding a job adds up to approximately $4,000 per person. Referring to the non-refundable application fees that the U.S. embassy received for the large number of Togolese applicants, one interviewee in Togo surmised that "the revenue for application fees supports the U.S. embassy staff."

19. By way of comparison, in 2010 a public school teacher in Lomé earned $100 per month.

20. The scale of "brain drain" was highlighted by Gwaradzimba and Shumba (2010) who report that according to the Institute of International Education "an estimated 23,000 university lecturers leave African universities annually to join the diaspora, [but] only 2,256 African scholars were teaching in American universities compared to 35,620 from Asia, 26,688 from Europe and 4,676 from Latin America" (229). These proportions are not reflected in the sectors of the diaspora where African intellectuals work.

5. DETROIT: "THE FIRST THIRD WORLD CITY OF THE U.S."

1. See Bluestone and Harrison (1982) and Harrison and Bluestone (1990).

2. To understand the "leaner meaner" policies, the words of Carol and Aaron, Detroiters I interviewed in 2012 in Beardstown, are instructive: "Summer of 2011 they cut that off, if you been on it—Social Service, for more than five years, they cut you off. So that's why it's so bad right now, because there's no work, and the government not helping. . . . No more food stamps, no more paying your rent, no more light bill, no more child care. . . . So that's why it got crazy over there. Man! That's why it got wild. So this would push people out. . . . They can't pay their rent no more, everything. . . . Man, and it's making people do crimes that they ordinarily would not have done, just to feed their families."

6. GLOBAL RESTRUCTURING OF SOCIAL REPRODUCTION

1. Unfortunately, my efforts to speak with him over the phone or in person were unsuccessful, and my calls were not returned.

2. See Sørensen (2012); Leighton (2013); Geiger and Pécoud (2013); Borje (2013).

3. Some scholars argue that remittances lead to increased social inequities based on connections individuals may have to international migrants. This argument also holds that remittances create dependencies and are counterproductive since recipients spend the money on conspicuous consumption (Binford 2003; Sana and Massey 2005; Sandoval 2007). Others argue that remittances lead to development because recipients invest the money in

employment-creating activities such as construction of new homes or the improvement of existing housing (Cohen and Conway 2005; Durand, Kandel, and Parrado 1996; Rose and Shaw 2008; Sana and Massey 2005 in reference to Mexico specifically; Hugo 2009 for Asia Pacific). This argument further holds that resources often flow to families left behind in the country of origin to support education and health care as well as overall social and economic development.

4. This is a particularly understudied relationship. Raghuram (2009) refers to the problem and how the migration-development Nexus creates certain blind spots in migration studies. Levitt (2001) in her study of social remittances calls attention to the important contributions made by communities of origin. There are also some high-profile, recent commentaries such as Leighton (2013) of the International Labor Organization and Castles (2014), which are critical of the migration-development nexus's focus on remittance, but they still fall short in recognizing the particular relationship I discuss here. Also see Muniandy and Bonatti (2014).

5. In a certain way, they were lucky to afford to travel together. In many instances, only the winning applicant goes to the United States, leaving the spouse behind. According to several interviewees, many people deal with this predicament. One Togolese I interviewed in Beardstown in 2008 explained a case in which a Togolese lottery visa winner, who lived in Beardstown but had a spouse back in Togo, made arrangement with a single man who had recently won the lottery visa in Togo. The single man claimed the wife of the husband who was already in Beardstown as his own wife in order to enable her to immigrate. In return, the husband and wife paid the travel expenses of the single man. These arrangements can lead to problems when the single man is living in the United States and decides he wants to marry.

6. Among West Africans surveyed in Rushville and Beardstown who had children, 67 percent had to leave at least one child behind when they emigrated; this was the case for 16 percent of Mexican immigrants surveyed in Beardstown. See chapters 2, 3, and 4 for an explanation of these differential migration and settlement patterns among Mexicans and Togolese.

7. On "affect," see McKay (2014) and Anderson (2014).

8. One Togolese interviewed in Illinois explained this Ewe expectation in the following terms: "Everyone has to have a place to go to, a village of origin, everyone has to. A lot of people don't have one when they come [to the United States]. They save here and build it [there]. Before cement was cheaper but now expensive so harder to build the 'place' a home. Since 1975 price has been going up 600 CFA [francs] to 1,500 CFA [francs] in early 1980s to now almost 4,500 CFA [francs]." She explained further that "the home in place of origin is about confidence, if you have someone to trust that they will use the money for construction, you'll do it, otherwise you wait till you can go back to build your home."

9. One Mexican in Beardstown who helped me understand the importance of *quinceañeras* told me that "people borrow money and undergo debt on their credit card even refinance home to pay for impressive celebration of *quinceañera*."

10. Genevieve le Baron and Adrienne Roberts (2010) draw on the notion of carceral relationships in discussing how labor through invisible means might be constrained in its physical and social mobility. While freedom of capital is secured through state institutions, the freedom of labor to move is highly controlled through immigration policies and other mechanisms. Carceral relations, they argue, have become a central means for containing not

only contradictions and insecurities but also resistances that are generated by shifting relations of production and social reproduction. Focusing on the societies of the global North, namely, those of the United States and Canada, they highlight the carceral relations that are produced through prisons, debt structures, and households. They argue that whereas previously the state managed tensions and insecurities of capitalist society through a combination of macroeconomic and social policies—for example, welfare programs—in the contemporary era capitalism prefers to manage its contradictions through carceral social relations and institutions. Those are relations that weigh down people's mobility and their future life choices, facilitating unequal and un-free capitalist social relations within which people have limited social and physical mobility. Examples of this include locking people up (e.g., the literal incarceration of African American youth in the United States) or by creation of debt and family obligations.

11. Most migration studies explain the movement of people in terms of economic rationalities. But few have started to pay attention to the role that imaginations, of both nonmaterial and material possibilities, play in this movement. For example, see Dannecker (2013) for how the seductive imagination of destination motivates immigrants' movement, and Jackson (2008) for how the negative imagination of the home country keeps immigrants in places of destination.

12. See Table 1.1 in this volume for 2014 U.S. Bureau of Labor Statistics data.

13. See Wilson and Miraftab (2015) on new rounds of accumulation in the rust belt. We write that "global capital, like vultures, having recently wreaked havoc on vast disadvantaged populations in America and around the world in cycles of accumulation, now comes back to feast on the ruins (people, physical infrastructures, unstable economic bases, neighborhoods). In less metaphorical terms, capital continues its relentless pursuit for profit that takes it, in one more round of activity, to communities across the globe only to abandon them and later come back. Though much has been written about the behavior and logic of footloose capital in its earlier rounds of global relocation, less explored is how global capital today finds new opportunities in these left-behind spaces" (28). Wilson and I highlight how the new round is facilitated through parasitic industries like payday lenders, pawn shops, check cashers in the urban rust belt, and highly hazardous industries like meatpacking in rural rust belt.

14. See Neil Smith (1984) and David Harvey (2006).

15. We know that disparities between developing and developed nations have accelerated with globalization. In 1900, the ratio of the average income of the five richest countries in the world to the five to ten poorest countries was about 9:1. Today that ratio is 100:1. See Pramila Jayapal, "Root Causes of Immigration—NAFTA," February 13, 2011, http://www.weareoneamerica.org/root-causes-immigration-nafta (accessed December 2014).

16. Companies not only seek to transfer risks and costs, but also to keep benefits within. This is commonly practiced through creation of tax increment fund (TIF) districts, where taxes are reinvested in the district where certain businesses or companies are located. A less common practice by larger manufacturing companies is to create an incorporated "city" that includes only their production site. Such an incorporated city would include in its borders the plant and no more—no residence, no school, no hospital. In the United States, this is referred to as "club goods" (on the model of golf clubs). The companies transfer risk and costs associated with workers and their families to other towns and keep the benefits within the production site. Monsanto, Illinois (now Sauget), near St. Louis, is a prime example of this phenomenon.

Theising (2003) calls such configurations "industrial suburbs" and identifies additional examples such as National City, IL (National Stockyards), and Granite City, IL (Granite Iron
Rolling Mills).

17. See Allegretto et al. (2013); Dube and Jacobs (2004); Martin (2012).

18. See Peck (2002); Shipler (2005); Newman (1999); Theodore and Martin (2007).

19. The right to socialized care is stipulated by the Mexican Constitution (Article 4). This
does not mean that there is a strong form of public sector social protection, but as a legacy of
the 1910 Mexican revolution, social protection has had a strong presence in the political and
cultural consciousness of Mexican society and there is always a debate on how to improve
the guarantees for this right through public and private institutions. Maybe governmental
institutions are corrupt and some are quite ineffective, but the Mexican government at all
levels assigns resources for those purposes and oversees the affordability of private health
care. Against this broader backdrop there are several ways in which Mexican immigrants
in the United States and their families back home can count on social protection (health
care or old age pension). Returning migrants can receive governmental social services
directly through a range of governmental programs (see Mexico Secretaria de Desarrollo
Social [SEDESOL], "Programas Sociales," n.d., http://www.sedesol.gob.mx/en/SEDESOL
/Programas_Sociales, accessed December 2014), or indirectly through a family member's Instituto Mexicano del Seguro Social (IMSS) entitlements. If upon return, migrants are healthy
and can work, they qualify to be incorporated into the IMSS. If migrants return to Mexico at
an old age, they can be affiliated with other programs like Pensiones Para Adultos Mayores.
They can also receive medical attention for free at public health care clinics, like Centros de
Salud, which are available across the country. In addition, immigrants' families and returned
migrants can access other low-cost social programs, such as Seguro Popular (Popular Insurance Scheme); see http://www.seguro-popular.salud.gob.mx/index.php?option=com
_content&view=article&id=100&Itemid=137 (accessed December 2014) or low-price private
institutions such as *farmacias similares*, where consultation and medicines can be for as low
as two dollars per doctor visit; see http://healthmarketinnovations.org/program/farmacias
-similares (accessed December 2014).

20. See Medicina Digital, "Abre IMSS novena oficina en EU en apoyo a inmigrantes y
sus familias," February 23, 2007, http://www.medicinadigital.com/index.php/secciones
/empresa-medica-93528/4628-abre-imss-novena-oficina-en-eu-en-apoyo-a-inmigrantes-y-sus
-familias (accessed December 2014).

21. In the United States and Europe, this corresponds to the 1930s through 1970s, when the
ideal of a welfare state was prominent. In the global South, the state's role in social reproduction
has not been through welfare programs, but rather through developmental programs that
provision collective goods, such as infrastructures, schools, health care, housing, and the like.
Developmental programs emerged in distinct time periods, depending on when they moved
toward postcolonial state formation, but as in Europe and the United States, they diminished
in the 1970s.

22. See Hochschild (2003); Parreñas (2003); Hontagneu-Sotelo (2001); Romero (2002),
among others.

23. In Tejaro, I learned from the public works project labor force that remittances from
places like Beardstown funded much of the infrastructure improvement. Typically, the municipality pays half and residents pay the other half. Each homeowner pays for the infrastructure costs in front of his or her lot. The share of those who cannot pay is picked up by others

who live on the street. Effectively, this means emigrants pay not only for their own share of infrastructure costs but also subsidize neighbors who have less economic means.

7. WE WANTED WORKERS

1. Cargill, "Our Responsibility in a Changing World," 2012, http://www.cargill.com/wcm /groups/public/@ccom/documents/document/na3066211.pdf (accessed December 2014).

2. Cargill, "Ethics and Values," n.d., http://www.cargill.com/careers/why-better -together/ethics-values/index.jsp (accessed December 2014). See also Cargill, *Our Guiding Principles: Cargill Code of Conduct,* 2012, http://www.cargill.com/wcm/groups/public/ @ccom/documents/document/na3064473.pdf (accessed October 20, 2014).

3. Article 1904.7 of the OSHA Act defines recordable injury in terms of "an injury or ill-ness [that] involves one or more days away from work." See OSHA, 1904.C, n.d., https://www .osha.gov/pls/oshaweb/owadisp.show_document?p_table=STANDARDS&p_id=9638 (ac-cessed December 2014).

4. See Cargill, "Workplace Safety," n.d., http://www.cargill.com/corporate-responsibility /workplace-safety/ (accessed December 2014).

5. See Cargill, "Enriching Our Communities," n.d., http://www.cargillfoods.com /emea/en/products/Malt-2/Our-Global-Commitment/Operating-Responsibly/Enriched -Communities/index.jsp (accessed December 2014).

6. See Cargill, *Our Guiding Principles.*

7. Cargill, "Our Responsibility in a Changing World," 12.

8. List from ibid., 16.

9. See Cargill, "Cargill Beardstown," n.d., http://www.cargill.com/wcm/groups/public /@ccom/documents/document/na3068946.pdf (accessed December 2014).

10. See U.S. Department of Labor, U.S. Bureau of Labor Statistics, 2011. "TABLE 1. Inci-dence rates of nonfatal occupational injuries and illnesses by industry and case types, 2010." http://www.bls.gov/iif/oshwc/osh/os/ostb2813.pdf (accessed June 2015).

11. For example, closer to Christmas, they find the lines move faster. Interviewees men-tioned that closer to the contract deadline, for example, closer to the Olympic Games in China, the company, which had already changed to a six-day work week several months ear-lier, also made the lines faster. Overtime payments are at a rate of one and a half.

12. Associated Press 1999.

13. United Food & Commercial Workers (UFCW), "Is the Meatpacking Industry Get-ting Safer?" January 10, 2012, http://www.ufcw.org/2012/01/10/is-the-meatpacking-industry -getting-safer/ (accessed December 2014).

14. "Recent efforts by business groups to 'reform' workers' comp have made it more dif-ficult for injured employees to obtain payments. In Colorado, the first 'workers' comp reform' bill was sponsored in 1990 by Tom Norton, a conservative state senator from Greeley. His wife, Kay, was a vice president at ConAgra Red Meat at the time. Under Colorado's new law, which places limits on compensation, the maximum payment for losing an arm is $37,738. Losing a digit brings you anywhere from $2,400 to $9,312, depending on whether it's a middle finger, a pinkie, or a thumb" (Schlosser 2001, 42).

15. According to an article in the *State Journal-Register,* "Several state and local agencies are still trying to aid the former Oscar Mayer employees who were not hired back. When Os-car Mayer closed in April, there were about 819 employees. About 200 of those workers found

jobs on their own or retired, while the remainder applied for jobs with Excel, said Kathleen McCullough, administrator for the Land of Lincoln Consortium. About 90 of those workers are attending Lincoln Land Community College, trucking schools or taking other training through the assistance of the consortium. The consortium also has subcontracted with former Oscar Mayer union officials to form 'Project Assist,' which helps laid-off workers with their job search. . . . The consortium . . . receive[d] a $215,000 grant in July, which will be used to retrain the workers. . . . . Under that program, employers who hire former Oscar Mayer workers will temporarily be reimbursed for about 50 percent of the trainee's wages" (Hebron 1987b, 47).

16. For the current map of Beardstown's EZ and TIF (Tax Increment Financing) district, see http://www.cityofbeardstown.org/index.aspx?NID=1019 (accessed June 2015).

17. See Story (2012) for an extensive database of business incentives and tax deals awarded by state and local governments to companies and what they receive in return—in fact very little. Also see Brunori (1997), Harrison and Kanter (1978), and Knaap and Simon (1994).

18. For detailed coverage of Cargill-PTAB negotiation, see Ursch (2007).

19. On April 5, 2007, the *Star Gazette*, the local newspaper of Beardstown, published an interesting report which revealed the irony of Cargill's "community giving." Written cleverly by the late Bill Beard, the newspaper's then chief editor, the article reported on a meeting sponsored by Cargill in the aftermath of the ICE raid the previous day. Calling it a "leadership conference," Cargill brought together the concerned residents, plant managers, and community leaders and made a presentation of company's economic benefits to the community. Steve Pirkle, the Beardstown plant's general manager praised the company's community giving and cited "the plant's donations to the community through its donation committee ($100,0000 annual budget) and cultural fund in partnership with the United Food & Commercial Workers Local 431 ($20,000 annual budget)." The company's recent donations "included $150,000 to the Beardstown school district" (Beard 2007, 1). Beard then went on to state that this presentation was immediately followed by a thorny question raised by a member of the audience concerning "the company's request for a property reassessment from the Cass County Board of Review." In response Pirkle dodged the question and stated, "The plant is presently being appraised by an independent source and an announcement can be expected in mid-April." Discussion was limited at that meeting, Beards writes, as the only county board member in attendance had left early due a previous engagement.What is curious is that the report then goes on to indicate that Tom Daniels, vice president and general manager of QSI, the sanitation company that Cargill subcontracted to clean the Beardstown plant and was later fired for illegal employment of undocumented workers that were arrested the very previous night, presented Beardstown School District Superintendent Robert Bagby with a four-thousand-dollar donation. As to the intended purpose of this donation, Daniel stated it was to help the district employ Beardstown Police Department officers to monitor the middle and high school on a part-time daily basis. The juxtaposition of the company's presentation of community giving, the community's questioning of tax avoidance, and the contractor who makes the donation at that meeting are quite suggestive in the context of the ensuing discussion of patronage.

20. See, among many others, Stull et al. (1995) and Broadway (1995) for Kansas; Grey (1995) for Iowa; Griffith (1995) for North Carolina; and Fennelly (2005) for Minnesota.

21. See Grey (2009); Erickson (1990); Fennelly (2005); Gozdziak (2005); Griffith (2008).

22. The owners' sentence of twenty-seven years in prison was based not only on breaking immigration laws, but also financial fraud and a range of labor practices including sexual ha-

rassment and child labor (Preston 2010). Postville has been the subject of a range of studies. For a journalistic account, see Stephen Bloom (2000) as well as *New York Times* (2008); for an academic account, which concerns transnational dimensions of immigrants' placemaking in Postville and in Guatemala, see Sandoval (2012; 2014); for a practice-oriented account of "lessons to be learned," see Grey (2009).

23. Sometimes these events and the corporate giving could become contentious. Such was the case with a Congolese fundraiser, a raffle in which Cargill put up a thousand-dollar flat-screen TV as a prize, and which fueled tension between Congolese and other Africans, in particular the Togolese. In terms of numbers, they were the largest group of Africans in the area as of 2012 and had worked through the African Association which is for all Africans, rather than being an ethnically or nationally specific organization. The African Association, which was founded in 2003, had instituted the annual Africa Day celebrations but never received the kind of support for its activities as the Congolese did for their separate nationally specific organizing effort. In addition to the annual Africa Day celebration, the African Association also helps "the new comers to find their way," as one of the founders of the group said. "If emergency we help, someone loses job or has death in family and we collect money to help."

24. De Genova (2002) points out how the constant threat of deportation, even if it is not real, renders "undocumented migrant labor a distinctly disposable commodity" (438). Licona and Maldonado (2013), building on De Genova's concept of a "deportability regime," uncover the "'micro' interactions that (re)produce a real and/or perceived threat of deportability in everyday contexts" (534). Understood in such terms, the interaction that demobilized the Committee for Intercultural Understanding is precisely how a regime of deportability functions—producing "borders within."

25. A more recent organization, the Beardstown Rushville Immigrants United (BRIFU), started in Beardstown in spring of 2008 with the support of Gamaliel Foundation. BRIFU, as a community-based NGO-sponsored group, was initiated to bring the French- and Spanish-speaking immigrants in Beardstown and Rushville together to discuss issues of importance to both groups. But over time its focus shifted to West African immigrants' concerns with legal residency and continued higher education. In BRIFU's now all French-speaking membership, meetings and workshops concern the mobility of West Africans, how to bring family members in for lottery visa holders, how to apply to obtain U.S. citizenship, and how to pursue certification of their academic credentials or apply to universities.

26. Labor studies that focus on workplace dynamics among different ethnic groups help us understand the role of ethnic minorities' recruitment in creating division within the working class. Recruitment of ethnicized labor, some stress, constructs a dual labor market which sets one group against the other, weakening labor's collective bargaining power (Bonacich 1972; Farley 2005 [1982]). Others argue that white and more senior members of the labor force are beneficiaries of splitting or segmenting the labor market, as they gain in various ways from industry's use of more exploited ethnicized minority workers (Edwards 1973). Roediger and Esch (2013) argue that the white working class did not merely benefit from this process, but actively took part in the production of ethnic and racial differences that privilege them in the labor market.

27. See Nast with Pulido (2000); Gómez-Peña (2001).

28. The literature focused on the interracial, interethnic dynamics of workers at the workplace has featured ethnographic research in manufacturing firms including the meat industry. These studies indicate that a corporation's transnational and translocal recruitment

strategies are often designed to create a dual labor market which sets one group against the other and weakens labor's collective bargaining power to accept the low wages for risky and back-breaking jobs (Bonacich 1972; Fink 1998; Gordon, Edwards, and Reich 1996; Roediger and Esch 2012; Dunn, Argones, and Shiver 2005). Labor segmentation and stratification are pointed out in this literature as a means of effective control of labor to diminish possibilities of labor solidarity and organizing and to increase the pressure on a divided workforce. Capitalizing on their linguistic, ethnic, racial, and religious differences, as well as their legal status and historically produced social prejudice and stereotypes about each minority group, companies use the diverse workforce to manage and control the wages and the conditions of work—that is to press down the wages and speed up production. See for example Gordon, Edwards, and Reich (1996); Bonacich (1972); Fink (1998); Barrett (2002); and Roediger and Esch (2012).

8. WE GOT PEOPLE

1. In this chapter the experience of African Americans does not feature for various reasons. Sites of mediation discussed in this chapter emerged out of the observations among Mexicans, West Africans, and white locals during my Illinois fieldwork in 2005–2012. African Americans, however, too few in numbers, did not take stable local residence in Rushville or Beardstown until 2010–2011, and I connected with them only at the tail end of the fieldwork in 2012 (see chapter 5). In the course of Beardstown fieldwork, I therefore did not have the opportunity to observe specific sites through which Detroiters might or might not (re)negotiate interracial relationships in this local context, nor are we to assume that the observations made among the other groups can be extended to Detroiters.

2. The 2010 population census reported that 43 percent of Hispanics in Beardstown lived in owner-occupied housing units. For non-Hispanic whites in Beardstown the percentage of households living in owner-occupied units was 71 (Table H15 and H17I, U.S. Bureau of Census 2010). For comparison, the data for the country as a whole indicates that respective percentages are 47.3 percent Hispanic household and 72.2 percent non-Hispanic white households (table H15 and H17I, U.S. Bureau of Census 2010). Considering the recent arrival of Latinos to Beardstown, this comparative data is quite impressive.

3. McConnell and Miraftab (2008, 2009) argue that the high rate of homeownership among Spanish-speaking, predominantly Mexican immigrants has been made possible by various circumstances. One is the affordability of homeownership in this small town. The house prices are relatively low, the employment at the plant secure and year-round, and the mortgage market that developed in the early 2000s favorable to immigrants. The large local and translocal network of Mexican immigrants was a source of information about the processes and conditions of homeownership. The Beardstown native and entrepreneurial realtor, Buffy Tillitt, mentioned in chapter 2, who took intensive Spanish classes and conducted home ownership workshops at the plant in Spanish, was also instrumental in locally facilitating the national shift in the housing market and private banks' lending practices. We also discussed in those publications how the absence of zoning and prior planning regulations might have contributed to the residential integration we observe in town today. The absence of any preexisting, residentially segregated spatial structure in town means that newcomers can find places to live wherever there is a landlord or owner willing to rent or sell to them.

4. The 2010 census indicates that 15.63 percent of Africans and blacks, grouped together by census data, lived in owner occupied units. U.S. Bureau of the Census 2010, 2010 Census

of Population and Housing, Summary File 1, Table H11B. Total Population in Occupied Housing Units by Tenure (Black or African American Alone Householder), www.factfinder2 .census.gov (accessed January, 2012).

5. Africans' lower rate of homeownership also has to do with their greater levels of debt, their thinner social support networks in the United States, their greater remittance obligations to support family members left behind, and their more recent immigration to Beardstown.

6. For more on this, see McConnell and Miraftab (2009).

7. Spatial residential integration calculated by the index of dissimilarity between whites and Latinos in 2000 was 59.4 for Beardstown compared to 62 for Chicago, 63 for Los Angeles-Long Beach, and 67 for New York (American Communities Project 2001, cited in McConnell and Miraftab 2009, 611). According to the 2010 population census block-level data, Beardstown was even more integrated than it had been in 2000. The index of dissimilarity dropped from 59.4 in 2000 to 54 in 2010. Such block-level census information is unavailable for Africans or African Americans in Beardstown due to their small numbers, but from what one can see and hear from residents, no neighborhood is designated black or white or Latino. For more on specifics of index of dissimilarity calculation, see McConnell and Miraftab (2009). Values for 2000 are calculated from the U.S. Bureau of the Census 2000, Summary File 1, http://factfinder2.census.gov (accessed December 2014). Value for 2010 calculated from the U.S. Bureau of the Census 2010, Summary File 1, http://factfinder2.census.gov (accessed December 2014).

8. National Center for Education Statistics, 2012. In the 2010 NCES survey, this data is identified with "English Language Learner Students." Limited English Proficient Students grew from 17 percent in 2000 to over 25 percent in 2010.

9. Illinois State Board of Education. 2010.

10. Illinois State Board of Education. 2013.

11. "Since 1973, Illinois has mandated a Transitional Bilingual education (TBE) policy, required in schools with 20 or more students speaking a common minority language. TBE must be provided for a period of 3 years until such time as [a student] achieves a level of English language skills which will enable him to perform successfully in classes in which instruction is given only in English" (Illinois State Board of Education 2008, cited in Paciotto and Delany-Barmann 2011, 226). Paciotto and Delany-Barmann note that most English Language Learners programs meet the state's minimum transitional requirement, reflecting the perspective of language as a problem "perpetuating the low performance of ELLs" (ibid.).

12. The Dual Language program can follow a 90 percent–10 percent, 80 percent–20 percent, and 50 percent–50 percent instructional language allocation model, with the higher percentage being in the minority language. In Beardstown they elected the 50 percent–50 percent program. This might help better recognize the boldness of the approach in Beardstown (see Paciotto and Delany-Barmann 2011).

13. In 2012 Beardstown High School started a soccer team, which is quite strong and has made soccer more popular in town among white youth. According to Adam Hamilton, the team coach, the players' diversity has given the team advantage over other schools because even though all players on the team know English, "when the boys speak Spanish or French, the other team might not know what we're talking about" (Kane 2014).

14. Africa Day has been celebrated in Rushville because that is where most of the area's Africans used to live when these celebrations were initiated. In addition, Rushville, despite its sundown town history, at the time had a supportive mayor who had been at the forefront of

promoting integration and appreciation of the cultural diversity West Africans had brought to town.

15. See the Beardstown Community Unit School District #15 demographic information at Illinois State Board of Education (2007).

16. See the Beardstown Community Unit School District #15 demographic information at Illinois State Board of Education (2007) and Illinois State Board of Education (2013).

17. This reflects the situation in 2012. In the last elections, Walters was not a candidate, and a new mayor, also white, male, and U.S.-born, was elected to office.

18. As in most other small towns, in Beardstown there is no specific planning agency or entity that makes the development decisions. The City Council's committees, such as the Finance Committee, the Roads and Streets Committee, and the Cemetery Committee, are headed by aldermen the mayor appoints. The professional staff of these committees are engineers, none of whom are formally trained as planners. The existing zoning dates back to 1980, was revised in 2003 and approved at a town council meeting, and is enforced by a zoning enforcement officer who used to be the town's chief of police. The main agency involved in spatial development—namely, infrastructure development or the recent zoning revision to designate specific sites for the town's growing number of mobile homes—is the Public Works department, headed by an engineer who works at that office only part-time.

19. I should clarify here the interviewee is referring not necessarily to the actual council members but to a mix of council members and influential farmers in the community.

20. Lamphere and colleagues (1992) distinguish mediating arenas, institutions, and sites, whereby, for example, the workplace is a mediating arena, the corporation is a mediating institution, and a particular plant is a mediating site.

21. An insightful example is offered through ethnographic study of the Collingwood Neighborhood House in Vancouver. See Sandercock and Cavers (2009) and Sandercock and Attili (2009).

22. Aiming for inclusive planning in multicultural societies, planning scholarship has made important advances in recent years. Careful ethnographic research has exposed the cultural bias of seemingly banal planning decisions—e.g., building permits, occupancy rates, and street and shopping signs. Thus in multicultural societies, controversies about planning decisions can indeed be about cultural and material domination/subjugation. The examples are many; to list a few: the work on multiculturalism and planning in Australian cities by Sandercock and Kliger (1998a; 1998b) and Thompson (2003); in California by Lung-Amam (2013), Harwood and Myers (2002) and Harwood (2005); in Canada by Sandercock and Attili (2009), Miraftab (2000), Qadeer (1997), Qadeer and Agrawal (2011) and Milroy and Wallace (2002). See also contributions to Burayidi (2015).

While this multicultural perspective has made significant contributions to planning scholarship, in its analytical formation two related shortcomings persist. First, although not explicit, the assumption is that multiracial, multicultural dynamics are principally the concerns of large cities and their suburbs. Second (and consequently), it is taken for granted that the planning profession is omnipresent. All urban objects of the planning theories are assumed to enjoy pre-existing planning processes and structures within which progressive planning professionals can apply inclusive methods. These are troubling assumptions for both planning scholarship and pedagogy, considering the recent demographic reality that shows the growth of immigrant populations in small communities across the country. Many of these small towns are not detected in the urban radar of these theories.

23. In respect to the materiality of globalization, Gille (2013) encourages us to start "understanding materiality as not just something that resides in and is limited to a particular place, but also as something that transcends the boundaries of the local. We used to think that in order to understand the role the nonhuman world plays in the human world we had to stay in one place and study the local manifestations of materiality." In contrast, she suggests the need "to understand materiality as simultaneously local, translocal, and transnational" (162–63).

CONCLUSION

1. See Brenner (2009) and Glick Schiller and Caglar (2011).

2. For example, see Peirce, Johnson, and Peters (2008).

3. See Lefebvre (2003), Merrifield (2013), and contributors to Brenner (2014).

4. Lefebvre (2003) writes, "in the complete urbanization of society we should stop using the term city" and adopt instead the terminology "urban society." Urban society "constitutes itself on the ruins of the city.... The city exists only as a historical entity, ... [it] no longer corresponds to a social object. Sociologically, the city is a pseudo-concept."

5. Elsewhere (2006 and 2009) I have discussed these ideas at length.

REFERENCES

Achebe, Chinua. 1986 [1967, c1964]. *Arrow of God*. New York, John Day.

Aguayo, Beatriz Eugenia Cid. 2008. "'Localities': Global Villages and Rural Cosmopolitanism: Exploring Global Ruralities." *Globalizations* 5 (4): 541–54.

Ahmed, Sara. 2004. "Affective Economies." *Social Text* 22 (2): 121–39.

Akins, Shelly. 2008. "West Africans Meet to Discuss Immigrant Issues." *Rushville Times*, April 30.

Akyeampong, Emmanuel. 2000. "Africans in the Diaspora: The Diaspora and Africa," *African Affairs* 99: 183–215

Akyemang-Konadu, Kwado, and Baffour K. Takyi. 2001. "African Immigrants in the U.S.A.: Some Reflections on Their Pre- and Post-Migration Experiences." *Arab World Geographer* 4 (1): 31–47.

Alarcón, Rafael. 1995. "Transnational Communities, Regional Development, and the Future of Mexican Immigration." *Berkeley Planning Journal* 10: 36–54.

Alexander, Peter, and Anita Chan. 2004. "Does China Have an Apartheid Pass System?" *Journal of Ethnic and Migration Studies* 30 (4): 609–29.

Allegretto, Sylvia, Marc Doussard, Dave Graham-Squire, Ken Jacobs, Dan Thompson, and Jeremy Thompson. 2013. *Fast Food, Poverty Wages: The Public Cost of Low-Wage Jobs in the Fast-Food Industry*. Berkeley, CA: Center for Labor Research and Education, University of California.

Allegro, Linda, and Andrew Grant Wood. 2013. "Introduction: Heartland North, Heartland South." In *Latin American Migrations to the Heartland: Changing Social Landscapes in Middle America*, edited by Linda Allegro and Andrew Grant Wood, 1–24. Chicago: University of Illinois Press.

American Communities Project. 2001. *Sortable List of Dissimilarity Scores*. Presented jointly by the Initiative in Spatial Structures in the Social Sciences, Brown University, and the Lewis Mumford Center, University at Albany. http://www.s4.brown.edu/cen2000 /WholePop/WPsort.html (accessed June 2012).

Amin, Ash. 2004. "Regions Unbound: Towards a New Politics of Place." *Geografiska Annaler. Series B, Human Geography* 86 (1), Special Issue: *The Political Challenge of Relational Space*, 33–44.

Anderson, Ben. 2014. *Encountering Affect: Capacities, Apparatuses, Conditions*. Burlington, VT: Ashgate.

Appadurai, Arjun. 2001. "Deep Democracy: Urban Governability and the Horizon of Politics." *Environment and Urbanization* 13 (2): 23–43.

Arat-Koc, Sedef. 2006. "Whose Social Reproduction? Transnational Motherhood and Challenges to Feminist Political Economy." In *Social Reproduction: Feminist Political Economy Challenges Neo-Liberalism,* edited by Meg Luxton and Kate Bezanson, 75–92. McGill, Canada: Queens University Press.

Arthur, John A. 2000. *Invisible Sojourners: African Immigrant Diaspora in the United States.* Westport, CT: Praeger.

———. 2008. *The African Diaspora in the United States and Europe.* Burlington, VT: Ashgate.

———. 2010. *African Diaspora Identities: Negotiating Culture in Transnational Migration.* Plymouth, UK: Lexington Books.

Arthur, John A., and Joseph Takougang. 2012. "Africans in Global Migration: Still Searching for Promised Lands." In *Africans in Global Migration: Searching for Promised Lands,* edited by John A. Arthur, Joseph Takougang, and Thomas Owusu, 307–14. Plymouth, UK: Lexington Books.

Associated Press. 1999. "Out of Court Settlement in Lawsuit by Disabled Former Workers." *Associated Press State and Local Wire,* Nov 24.

Bacon, David. 2008a. *Illegal People: How Globalization Creates Migration and Criminalizes Immigrants.* Boston: Beacon Press.

———. 2008b. "Displaced Peoples: NAFTA's Most Important Product." North American Congress on Latin America (NACLA), September 3. http://nacla.org/news/displaced -people-nafta%E2%80%99s-most-important-product (accessed October 2014).

Bailey, Benjamín. 2001. "Dominican American Ethnic/Racial Identities and United States Social Categories." *International Migration Review* 35: 677–708.

Bailey, Rayna. 2008. *Immigration and Migration.* New York: Infobase Publishing.

Bakker, Isabella. 2003. "Neo-Liberal Governance and the Reprivatization of Social Reproduction: Social Provisioning and Shifting Gender Orders." In *Power, Production and Social Reproduction,* edited by Isabella Bakker and Stephen Gill, 66–82. London: Macmillan-Palgrave.

Bakker, Isabella, and Stephen Gill. 2003. "Global Political Economy and Social Reproduction." In *Power, Production and Social Reproduction,* edited by Isabel Bakker and Stephen Gill, 3–16. London: Macmillan-Palgrave.

Banjo, Adewale. 2008. "The Politics of Succession Crisis in West Africa: The Case of Togo." *International Journal on World Peace* 25 (2): 33–55.

Barker, Dale. 1986. "Living on 'Borrowed Time.'" *Illinoian StarDaily.* October 3.

Barnes, Teresa. 1999. *We Women Worked So Hard: Gender, Urbanization and Social Reproduction in Colonial Harare, Zimbabwe, 1930–1956.* Portsmouth, NH: Heinemann.

Barrett, James. 2002. *Work and Community in the Jungle.* Chicago: University of Illinois Press.

Bayat, Asef. 2010. *The Art of Presence.* Palo Alto, CA: Stanford University Press.

Bean, Frank F., Rodolfo Corona, Rodolfo Tuiran, and Karen Woodrow-Lafield. 2001. "Circular, Invisible, and Ambiguous Migrants: Components of Difference in Estimates of the Number of Unauthorized Mexican Migrants in the United States." *Demography* 38 (3): 411–22.

Beard, Bill. 2007. "Cargill Sponsors Leadership Conference." *Cass County Star Gazette,* Beardstown, IL, April 5, page 1.

Beard, Victoria, and Carolina Sarmiento. 2010. "Ties that Bind: Transnational Community-Based Planning in Southern California and Oaxaca." *International Development Planning Review* 32 (3): 207–24.

Beardstown Gazette. 1979. *Beardstown Yesterday and Today: 1829 to 1979.* Beardstown, IL.

Beardstown (IL) *Illinoian-Star Newspaper.* 1946. "Wels Lamont Comes Through." January 14, page 2.

Beardstown (IL) *Illinoian Star Daily.* 1985. "For New Business and Industry, Mayor Says, 'I'd Negotiate with the Devil.'" May 14, page 1.

Beardstown (IL) *Illinoian Star Daily.* 1986a. "Keep Cool and Align." October 1.

Beardstown (IL) *Illinoian Star Daily.* 1986b. "Mayor Walters: 'Go Forward and Not Stop.'" October 4, page 1.

Beardstown (IL) *Illinoian Star Daily.* 1986c. "OM Offers Contract Extensions to Local 431." October 17, page 1.

Beardstown Ladies. 1994. *The Beardstown Ladies' Common-Sense Investment Guide.* New York: Hyperion.

Benería, Lourdes. 2008. "The Crisis of Care, International Migration, and Public Policy." *Feminist Economics* 14 (3): 1–21.

Benería, Lourdes, and Shelly Feldman, eds. 1992. *Unequal Burden: Economic Crises, Persistent Poverty and Women's Work.* Boulder, CO: Westview Press.

Binford, Leigh. 2009. "From Fields of Power to Fields of Sweat: The Dual Process of Constructing Temporary Migrant Labour in Mexico and Canada." *Third World Quarterly* 30 (3): 503–17.

Blocker, Jack S. 2008. *A Little More Freedom: African Americans Enter the Urban Midwest, 1860–1930.* Columbus: Ohio State University Press.

Bloom, Stephen. 2000. *Postville: A Clash of Cultures in Heartland America.* New York: Harvest Books Harcourt.

Bluestone, Barry, and Bennett Harrison. 1982. *The Deindustrialization of America: Plant Closings, Community Abandonment, and the Dismantling of Basic Industry.* New York: Basic Books.

Blyden, Nemata. 2012. "Relationships among Blacks in the Diaspora: African and Caribbean Immigrants and American-Born Blacks." In *Africans in Global Migration: Searching for Promised Lands,* edited by John A. Arthur, Joseph Takougang, and Thomas Owusu, 161–74. Plymouth, UK: Lexington Books.

Bolina-Silva, Eduardo. 2009 [2003, 2006]. *Racism without Racists: Color-Blind Racism and the Persistence of Racial Inequality in America.* New York: Rowman & Littlefield Publishers.

Bonacich, Edna. 1972. "A Theory of Ethnic Antagonism: The Split Labor Market." *American Sociological Review* 37 (5): 547–59.

Borchert, James. 2004. "Deindustrialization." In *Encyclopedia of Homelessness,* edited by David Levinson, 106–11. Thousand Oaks, CA: SAGE Publications.

Borje, Eva Akerman. 2013. "Unlocking the Potential of Migration for Inclusive Development." *Migration Policy Practice* 3 (1): 3–5. Geneva: International Organization for Migration (IOM).

Brenner, Neil. 2009. "Restructuring, Rescaling, and the Urban Question." *Critical Planning* 16: 60–79.

———. 2011. "The Urban Question and the Scale Question: Some Conceptual Clarifications." In *Locating Migration: Rescaling Cities and Migrants,* edited by Nina Glick Schiller and Ayse Caglar, 23–41. Ithaca, NY: Cornell University Press.

———. 2013. "Theses on Urbanization." *Public Culture* 25 (1): 85–114.

Brenner, Neil (ed.). 2014. *Implosions/Explosions: Towards a Study of Planetary Urbanization.* Berlin: JOVIS.

Broadway, Michael. 1995. "From City to Countryside: Recent Changes in the Structure and Location of the Meat- and Fish-Processing Industries." In *Any Way You Cut It: Meat*

Processing and Small-Town America, edited by Donald Stull, Michael Broadway, and David Griffith, 17–40. Lawrence: University Press of Kansas.

Brown, Lawrence A., Tamar E. Mott, and Edward J. Malecki. 2007. "Immigrant Profiles of U.S. Urban Areas and Agents of Resettlement." *Professional Geographer* 59 (1): 56–73.

Brunori, David. 1997. "Principles of Tax Policy and Targeted Tax Incentives." *State & Local Government Review* 29 (1): 50–61.

Burawoy, Michael. 2001. "Manufacturing the Global." *Ethnography* 2: 147–59.

Burawoy, Michael, Joseph A. Blum, Sheba George, Zsuzsa Gille, and Millie Thayer. 2000. *Global Ethnography: Forces, Connections and Imaginations in a Postmodern World.* Berkeley: University of California Press.

Burayidi, Michael (ed). 2015. *Cities and the Politics of Difference: Multiculturalism and Diversity in Urban Planning,* Toronto: University of Toronto Press.

Bustamante, Jorge A. 1992. "Migración indocumentada México-Estados Unidos: Tendencias recientes de un mercado internacional de mano de obra." In *Coloquio de antropología e historia regional,* edited by Cecilia Noriega Elío, 587–614. Zamora, Mexico: Colegio de Michoacán.

Butler, Judith, and Anthena Athanasiou. 2013. *Dispossession: The Performative in the Political.* Malden, MA: Polity Press.

Bybee, Roger, and Carolyn Winter. 2006. "Immigration Flood Unleashed by NAFTA's Disastrous Impact on Mexican Economy." CommonDreams.org, April 25. http://www .commondreams.org/views06/0425-30.htm (accessed October 2014).

Caglar, Ayse, and Nina Glick Schiller. 2011. "Introduction: Migrants and Cities." In *Locating Migration: Rescaling Cities and Migrants,* edited by Nina Glick Schiller and Ayse Caglar, 1–22. Ithaca, NY: Cornell University Press.

Capps, Randy, Kristen McCabe, and Michael Fix. 2012. *Diverse Streams: Black African Migration to the United States.* Washington, DC: Immigration Policy Institute.

Cargill Incorporated. 2013a. *Cargill 2014 Fact Sheet.* Minneapolis: Cargill. http://www.cargill .com/wcm/groups/public/@ccom/documents/document/na3054921.pdf(accessed May 2015).

———. 2013b. *Corporate Responsibility Report.* Minneapolis: Cargill.

Carter, Scott. 2013. "Latin American Migrations to the US Heartland: Demographic and Economic Activity in Six Heartland States, 2000–2007." In *Latin American Migrations to the Heartland: Changing Social Landscapes in Middle America,* edited by Linda Allegro and Andrew Grant Wood, 271–306. Chicago: University of Illinois Press.

Castells, Manuel. 1983. *The City and the Grassroots.* Berkeley: University of California Press.

———. 1998. *The Informational City: Information Technology, Economic Restructuring, and the Urban Regional Process.* Oxford, UK: Basil Blackwell.

———. 2005. "Space of Flows, Space of Places: Materials for a Theory of Urbanism in the Information Age." In *Comparative Planning Culture,* edited by B. Sanval, 45–65. New York: Routledge.

Castles, Stephen. 2014. "International Migration at a Crossroads." *Citizenship Studies* 18 (2): 190–207.

Chafets, Ze'ev. 1990a. "The Tragedy of Detroit." *New York Times Magazine,* July 29, p. 23.

———. 1990b. *Devil's Night: And Other True Tales of Detroit.* New York: Random House.

Chant, Silvia. 2010. "Gendered Poverty across Space and Time: Introduction and Overview." In *The International Handbook on Gender and Poverty: Concepts, Research and Policy,* edited by Sylvia Chant, 1–28. Northampton, MA: Edward Elgar.

Charles, Camille Zubrinsky. 2001. "Socio Economic Status and Segregation: African American, Hispanics and Asians in Los Angeles." In *Problem of the Century: Racial Stratification in the United States*, edited by Elijah Anderson and Douglass Massey, 271–89. New York: Russell Sage Foundation.

Cohen, Deborah. 2011. *Braceros: Migrant Citizens and Transnational Subjects in the Postwar United States and Mexico*. Chapel Hill: University of North Carolina Press.

Cohen, J., R. Jones, and D. Conway. 2005. "Why Remittances Shouldn't Be Blamed for Rural Underdevelopment in Mexico: A Collective Response to Leigh Binford." *Critique of Anthropology* 25 (1): 87–96.

Colen, Shellee. 1986. " 'With Respect and Feelings': Voices of West Indian Child Care and Domestic Workers in New York City." In *All American Women: Lines that Divide, Ties that Bind*, edited by Johnetta B. Cole, 46–70. New York: Free Press.

Cornelius, Wayne A. 1989. "Mexican Migration to the United States: Introduction." In *Mexican Migration to the United States: Origins, Consequences, and Policy Options*, edited by Wayne A. Cornelius and Jorge Bustamante, 1–21. La Jolla: Center for U.S.-Mexican Studies, University of California, San Diego.

Cottle, Trevor, Rochelle Galvez, Connie Starkey, and Edwin Úbeda. 2007. "Seeds of Change in a Small Town: Cultivating Second Language Acquisition." La Cosecha, Dual Language Conference. Albuquerque, NM, November 17.

Crowley, Martha, and Daniel T. Lichter. 2009. "Social Disorganization in New Latino Destinations." *Rural Sociology* 74: 573–604.

Dannecker, Petra. 2013. "Rationalities and Images Underlying Labour Migration from Bangladesh to Malaysia." *International Migration* 51 (1): 40–60.

Davis, Mike. 2001. *Magical Urbanism: Latinos Reinvent the U.S. Big City*. New York: Verso.

Dear, Michael, and Allen Scott. 1981. "Towards a Framework for Analysis." In *Urbanization and Urban Planning in Capitalist Society*, edited by Michael Dear and Allen Scott, 3–18. New York: Methuen.

Decalo, Samuel. 1976. "The Benevolent General: Military Rule in Togo." In *Coups and Army Rule in Africa: Studies in Military Style*, New Haven, CT: Yale University Press.

De Genova, Nicholas. 2002. "Migrant 'Illegality' and Deportability in Everyday Life." *Annual Review of Anthropology* 31: 419–47.

———. 2005. *Working the Boundaries: Race, Space, and "Illegality" in Mexican Chicago*. Durham, NC: Duke University Press.

De Genova, Nicholas, and Ana Y. Ramos-Zayas. 2003. *Latino Crossings*. New York: Routledge.

de Haas, Hein. 2010. "Migration and Development: A Theoretical Perspective." *International Migration Review* 44 (1): 227–64.

de Janvry, Alain. 1975. "The Political Economy of Rural Development in Latin America: An Interpretation." *American Journal of Agricultural Economics* 57 (3): 490–99.

Delany-Barmann, Gloria, and Carla Paciotto. 2009. "Educational Reform in a Midwestern Elementary School: A Teacher Movement for Interethnic Integration." Immigration and Race Symposium, Center for Democracy in a Multicultural Society, Urbana, University of Illinois.

Denton, Nancy A., and Douglas S. Massey. 1989. "Racial Identity among Caribbean Hispanics: The Effect of Double Minority Status on Residential Segregation." *American Sociological Review* 54: 790–808.

Diaz, David R., and Rodolfo D. Torres, eds. 2012. *Latino Urbanism: The Politics of Planning, Policy and Redevelopment*. New York: New York University Press

Dixon, David. 2006. "Characteristics of the African Born in the United States." Migration Information Migration Policy Institute, January. http://www.migrationinformation.org /USfocus/display.cfm?ID=366 (accessed December 2014).

Domosh, Mona. 2014. "Commentary on 'The Lives of Others': Body Work, the Production of Difference, and Labor Geographies." *Economic Geography* 91(1): 25–28.

Donato, Katharine M., Michael Aguilera, and Chizuko Wakabayashi. 2005. "Immigration Policy and Employment Conditions of US Immigrants from Mexico, Nicaragua, and the Dominican Republic." *International Migration* 43 (5): 5–29.

Donato, Katharine M., Charles M. Tolbert II, Afred Nucci, and Yukio Kawano. 2007. "Recent Immigrant Settlement in the Nonmetropolitan United States: Evidence from Internal Census Data." *Rural Sociology* 72: 537–59.

Doussard, Marc, Jamie Peck, and Nick Theodore. 2009. "After Deindustrialization: Uneven Growth and Economic Inequality in 'Postindustrial' Chicago." *Economic Geography* 85 (2): 183–207.

Driscoll, Barbara. 1999. *The Tracks North: Program of World War II.* Austin: CMAS Books.

Dube, Arindrajit, and Ken Jacobs. 2004. "Hidden Cost of Wal-Mart Jobs: Use of Safety Net Programs by Wal-Mart Workers in California." Briefing paper series, University of California, Berkeley, Labor Center, August.

Dunn, Timothy, Ana Maria Argones, and George Shivers. 2005. "Recent Mexican Migration in the Rural Delmarva Peninsula: Human Rights versus Citizenship Rights in a Local Context." In *New Destinations: Mexican Immigration in the United States,* edited by Victor Zúñiga and Ruben Hernández-León, 155–86. New York: Russell Sage Foundation.

Durand, Jorge, William Kandel, Emilio A. Parrado, and Douglas S. Massey. 1996. "International Migration and Development in Mexican Communities." *Demography* 33 (2): 249–64.

Durand, Jorge, Douglas Massey, and Chiara Capoferro. 2005. "The New Geography of Mexican Immigration." In *New Destinations: Mexican Immigration in the United States,* edited by Victor Zúñiga and Rubén Hernández-León, 1–20. New York: Russell Sage Foundation.

Durand, Jorge, Douglass Massey, and Fernando Charvet. 2000. "The Changing Geography of Mexican Migration to the United States, 1910–1996." *Social Science Quarterly* 8: 1–15.

Durand, Jorge, Douglas S. Massey, and René M. Zenteno. 2001. "Mexican Immigration to the United States: Continuities and Changes." *Latin American Research Review* 36 (1): 107–27.

Edwards, Richard 1973. "The Labor Process." In *Labor Market Segmentation,* edited by Michael Edwards, Richard Reich, and David M. Gordon. Lexington, MA: DC Heath.

Ehrenreich, Barbara. 2001. *Nickeled and Dimed: On (Not) Getting By in America.* New York: Metropolitan Books.

Ehrenreich, Barbara, and Arlie Hochschild. 2003. "Introduction." In *Global Woman: Nannies, Maids, and Sex Workers,* edited by Barbara Ehrenreich and Arlie Hochschild, 1–15. New York: Henry Holt.

Ellingwood, Ken. 2008. "Migrants Send Less Money Back to Mexico." *Los Angeles Times,* April 20. http://www.latimes.com/world/la-fg-migrant20apr20-story.html#page=1 (accessed October 2014).

Engels, Friedrich. 2010 [1884]. *The Origin of the Family, Private Property and the State.* London: Penguin Classics.

Erickson, Ken. 1990. "New Immigrants and the Social Service Agency: Changing Relations at SRS." *Urban Anthropology* 19 (4): 321–44.

Fainstein, Norman I., and Susan S. Fainstein. 1986. *Restructuring the City: The Political Economy of Urban Redevelopment.* London: Longman Group United Kingdom.

Farley, John E. 2005 [1982]. *Majority-Minority Relations,* 6th ed. Upper Saddle River, NJ: Prentice Hall.

Feagin, Joe. 2002. "White Supremacy and Mexican Americans: Rethinking the 'Black-White Paradigm.'" *Rutgers Law Review* 54: 959–84.

Fennelly, Katherine. 2005. "Latinos, Africans, and Asians in the North Star State: Immigrant Communities in Minnesota." In *Beyond the Gateway: Immigrants in a Changing America,* edited by Elzbieta M. Gozdziak, Susan F. Martin, Raleigh Bailey, and Micah N. Bump, 111–35. New York: Lexington Books.

———. 2008. "Prejudice Towards Immigrants in the Midwest." In *New Faces in New Places: The Changing Geography of American Immigration,* edited by Douglas Massey, 151–78. New York: Russell Sage Foundation.

Fennelly, Katherine, and Helga Leitner. 2003. "How the Food Processing Industry Is Diversifying Rural Minnesota." JSRI Working Paper. Lansing: Michigan State University.

Ferguson, James. 2006. *Global Shadows: Africa in the Neoliberal World Order.* Durham, NC: Duke University Press.

Fernandes, Deepa. 2007. *Targeted: Homeland Security and the Business of Immigration.* New York: Seven Stories.

Fernandez-Kelly, Maria Patricia. 1984. *For We Were Sold, I and My People: Women and Industry in Mexico's Frontier.* New York: State University of New York Press.

Fernandez-Kelly, Maria Patricia, and Douglas Massey. 2007. "Borders for Whom? The Role of NAFTA in Mexico-US Migration." *Annals of the American Academy of Political and Social Science* 610 (1): 98–118.

Fink, Deborah. 1998. *Cutting into the Meatpacking Line: Workers and Change in the Rural Midwest.* Chapel Hill: University of North Carolina Press.

Fitzgerald, Karen. 2006. "Welcome to America: African Immigrants at Cargill Are the Latest to See the Underside of the American Dream." *Illinois Times* (Springfield), June 29. http://illinoistimes.com/mobile/articles/articleView/id:3191 (accessed December 2014).

Flynn, James R. 1993. "The Railroad Shopmen's Strike of 1922 on the Industry, Company, and Community Levels." Ph.D. dissertation, Northern Illinois University.

Fraser, Nancy 2013. "How Feminism Became Capitalism's Handmaiden and How to Reclaim It." *Guardian,* Oct. 13. http://www.theguardian.com/commentisfree/2013/oct/14/feminism-capitalist-handmaiden-neoliberal?CMP=twt_gu (accessed December 2014).

Freeman, Richard. 2004. "Death of Detroit: Harbinger of Collapse of Deindustrialized America." *Executive Intelligence Review* 31 (16): 21–35.

Frey, William H. 2006. *Diversity Spreads Out: Metropolitan Shifts in the Hispanic, Asian, and Black Populations since 2000.* Washington, DC: Brookings Institute.

Friedmann, John. 1992. Empowerment: The Politics of Alternative Development. Oxford, UK: Wiley-Blackwell.

———. 2002. *The Prospect of Cities.* Minneapolis: University of Minnesota Press.

———. 2010. "Place and place-making in cities: A global perspective." *Planning Theory and Practice* 11(2): 149–65.

Friedmann, John, and G. Wolff. 1982. "World City Formation: An Agenda for Research and Action." *International Journal of Urban and Regional Research* 6 (3): 309–44.

Fudge, Judy. 2010. "Global Care Chains: Transnational Migrant Care Workers." International Association of Law Schools Conference on Labour Law and Labour Market in the New World Economy, Milan, May 20–22.

Gans, Herbert J. 1999. "The Possibility of a New Racial Hierarchy in the Twenty-First-Century United States." In *The Cultural Territories of Race: Black and White Boundaries,* Michéle Lamont, editor, 371–90. Chicago: University of Chicago Press.

García, Juan R. 1996. *Mexicans in the Midwest, 1900–1932.* Tucson: University of Arizona Press.

Geiger, Martin, and Antoine Pécoud. 2013. "Migration, Development and the 'Migration and Development Nexus.'" *Population, Space and Place* 19 (4): 369–74.

Gerstle, Gary. 2001. *American Crucible: Race and Nation in the Twentieth Century.* Princeton, NJ: Princeton University Press.

Gille, Zsuzsa. 2001. "Critical Ethnography in the Time of Globalization: Toward a New Concept of Site." *Cultural Studies—Critical Methodologies* 1 (3): 319–34.

———. 2012. "Global Ethnography 2.0: Materializing the Transnational." In *Beyond Methodological Nationalism: Research Methodologies for Cross-Border Studies,* edited by Anna Amelina, Devrimsel D. Nergiz, Thomas Faist, and Nina Glick Schiller, 93–110. London: Routledge.

———. 2014. "Materiality: Transnational Materiality." In *Framing the Global: Entry Points for Research,* edited by Hillary Kahn, 157–81. Bloomington: Indiana University Press.

Glick Schiller, Nina. 2012. "Transnationality and the City." In *The Transnationalism and Urbanism,* edited by Stefan Kratke, Kathrin Wildner, and Stephan Lanz, 31–45. London: Routledge.

Glick Schiller, Nina, and Ayse Caglar, eds. 2011a. *Locating Migration: Rescaling Cities and Migrants.* Ithaca, NY: Cornell University Press.

———. 2011b. "Locality and Globality: Building a Comparative Analytical Framework in Migration and Urban Studies." In *Locating Migration: Rescaling Cities and Migrants,* edited by Nina Glick Schiller and Ayse Caglar, 60–84. Ithaca, NY: Cornell University Press.

———. 2011c. "Downscaled Cities and Migrant Pathways: Locality and Agency without an Ethnic Lens." In *Locating Migration: Rescaling Cities and Migrants,* edited by Nina Glick Schiller and Ayse Caglar, 190–212. Ithaca, NY: Cornell University Press.

Goldman, Michael. 2011. "Speculating on the Next World City." In *Worlding Cities: Asian Experiments and the Art of Being Global,* edited by Ananya Roy and Aiwa Ong, 229–58. Oxford, UK: Wiley-Blackwell.

Gómez-Peña, Guillermo. 2001. "The New Global Culture Somewhere between Corporate Multiculturalism and the Mainstream Bizarre (a Border Perspective)." *TDR: The Drama Review* 45 (1): 7–30.

Gordon, David M., Richard Edwards, and Michael Reich. 1996. *Segmented Work, Divided Workers: The Historical Transformation of Labor in the United States.* Cambridge, UK: Cambridge University Press.

Gordon, Lewis R. 2007. "Thinking through Identities: Black Peoples, Race Labels, and Ethnic Consciousness." In *The Other African Americans: Contemporary African and Caribbean Families in the United States,* edited by Yoku Shaw-Taylor and Steven A. Tuch, 69–92. New York: Rowman and Littlefield.

Gouveia, Lourdes, and Donald Stull. 1995 "Dances with Cows: Beef Packing's Impact on Garden City, Kansas, and Lexington, Nebraska." In *Any Way You Cut It: Meat Processing and Small-Town America,* edited by Donald Stull, Michael Broadway, and David Griffith, 85–107. Lawrence: University Press of Kansas.

Government Accounting Office. 2005. "Workplace Safety and Health: Safety in the Meat and Poultry Industry, while Improving, Could Be Further Strengthened." Washington, DC: United States General Accounting Office.

Gozdziak, Elzbieta M. 2005. "New Immigrant Communities and Integration." In *Beyond the Gateway: Immigrants in a Changing America,* edited by Elzbieta M. Gozdziak, Susan F. Martin, Raleigh Bailey, and Micah N. Bump, 3–18. New York: Lexington Books.

Gozdziak, Elzbieta M., and Susan F. Martin, eds. 2005. *Beyond the Gateway: Immigrants in a Changing America.* Lanham, MD: Lexington Books.

Graham, S., and S. Marvin. 2001. *Splintering Urbanism: Networked Infrastructures, Technological Mobilities and the Urban Condition.* London: Routledge.

———. 2009. *Postville, USA: Surviving Diversity in Small-Town America.* Boston: GemmaMedia.

Grey, Mark. 1995. "Pork, Poultry, and Newcomers in Storm Lake, Iowa." In *Any Way You Cut It: Meat Processing and Small-Town America,* edited by Donald Stull, Michael Broadway, and David Griffith, 109–28. Lawrence: University Press of Kansas.

Grey, Mark, and Anne Woodrick. 2005. "Latinos Have Revitalized Our Community: Mexican Migration and Anglo Responses in Marshalltown, Iowa." In *New Destinations: Mexican Immigration in the United States,* edited by Victor Zúñiga and Rubén Hernández-León, 133–54. New York: Russell Sage Foundation.

Grieco, Elizabeth. 2004. "The African Born in the United States." Migration Information Migration Policy Institute, September 1. http://www.migrationinformation.org/USFocus /display.cfm?ID=250 (accessed December 2014).

Griffis, Ryan, and Sarah Ross. 2012. "Bottomlands and World: An Abbreviated Glossary of Experiences in and Around Beardstown, IL," in *Deep Routes: The Midwest in all Directions,* edited by Rozalinda Borcila, Bonnie Fortune, and Sarah Ross, 80–92. Iowa City, IA: White Wire.

———. 2014. "Between the Bottomland & the World." http://regionalrelationships.org /bottomlands/glossaryTOC.html (accessed December 2014).

Griffith, David. 1995. "New Immigrants in an Old Industry: Blue Crab Processing in Palmico County, North Carolina." In *Any Way You Cut It: Meat Processing and Small-Town America,* edited by Donald Stull, Michael Broadway, and David Griffith, 153–86. Lawrence: University Press of Kansas.

———. 2005. "Rural Industry and Mexican Immigration and Settlement in North Carolina." In *New Destinations: Mexican Immigration in the United States,* edited by Victor Zúñiga and Ruben Hernández-León, 50–75. New York: Russell Sage Foundation.

———. 2008. "New Midwesterners, New Southerners: Immigration Experiences in Four Rural American Settings." In *New Faces in New Places: the Changing Geography of American Immigration,* edited by Douglas Massey, 179–210. New York: Russell Sage Foundation.

Griffith, David, Michael Broadway, and Donald Stull. 1995. "Introduction: Making Meat." In *Any Way You Cut It: Meat Processing and Small-Town America,* edited by Donald Stull, Michael Broadway, and David Griffith, 1–15. Lawrence: University Press of Kansas.

Guarnizo, Luis, and Michael Peter Smith. 1998. "The Locations of Transnationalism." In *Transnationalism from Below,* edited by Michael Peter Smith and Luis Guarnizo, 3–34. New Brunswick, NJ: Transaction Publishers.

Gwaradzimba, Ellen, and Almon Shumba 2010. "The Nature, Extent and Impact of the Brain Drain in Zimbabwe and South Africa." *Acta Academica* 42 (1): 209–41.

Gyory, Andrew. 1998. *Closing the Gate: Race, Politics, and the Chinese Exclusion Act.* Chapel Hill: University of North Carolina Press.

Hackenberg, Robert, and Gary Kokulka. 1995. "Industries, Immigrants, and Illness in the New Midwest." In *Any Way You Cut It: Meat Processing and Small-Town America,* edited by

Donald Stull, Michael Broadway, and David Griffith, 187–211. Lawrence: University Press of Kansas.

Hansen, Karen Tranberg. 1989. *Distant Companions: Servants and Employers in Zambia, 1900–1985.* Ithaca, NY: Cornell University Press.

Harris, Collin. 2010. "NAFTA and the Political Economy of Mexican Immigration." ZNet, June 8. http://zcomm.org/znetarticle/nafta-and-the-political-economy-of-mexican-immigration-by-collin-harris/ (accessed December 2014).

Harrison, Bennett, and Barry Bluestone. 1990. *The Great U-Turn: Corporate Restructuring and the Polarizing of America.* New York: Basic Books.

Harrison, Bennett, and Sandra Kanter. 1978. "The Political Economy of States' Job-Creation Business Incentives." *Journal of the American Institute of Planners* 44 (4): 424–35.

Hart, Gillian. 2006. "Denaturalizing Dispossession: Critical Ethnography in the Age of Resurgent Imperialism." *Antipode* 38 (5): 977–1004.

Harvey, David. 1984. *Uneven Development: Nature, Capital, and the Production of Space.* Athens: University of Georgia Press.

———. 1985. *The Urbanisation of Capital.* Oxford, UK: Blackwell.

———. 2005. *New Imperialism.* Oxford, UK: Oxford University Press.

———. 2006. *Spaces of Global Capitalism: A Theory of Uneven Geographical Development.* New York: Verso.

———. 2009. *Social Justice and the City (Geographies of Justice and Social Transformation).* Athens: University of Georgia Press.

Harwood, Stacy. 2005. "Struggling to Embrace Difference in Land-Use Decision Making in Multicultural Communities." *Planning Practice and Research* 20 (4): 355–71.

Harwood, Stacy Anne, and Dowell Myers. 2002. "The Dynamics of Immigration and Local Governance in Santa Ana: Neighborhood Activism, Overcrowding and Land-Use Policy." *Policy Studies Journal* 30 (1): 70–91.

Hebron, Anthony. 1986. "Oscar Mayer to Close Beardstown Plant." *State Journal-Register* (Springfield, IL), October 3, page 15.

———. 1987a. "Excel Agrees to Buy Oscar Mayer Plant." *State Journal-Register* (Springfield, IL), January 29, page 1.

———. 1987b. "Hog-Slaughtering Plant Reopens in Beardstown." *State Journal-Register* (Springfield, IL), June 28, page 47.

Heilbrunn, John R. 1997. "Commerce, Politics, and Business Associations in Benin and Togo." *Comparative Politics* 29 (4): 473–92.

Hernández-León, R., and V. Zúñiga. 2003. "Mexican Immigrant Communities in the South and Social Capital: The Case of Dalton, Georgia." *Southern Rural Sociology* 19 (1): 20–45.

Hiheta, Ed Yao. 2005. "The Ewe Diaspora." In *A Handbook of Eweland: The Ewe of Togo and Benin,* edited by Benjamin N. Lawrance, 337–51. Accra, Ghana: Woeli Publishing Services.

Hjort, Mette. 2005. "Between Conflict and Consensus: Multiculturalism and the Liberal Arts." In *Concepts of Culture: Art, Politics, and Society,* edited by Adam Muller. Alberta: University of Calgary Press. http://www.uqtr.uquebec.ca/AE/vol_4/mette2.htm (accessed December 2014).

Hochschild, Arlie Russell. 2000. "Global Care Chains and Emotional Surplus Value." In *On the Edge: Living with Global Capitalism,* edited by William Hutton and Anthony Giddens, 130–46. London: Jonathon Cape.

————. 2003. *The Commercialization of Intimate Life: Notes from Home and Work*. San Francisco: University of California Press.

————. 2012. *The Outsourced Self: Intimate Life in Market Times*. New York: Metropolitan Press.

Holmes, Seth. 2013. *Fresh Fruit, Broken Bodies: Migrant Farmworkers in the United States*. Berkeley: University of California Press.

Hondagneu-Sotelo, Pierrette. 2001. *Domestica: Immigrant Workers Cleaning and Caring in the Shadow of Affluence*. Berkeley: University of California Press.

Hondagneu-Sotelo, Pierrette, and Ernestine Avila. 1997. "'I'm Here, but I'm There': The Meanings of Latina Transnational Motherhood." *Gender and Society* 11: 548–71.

Horowitz, Roger. 1997. *Negro and White, Unite and Fight: A Social History of Industrial Unionism in Meatpacking, 1930–90*. Urbana: University of Illinois Press.

Hou Jeffrey (ed.). 2013. *Transcultural Cities: Border-Crossing and Placemaking*. New York: Routledge.

Hubbard, William. 1975. William Hubbard Interview and Memoir. Interviewed by Reverend Negil McPherson. Oral History, University of Illinois at Springfield; Norris L Brookens Library Archives/Special Collections. 2 tapes, 180 minutes, 67pp.

Hugo, Graeme. 2009. "Best Practice in Temporary Labour Migration for Development: A Perspective from Asia and the Pacific." *International Migration* 47 (5): 23–74.

Human Rights Watch. 2004. *Blood, Sweat, and Fear: Workers' Rights in U.S. Meat and Poultry Plants*. New York: Human Rights Watch.

————. 2007. *Forced Apart: Families Separated and Immigrants Harmed by United States Deportation Policy*. New York: Human Rights Watch.

————. 2008. "Submission to the Committee on the Elimination of Racial Discrimination." *Human Rights Report* 20 (2).

Illinois State Board of Education.2007. Illinois District Report Card 2007. http://webprod .isbe.net/ereportcard/publicsite/getSearchCriteria.aspx (accessed December 2014).

————.2010. Illinois District Report Card 2010: Beardstown CUSD 15. http://webprod.isbe .net/ereportcard/publicsite/getSearchCriteria.aspx (accessed November 2014).

————. 2013. Illinois District Report Card 2013: Beardstown CUSD 15. http://webprod.isbe .net/ereportcard/publicsite/getSearchCriteria.aspx (accessed November 2014).

International Monetary Fund. 2007. "Togo: Staff-Monitored Program." *IMF Country Report*, July 22. Washington, DC: International Monetary Fund.

Instituto Nacional de Geografía y Estadística. 2012. "Población total por entidad federativa. Censo de población y vivienda, 1985–2010." http://www3.inegi.org.mx/sistemas/sisept /Default.aspx?t=mdemo148&s=est&c=29192 (October 2014).

Irazabal, Clara (ed.). 2012. "Beyond 'Latino New Urbanism': Advocating Ethnurbanisms." *Journal of Urbanism: International Research on Placemaking and Urban Sustainability* (special issue on Latino Urbanism: Placemaking in 21st Century American Cities) 5(2–3): 241–68.

————. 2014. *Transbordering Latin Americas: Liminal Places, Cultures, and Power (T)here*. New York: Routledge.

Irazábal, Clara, and R. Farhat. 2008. "Latino Communities in the United States: Place-Making in the Pre-World War II, Post-World War II, and Contemporary City." *Journal of Planning Literature* 22(3):207–28.

Iskandar, Natasha. 2010. *Creative State: Forty Years of Migration and Development Policy in Morocco and Mexico*. Ithaca, NY: Cornell University Press.

Jackson, Michael. 2008. "The Shock of the New: On Migrant Imaginaries and Critical Transitions." *Ethnos: Journal of Anthropology* 73(1): 57–72.

Jones-Correa, Michael. 1998. *Between Two Nations: The Political Predicament of Latinos in New York City*. Ithaca, NY: Cornell University Press.

Kamya, Hugo. 1997. "African Immigrants in the U.S.A.: The Challenges for Research and Practice." *Social Work* 42 (2): 154–65.

Kandel, William, and John Cromartie. 2004. *New Patterns of Hispanic Settlement in Rural America*. Washington, DC: Economic Research Service, USDA, RDRR 99.

Kandel, William, Jamila Henderson, Heather Koball, and Randy Capps. 2011. "Moving Up in Rural America: Economic Attainment of Nonmetro Latino Immigrants." *Rural Sociology* 76: 101–28.

Kandel, William, and Emilio A. Parrado. 2005. "Restructuring of the US Meat Processing Industry and New Hispanic Migrant Destinations." *Population and Development Review* 31 (3): 447–71.

Kane, Dave. 2014. "Diverse Beardstown Soccer Team Pulls Together to Start Season 4-1." *State Journal-Register* (Springfield, IL), Sept 9. http://www.sj-r.com/article/20140909 /Sports/140909473#ixzz3MBIRyCrX (accessed December 2014).

Katz, Cindi. 2001. "Vagabond Capitalism and the Necessity of Social Reproduction." *Antipode* 33: 709–28.

Keil, Roger, and Neil Brenner, eds. 2006. *The Global Cities Reader*. London: Routledge.

Kim, Moody. 1997. *Workers in Lean World: Unions in the International Economy*. London: Verso.

Klooster, Daniel J. 2005. "Producing Social Nature in the Mexican Countryside." *Cultural Geographies* 12 (3): 321–44.

Knaap, Geritt J., and Alison Simon. 1994. "Economic Development in Rural Illinois Communities: A Critical Assessment." *Community Development* 25 (1): 130–49.

Kneen, Brewster. 2002 [1995]. *Invisible Giant*. London: Pluto Press.

Kohnert, Dirk. 2011. "Togo: Thorny Transitions and Misguided Aid at the Roots of Economic Misery." In *Elections and Democratization in West Africa: 1990–2009*, edited by Abdoulaye Saine and Mathurin Houngnikpo, 181–212. Trenton, NJ: Africa World Press.

Kratke, Stefan, Kathrin Wildner, and Stephan Lanz, eds. 2012. *Transnationalism and Urbanism*. London: Routledge.

Krinsky, John, and Reese, Ellen. 2006. "Forging and sustaining labor-community coalitions: the workfare justice movement in three cities." *Sociological Forum* 21(4), 623–58.

Kudva, Neema. 2015. "Small Cities, Big Issues: Indian Cities in Debates on Urban Poverty and Inequality." In *Cities and Inequalities in a Global and Neoliberal World*, edited by F. Miraftab, D. Wilson, and K. Salo, 135–52. London: Routledge.

Kunz, Rahel. 2010. "The Crisis of Social Reproduction in Rural Mexico: Challenging the 'Reprivatization' of Social Reproduction." *Review of International Political Economy* 17:5.

LaFranchi, Howard. 1995. "Mexican State Sends More Workers to US than It Has at Home." *Christian Science Monitor* 87 (241), November 8, page 1.

Lamphere, Louise. 1992. *Structuring Diversity: Ethnographic Perspectives on the New Immigration*. Chicago: University of Chicago Press.

Latapi, Agustin, Philip Martin, Gustavo Lopez Castro, and Katharine Donato. 1998. "Factors that Influence Migration." In *Migration Between Mexico and the United States: A Binational Study*. Washington, DC: U.S. Commission on Immigration Reform. https://www.utexas .edu/lbj/uscir/binpapers/v1-3latapi.pdf (accessed December 2014).

Lay, J. Celeste. 2012. *A Midwestern Mosaic: Immigration and Political Socialization in Rural America*. Philadelphia: Temple University Press.

Lawson, Victoria, and Thomas Klak. 1990. "Conceptual Linkages in the Study of Production and Reproduction in Latin America." *Economic Geography* 66: 310–27.

le Baron, Genevieve, and Adrienne Roberts. 2010. "Toward a Feminist Political Economy of Capitalism and Carcerality." *Signs: Journal of Women in Culture & Society* 36 (1): 19–44.

Lee, Alana, and Andre Astrow. 1987. "Togo: In Search of Friends," *Africa Report* (March–April): 51–53.

Lefebvre, Henry. 2003. *The Urban Revolution.* Minneapolis: University of Minnesota Press.

Leighton, Michelle. 2013. "Labour Migration and Inclusive Development Setting a Course for Success." *UN Chronicle* 50 (3): 18–21.

Leitner, Helga, Eric Sheppard, and Kirstin Sziarto. 2008. "The Spatialities of Contentious Politics." *Royal Geographical Society* 33: 157–72.

Levitt, Peggy. 2001. *The Transnational Villagers.* Berkeley: University of California Press.

Lichter, D. T., and Johnson, K. M. 2009. "Immigrant Gateways and Hispanic Migration to New Destinations." *International Migration Review* 43: 496–518.

Lichter, Daniel T., and Kenneth M. Johnson. 2006. "Emerging Rural Settlement Patterns and the Geographic Redistribution of America's New Immigrants." *Rural Sociology* 71: 109–31.

Lichter, Daniel T., Dominico Parisi, Steven Grice, and Michael Taquino. 2007. "National Estimates of Racial Segregation in Rural and Small-Town America." *Demography* 44 (3): 563–81.

———. 2008. *Hispanic Residential Segregation in New Immigrant Destinations.* New Orleans: Population Association of America.

Licona, Adela C., and Marta Maria Maldonado. 2013. "The Social Production of Latina Visibilities and Invisibilities: Geographies of Power in Small Town America." *Antipode* 46 (2): 517–36.

Light, Ivan. 2006. *Deflecting Immigration: Networks, Markets, and Regulation in Los Angeles.* New York: Russell Sage Foundation.

Loewen, James. 2005. *Sundown Towns: A Hidden Dimension of American Racism.* New York: The New Press.

Longworth, Richard 2008. *Caught in the Middle: America's Heartland in the Age of Globalism.* New York: Bloomsbury.

Luden, Jennifer. 2007. "Meat Processors Look to Puerto Rico for Workers." NPR Morning Edition, December 6. http://www.npr.org/templates/story/story.php?storyId=16962455 (accessed December 2014).

Lung-Amam, Willow. 2013. "That 'Monster House' Is My Home: The Social and Cultural Politics of Design Reviews and Regulations." *Journal of Urban Design* 18 (2): 220–41.

Mahler, Sarah. 1998. "Theoretical and Empirical Contributions towards a Research Agenda for Transnationalism." In *Transnationalism from Below,* edited by Michael Peter Smith and Luis Guarnizo, 64–102. New Brunswick, NJ: Transaction Publishers.

Main, Kelly, and Gerardo Francisco Sandoval. 2015. "Placemaking in a Translocal Receiving Community: The Relevance of Place to Identity and Agency." *Urban Studies* 52 (1): 71–86.

Marcus, George. 1995. "Ethnography in/of the World System: The Emergence of Multi-Sited Ethnography." *Annual Review of Anthropology* 24: 95–117.

Marcuse, P., and R. van Kempen. 2000. "Introduction." In *Globalizing Cities: A New Spatial Order?,* edited by P. Marcuse and R. van Kempen, 1–21. Malden, MA: Blackwell.

Marrow, Helen. 2008. "Hispanic Immigration, Black Population Size, and Intergroup Relations in the Rural and Small-Town South." In *New Faces in New Places: The Changing Geography of American Immigration,* edited by Douglas Massey, 211–48. New York: Russell Sage Foundation.

———. 2009. "New Immigrant Destinations and the American Colour Line." *Ethnic and Racial Studies* 32: 1037–57.

———. 2011. *New Destination Dreaming: Immigration, Race, and Legal Status in the Rural American South*. Palo Alto, CA: Stanford University Press.

Martin, Nina. 2010. "The Crisis of Social Reproduction among Migrant Workers: Interrogating the Role of Migrant Civil Society." *Antipode* 42 (1): 127–51.

———. 2012. "'There Is Abuse Everywhere': Migrant Nonprofit Organizations and the Problem of Precarious Work." *Urban Affairs Review* 48 (3): 389–416.

Massey, Doreen. 1991. "A Global Sense of Place." *Marxism Today*, June. http://www.unz.org /Pub/MarxismToday-1991jun-00024 (accessed October 2014).

———. 1994. *Space, Place, and Gender*. Minneapolis: University of Minnesota Press.

———. 1995. "The Conceptualization of Place." In *A Place in the World?*, edited by Doreen Massey and Pat Jess, 45–86. Oxford, UK: Oxford University Press in association with the Open University.

———. 2004. "Geographies of Responsibility." Special issue, *The Political Challenge of Relational Space*, in *Geografiska Annaler*, Series B, *Human Geography* 86 (1): 5–18.

Massey, Douglas S. 1995. "The New Ethnicity in the U.S.A." *Population and Development Review* 21 (3): 631–52.

———, ed. 2008. *New Faces in New Places: The Changing Geography of American Immigration*. New York: Russell Sage Foundation.

Massey, Douglas, and Chiara Capoferro. 2008. "The Geographic Diversification of American Immigration" In *New Faces in New Places: The Changing Geography of American Immigration*, edited by Douglas Massey, 25–50. New York: Russell Sage Foundation.

Massey, Douglas S., and Nancy A. Denton. 1988. "The Dimensions of Residential Segregation." *Social Forces* 67 (2): 281–315.

———.1993. *American Apartheid: Segregation and the Making of the Underclass*. Cambridge, MA: Harvard University Press.

Massey, Douglas S., Jorge Durand, and Nolan J. Malone. 2002. *Beyond Smoke and Mirrors: Mexican Immigration in an Era of Economic Integration*. New York: Russell Sage Foundation.

Mather, Mark, and Kelvin Pollard. 2007. "Hispanic Gains Minimize Population Losses in Rural America." Population Reference Bureau. http://www.prb.org/Publications/Articles /2007/HispanicGains.aspx (accessed December 2014).

McCabe, Kristen. 2011. "African Immigrants in the United States." Migration Policy Institute online journal, July 21. http://www.migrationpolicy.org/article/african-immigrants-united -states (accessed October 2014).

McConnell, Eileen Diaz, and Faranak Miraftab. 2009. "Sundown Town to 'Mexican Town': Newcomers, Old Timers, and Housing in Small Town America." *Rural Sociology* 74 (4): 605–29.

McDonald, David. 2008. *World City Syndrome: Neoliberalism and Inequality in Cape Town*. London: Routledge.

McKay, Deirdre. 2014. "Affect: Making the Global through Care." In *Framing the Global: Entry Points for Research*, edited by Hilary Kahn, 18–36. Bloomington: Indiana University Press.

McNeil, May Carr. 1987. May Carr McNeil interview and Memoir. Interviewed by George Ingle. Oral History, University of Illinois at Springfield; Norris L Brookens Library Archives/Special Collections. 4 tapes, 345 mins., 2 vols., 146 pp.

Mercer, Claire, Ben Page, and Martin Evans. 2008. *Development and the African Diaspora: Place and the Politics of Home*. London: Zed Books.

Merrifield, Andy. 2013. "The Urban Question under Planetary Urbanization." *International Journal of Urban and Regional Research* 37(3):909–22.

———. 2014. *The New Urban Question*. London: Pluto Press.

Millard, A. V., and Jorge Chapa. 2004. "Aqui in the Midwest." In *Apple Pie and Enchiladas: Latino Newcomers in the Rural Midwest*, edited by A. V. Millard and Jorge Chapa, 1–21. Austin: University of Texas Press.

Milroy, Beth M., and M. L. Wallace. 2002. "Ethnoracial Diversity and Planning Practices in the Greater Toronto Area." Toronto, Joint Centre of Excellence for Research on Immigration and Settlement (CERIS).

Miraftab, Faranak. 2000. "Sheltering Refugees: The Housing Experience of Refugees in the Metropolitan Vancouver, Canada." *Canadian Journal of Urban Research* 9 (1): 42–63.

———. 2004. "Can you Belly Dance? Methodological Questions in the Era of Transnational Feminist Research." *Gender, Place and Culture: Journal of Feminist Geography* 11(4): 595–604.

———. 2006. "Feminist Praxis, Citizenship and Informal Politics: Reflections on South Africa's Anti-Eviction Campaign." *International Feminist Journal of Politics* 8 (2): 194–218.

———. 2009. "Insurgent Planning: Situating Radical Planning in the Global South." *Planning Theory* 8 (1): 32–50.

———. 2010. "Contradictions in the Gender-Poverty Nexus: Reflections on the Privatisation of Social Reproduction and Urban Informality in South African Townships." In *The International Handbook on Gender and Poverty: Concepts, Research and Policy*, edited by Silvia Chant. New York: Edward Elgar Publishers.

———. 2011 "Faraway Intimate Development: Global Restructuring of Social Reproduction." *Journal of Planning Education and Research* 31 (4):392–405.

———. 2012a. "Small-Town Transnationalism: Socio-Spatial Dynamics of Immigration to the Heartland." In *The Transnationalism and Urbanism*, edited by Stefan Kratke, Kathrin Wildner, and Stephan Lanz, 220–31. London: Routledge.

———. 2012b. "Planning and Citizenship" in Rachel Weber and Randall Crane (eds.) *Oxford Handbook of Urban Planning*. Oxford University Press. Chapter 38, pp. 1180–1204.

Miraftab, Faranak, and Eileen Diaz McConnell. 2008. "Multiculturalizing Rural Towns: Insights for Inclusive Planning." *International Planning Studies* 13 (4): 343–60.

Mitchel, Don. 1996. *The Lie of the Land: Migrant Workers and the California Landscape*. Minneapolis: University of Minnesota Press.

———. 2012. *They Saved the Crops: Labor, Landscape, and the Struggle over Industrial Farming in Bracero-Era California*. Athens: University of Georgia Press.

Mitchell, Katharyne, Sallie A. Marston, and Cindi Katz. 2004. "Life's Work: An Introduction, Review and Critique." In *Life Works: Geographies of Social Reproduction*, edited by Katharyne Mitchell, Sallie A. Marston, and Cindi Katz, 1–26. Malden, MA: Blackwell.

Mohan, Gill. 2006. "Embedded Cosmopolitanism and the Politics of Obligation: The Ghanaian Diaspora and Development." *Environment and Planning A* 38 (5): 867–83.

Moll, David. 1995. "Klan Group Plans Fulton Rally: Group Says It Got Letters from Beardstown Complaining about Illegal Immigrants." *Jacksonville Journal Star*, October 4, page A1.

Moody, Kim. 1997. *Workers in a Lean World: Unions in the International Economy*. London: Verso.

Mott, Tamar E. 2010. "African Refugee Resettlement in the US: The Role and Significance of Voluntary Agencies." *Journal of Cultural Geography* 27 (1): 1–33.

Moura, Colleen Lowe. 1990. "Africa's Switzerland," *Africa Report* (September–October): 36–38.

Muniandy, Parthiban, and Valeria Bonatti. 2014. "Are Migrants Agents or Instruments of Development? The Case of Temporary Migration in Malaysia." *Journal of Ethnic and Migration Studies* 40 (11): 1836–53.

Myers, Dowell. 2007. *Immigrants and Boomers.* New York: Russell Sage Foundation.

Nast, Heidi J., with Laura Pulido. 2000. "Resisting Corporate Multiculturalism: Mapping Faculty Initiatives and Institutional-Student Harassment in the Classroom." *Professional Geographer* 52 (4): 722–37.

National Center for Education Statistics. 2012. NCES Common Core Data (CCD), Local Education Agency (School District) Universe Survey Data. http://nces.ed.gov/ccd/pubagency.asp (accessed November 2014).

Nederveen Pieterse, Jan. 2007. *Ethnicities and Global Multiculture: Pants for an Octopus.* Plymouth, UK: Rowman & Littlefield.

Nelson, Lise, and Peter B. Nelson. 2010. "The Global Rural: Gentrification and Linked Migration in the Rural USA." *Progress in Human Geography* 35 (4): 441–59.

Newman, Katherine S. 1999. *No Shame in My Game: The Working Poor in the Inner City.* New York: Russell Sage Foundation.

New York Times. 1922. "Posse Kills Greek after Fatal Affray: Shooting of Illinois Sheriff and Two Deputies Blamed on Labor Agitators." April 30.

———.1953a. "General Gas Building Plant." June 9, page L37.

———.1953b. "Plant on 20-acre Site; Road Equipment Maker Plans Expansion in IL." December 27, page F5.

———.1998. "Beardstown Ladies Had the Wrong Results." March 18, page D2.

———.2008. "The Shame of Postville, Iowa." July 13. http://www.nytimes.com/2008/07/13/opinion/13sun2.html?module=Search&mabReward=relbias%3Ar&_r=0 (accessed December 2014).

Obeng, Cecilia Sem. 2007. "Immigrant Families and Childcare Preferences: Do Immigrants' Cultures Influence Their Childcare Decisions?" *Early Childhood Education Journal* 43 (4): 259–64.

Oduro, Abena D., and Ivy Aryee. 2003. *Investigating Chronic Poverty in West Africa.* Chronic Poverty Research Centre Working Paper No. 28. Accra-North, Ghana: Centre for Policy Analysis.

Olivos, Edward, and Gerardo Sandoval. 2015. "Latina/o Identities, the Racialization of Work, and the Global Reserve Army of Labor: Becoming Latino in Postville, Iowa." *Ethnicities* 15(2): 190–210.

Ong, Aihwa. 2003. *Buddha Is Hiding: Refugees, Citizenship, the New America.* Berkeley: University of California Press.

Orrenius, Pia M. 2004. "The Effect of U.S. Border Enforcement on the Crossing Behavior of Mexican Migrants." In *Crossing the Border: Research from the Mexican Migration Project,* edited by Jorge Durand and Douglass S. Massey, 281–98. New York, Russell Sage Foundation.

Pachirat, Timothy. 2011. *Every Twelve Seconds: Industrialized Slaughter and the Politics of Sight.* New Haven, CT: Yale University Press.

Paciotto, Carla, and Gloria Delany-Barmann. 2011. "Planning Micro-Level Language Education Reform in New Diaspora Sites: Two-Way Immersion Education in the Rural Midwest." *Language Policy* 10: 221–43.

Parisi, Domenico, and Daniel T. Lichter. 2007. "Hispanic Segregation in America's New Rural Boomtowns." Washington, DC: Population Reference Bureau. http://www.prb.org/Publications/Articles/2007/Hispanic Segregation.aspx (accessed December 2014).

Parisi, Domenico, Daniel T. Lichter, and Michael C. Taquino. 2011. "Multi-Scale Residential Segregation: Black Exceptionalism and America's Changing Color Line." *Social Forces* 89: 829–52.

Parreñas, Rachel Salazar. 2001. *Servants of Globalization: Women, Migration, and Domestic Work*. Palo Alto, CA: Stanford University Press.

Peck, Jamie. 2002. "Political Economies of Scale: Fast Policy, Interscalar Relations, and Neoliberal Workfare." *Economic Geography* 78 (3): 331–60.

Peirce, Neal R., and Curtis W. Johnson with Farley M. Peters. 2008. *Century of the City: No Time to Lose*. New York: Rockefeller Foundation.

Perrin, William Henry. 1882. *History of Cass County, Illinois*. Chicago: O. H. Baskin & Co., Historical Publishers.

Perry, Charles R., and Delwyn H. Kegley. 1989. *Disintegration and Change: Labor Relations in the Meat Packing Industry*. Philadelphia: Industrial Research Unit, Wharton School, University of Pennsylvania.

Piot, Charles D. 1999. *Remotely Global: Village Modernity in West Africa*. Chicago: University of Chicago Press.

———. 2010. *Nostalgia for the Future: West Africa after the Cold War*. Chicago: University of Chicago Press.

———. 2013. "Migration Stories: The U.S. Visa Lottery and Global Citizenship." Distinguished Africanist Lecture Series, University of Chicago. May 16.

Portes, Alejandro, and Robert Manning. 1986. "The Immigrant Enclave: Theory and Empirical Examples." In *Competitive Ethnic Relations*, edited by Susan Olzak and Joanne Nagel. Orlando: Florida University Press.

Portes, Alejandro, and Ruben Rumbaut. 2006. *Immigrant America: A Portrait*. Berkeley: University of California Press.

Preibisch, K., and Leigh Binford. 2007. "Interrogating Racialized Global Labour Supply: An Exploration of the Ethnic Replacement of Foreign Agricultural Workers in Canada." *Canadian Review of Sociology and Anthropology* 44 (1): 5–36.

Preston, Julia. 2010. "27-Year Sentence for Plant Manager." *New York Times*, June 22, page A18.

———. 2013. "Number of Illegal Immigrants in U.S. May Be on Rise Again, Estimates Say." *New York Times*, September 23, page A16.

Qadeer, Mohammad Abdul. 1997. "Pluralistic Planning for Multicultural Cities: The Canadian Practice." *Journal of the American Planning Association* 63 (4): 481–94.

Qadeer, Mohammad Abdul, and Sandeep Kumar Agrawal. 2011. "The Practice of Multicultural Planning in American and Canadian Cities." *Canadian Journal of Urban Research* 20 (1): 132–156.

Raghuram, Parvati. 2009. "Which Migration, What Development? Unsettling the Edifice of Migration and Development." *Population, Space and Place* 15 (2): 103–17.

Relinger, Rick. 2010. "NAFTA and U.S. Corn Subsidies: Explaining the Displacement of Mexico's Corn Farmers." *Prospect: Journal of International Affairs at UCSD*, April 19. http://prospectjournal.org/2010/04/19/nafta-and-u-s-corn-subsidies-explaining-the-displacement-of-mexicos-corn-farmers-2/ (accessed October 2014).

Rhodes, Dusty. 2012. "Study Finds Wide Global Impact in Beardstown: Distant Communities Support Local Town via 'Social Reproduction,' Professor Says." *Jacksonville Journal Courier*, February 5, page 1.

Rios, Michael. 2015. "Beyond "Place," Translocal Placemaking of the Hmong Diaspora." *Journal of Planning Education and Research* 35(2):209–19.

Rios, Michael, and Leonardo Vazquez (eds). 2012. *Diálogos: Placemaking in Latinos Communities*. New York: Routledge.

Roberts, Adrienne. 2008. "Privatizing Social Reproduction: The Primitive Accumulation of Water in an Era of Neoliberalism." *Antipode* 40 (4): 535–60.

Roberts, Bryan, and Reanne Frank. 1999. "Transnational Migrant Communities and Mexican Migration to the U.S." *Ethnic and Racial Studies* 22 (March): 238–67.

Roberts, Sam. 2005. "More Africans Enter the U.S than in Days of Slavery." *New York Times*, February 21. http://www.nytimes.com/2005/02/21/nyregion/21africa.html (accessed December 2014).

Robinson, Jennifer. 2006. *Ordinary Cities: Between Modernity and Development*. London: Routledge.

Rodriguez-Scott, Esmeralda. 2002. "Patterns of Mexican Migration to the United States." Southwestern Social Science Association, New Orleans, March 27–30. http://www1.appstate.edu/~stefanov/proceedings/rodriguez.htm (accessed December 2014).

Roediger, David. 1991. *The Wages of Whiteness: Race and the Making of the American Working Class*. London: Verso.

Roediger, David, and Elizabeth Esch. 2012. *The Production of Difference: Race and the Management of Labor in US History*. New York: Oxford University Press.

Rojas, James. 2010. "Latino Urbanism in Los Angeles: a Model for Urban Improvisation and Reinvention" in J. Hou (ed.) *Insurgent Public Space: Guerilla Urbanism and the Remaking of Contemporary Cities*, pp. 36–44. New York: Routledge.

Romero, Mary. 2002. *Maid in the USA*. New York: Routledge.

Rosas, Ana Elizabeth. 2011. "Breaking the Silence: Mexican Children and Women's Confrontation of *Bracero* Family Separation, 1942–64." *Gender & History* 23 (2): 382–400.

Rose, Susan, and Robert Shaw. 2008. "The Gamble: Circular Mexican Migration and the Return on Remittances." *Mexican Studies* 24 (1): 79–111.

Roy, Ananya. 2011. "The Blockade of the World-Class City: Dialectical Images of Indian Urbanism." In *Worlding Cities: Asian Experiments and the Art of Being Global*, edited by Ananya Roy and Aiwa Ong, 229–58. Oxford, UK: Wiley-Blackwell.

———. 2012. "Placing Planning in the World: Transnationalism as Practice and Critique." *Journal of Planning Education and Research* 31 (4): 416–22.

Ruggles, Steven, J., Trent Alexander, Katie Genadek, Ronald Goeken, Matthew B. Schroeder, and Matthew Sobek. 2010. Integrated Public Use Microdata Series: Version 5.0. [Machine-readable database]. Minneapolis: University of Minnesota. IPUMS-USA, University of Minnesota, www.ipums.org.

Ruiz, Ramon Eduardo. 2010. *Mexico: Why a Few Are Rich and the People Poor*. Berkeley: University of California Press.

Salo, Ken. 2015. "Local Practices and Translocal Solidarities: Reflections on Antieviction Practices on the Cape Flats, South Africa and Southside Chicago." In *Cities and Inequalities in a Neoliberal and Transnational Era*, edited by F. Miraftab, D. Wilson, and K. Salo, 217–26. London: Routledge.

Sampson, Steven. 2002 "Beyond Transition: Rethinking Elite Configurations in the Balkans." In *Postsocialism: Ideals, Ideologies and Practices in Eurasia,* edited by C. M. Hann, 297–316. New York: Routledge.

Sana, Mariano, and Douglas S. Massey. 2005. "Household Composition, Family Migration, and Community Context: Migrant Remittances in Four Countries." *Social Science Quarterly* 86 (2): 509–28.

Sander, Libby. 2007. "Immigration Raid Yields 62 Arrests in Illinois." *New York Times*, April 5, page A12.

Sandercock, Leonie. 1998. *Towards Cosmopolis*. New York: John Wiley and Sons.

———. 2003. *Cosmopolis II: Mongrel Cities of the 21st Century*. London: Continuum.

Sandercock, Leonie, and Giovanni Attili. 2009. *Where Strangers Become Neighbours: Integrating Immigrants in Vancouver, Canada*. Springer.

Sandercock, Leonie, and V. Cavers. 2009. "The Story of the Collingwood Neighbourhood House: A Unique Gathering Place." In Leonie Sandercock and Giovanni Attili, *Where Strangers Become Neighbours: Integrating Immigrants in Vancouver, Canada*. Springer.

Sandercock, Leonie, and B. Kliger. 1998a. "Multiculturalism and the Planning System, Part One." *The Australian Planner* 35 (3): 127–132.

———. 1998b. "Multiculturalism and the Planning System, Part Two." *The Australian Planner* 35 (4): 231–35.

Sanderson, Matthew R. 2013a. "Does Immigration Have a Matthew Effect? A Cross-National Analysis of International Migration and International Income Inequality, 1960–2005." *Social Science Research* 42 (3): 683–97.

———. 2013b. "Does Immigration Promote Economic Development? A Cross-National and Regional Analysis, 1965–2005." *Journal of Ethnic and Migration Studies* 39 (1): 1–30.

Sandoval, Gerardo Francisco. 2013. "Shadow Transnationalism: Cross-Border Networks and Planning Challenges of Transnational Unauthorized Immigrant Communities." *Journal of Planning Education and Research* 33 (2): 176–93.

———. 2014. "Immigrant Integration Models in 'Illegal' Communities: Postville Iowa's Shadow Context." *Local Environment: The International Journal of Justice and Sustainability*. doi: 10.1080/13549839.2014.963839.

Sandoval, Gerardo Francisco, and Marta Maria Maldonado. 2012. "Latino Urbanism Revisited: Placemaking in New Gateways and the Urban-Rural Interface." *Journal of Urbanism: International Research on Placemaking and Urban Sustainability* 5 (2–3): 193–218.

Sarmiento, Carolina, and Victoria Beard. 2013. "Traversing the Border: Community-Based Planning and Transnational Migrants." *Journal of Planning Education and Research* 33(3):336–47.

Sassen, Saskia. 1991. *Global City: New York, London, Tokyo*. Princeton, NJ: Princeton University Press.

———. 2000. "Spatialities and Temporalities of the Global: Elements for a Theorization." *Public Culture* 12 (1): 215–32.

———. 2014. *Expulsions: Brutality and Complexity in the Global Economy*. Cambridge, MA: Harvard University Press/Belknap.

Schlosser, Eric. 2001. "Chain Never Stops." *Mother Jones* 26 (4): 38–50.

Schneider, Daniel. W. 1996. "Enclosing the Floodplain: Resource Conflict on the Illinois River, 1880–1920." *Environmental History* 1 (2):70–96.

Schwartzman, Kathleen. 2013. *The Chicken Trail: Following Workers, Migrants, and Corporations across the Americas*. Ithaca, NY: Cornell University Press.

Schweer, T. J. 1925. *History of Beardstown and Cass County*. Beardstown, IL: n.p.

Sears, David O., and Victoria Savalei. 2006. "The Political Color Line in America: Many' Peoples of Color' or Black Exceptionalism?" *Political Psychology* 27(6):895–924.

Shapira, Harel. 2013. "The Border: Infrastructure of the Global." *Public Culture* 25 (2): 249–60.

Shatkin, Gavin. 2007. "Global Cities of the South: Emerging Perspectives on Growth and Inequality." *Cities* 24 (1): 1–15.

Shaw-Taylor, Yoku. 2007. "The Intersection of Assimilation, Race, Presentation of Self and
    Transnationalism in America." In *The Other African Americans: Contemporary African and
    Caribbean Families in the United States,* edited by Yoku Shaw-Taylor and Steven A. Tuch,
    1–48. New York: Rowman and Littlefield.
Shaw-Taylor, Yoku, and Steven A. Tuch, eds. 2007. *The Other African Americans: Contem-
    porary African and Caribbean Families in the United States.* New York: Rowman and
    Littlefield.
Sheppard, Eric. 2002. "The Spaces and Times of Globalization: Place, Scale, Networks and
    Positionality." *Economic Geography* 78: 307–30.
Shipler, David K. 2005. *The Working Poor, Invisible in America.* New York: Vintage Books.
Sinclair, Upton. 1906. *The Jungle.* New York: The Jungle Publishing Co.
Smith, Michael Peter. 2001. *Transnational Urbanism: Locating Globalization.* Malden, MA:
    Blackwell Publishers.
Smith, Michael Peter, and Luis Guarnizo, eds. 1998. *Transnationalism from Below.* New Bruns-
    wick, NJ: Transaction Publishers.
Smith, Neil. 1984. *Uneven Development: Nature, Capital, and the Production of Space.* Athens:
    University of Georgia Press.
———. 2002. "New Globalism, New Urbanism: Gentrification as Global Urban Strategy."
    Antipode 34 (3): 427–50.
Smith, Wes. 1995. "Beardstown Ladies Bask in a Bonanza." *Chicago Tribune,* March 14.
Sørensen, Ninna Nyberg. 2012. "Revisiting the Migration-Development Nexus: From Social
    Networks and Remittances to Markets for Migration Control." *International Migration* 50
    (3): 61–76.
State Journal-Register (Springfield, IL). 1989. "Rushville Chamber Backs Prison Work Camp
    Plan." November 22, page 18.
Stiglitz, Joseph. 2004. "The Broken Promise of Nafta." *New York Times,* Op Ed. January 6.
Story, Louise. 2012. "The Empty Promise of Tax Incentives." *New York Times,* December 2,
    page A1.
Stull, Donald. 1990. "'I Come to the Garden': Changing Ethnic Relations in Garden City,
    Kansas." *Urban Anthropology* 1 (4): 303–20.
Stull, Donald, Michael Broadway, and David Griffith, eds. 1995. *Any Way You Cut It: Meat Pro-
    cessing and Small-Town America.* Lawrence: University Press of Kansas.
Sugrue, Thomas J. 1996. *The Origins of the Urban Crisis: Race and Inequality in Postwar Detroit.*
    Princeton, NJ: Princeton University Press.
Terrazas, Aaron. 2009. "African Immigrants in the United States." Migration Policy Institute.
    http://www.migrationpolicy.org/article/african-immigrants-united-states-0 (accessed
    May 2009).
Theising, Andrew. 2003. *East St. Louis, Made in USA: The Rise and Fall of a River Town.*
    St. Louis: Virginia Publishing.
Theodore, Nik, and Nina Martin. 2007. "Migrant Civil Society: New Voices in the Struggle
    over Community Development." *Journal of Urban Affairs* 29 (3): 269–87.
Thomas, June Manning. 2013. *Redevelopment and Race: Planning a Finer City in Postwar
    Detroit.* Detroit: Wayne State University Press.
Thompson, Susan. 2003. "Planning and Multiculturalism: A Reflection on Australian Local
    Practice." *Planning Theory and Practice* 4 (3): 275–93.
Thornburgh, Nathan. 2007. "Immigration: The Case for Amnesty" *Time* 169 (25):
    38–42.

Toporowski, Jan. 1988. "Togo: A Structural Adjustment that Destabilizes Economic Growth." *IDS Bulletin* 19 (1): 17–23.

Trabalzi, Ferro and Sandoval, Gerardo. 2010. "The Exotic Other: Latinos and the Remaking of Community Identity in Perry, Iowa." *Community Development*, vol. 41, no. 1.

Tsing, Ana. 2005. *Friction: An Ethnography of Global Connection*. Princeton, NJ: Princeton University Press.

Ursch, John W. 2006. "Cargill Vexes Cass County Officials." *Jacksonville Journal-Courier*, November 24.

———. 2007. "Cass County, Ill., Officials, Meat Plant Agree on Lower Tax Assessment." *Jacksonville Journal-Courier*, May 8.

U.S. Bureau of the Census .1990. 1990 Census of Population and Housing, Summary File 1. www.socialexplorer.com (accessed December 2014).

———. 1993–.American Community Survey (ACS). http://www.census.gov/acs/www /library/by_year/2014 (accessed December 2014).

———. 2000. 2000 Census of Population and Housing, Summary File 1. http://factfinder2 .census.gov (accessed December 2014).

———. 2010. 2010 Census of Population and Housing, Summary File 1. http://factfinder2 .census.gov (accessed December 2014).

———. 2013. 2008–2012 American Community Survey 5-Year Estimates. http://factfinder2 .census.gov (accessed November 10, 2014).

———. 2014. Quarterly Workforce Indicators Data. Longitudinal-Employer Household Dynamics Program. http://lehd.ces.census.gov/data/#qwi (accessed June 2015).

U.S Department of Justice, 1997. *Statistical Yearbook of the Immigrant and Naturalization Service*. Washington, DC: U.S Government Printing Office.

U.S. Department of Labor, Bureau of Labor Statistics. 2011. "Incidence Rates of Nonfatal Occupational Injuries and Illnesses by Industry and Case Types, 2010." October. http://www .bls.gov/iif/oshwc/osh/os/ostb2813.pdf (accessed June 2015).

———. 2012. Labor Force Statistics, Table 18. http://www.bls.gov/cps/cpsaat18.htm (accessed December 2014).

———. 2013. *Workplace Injury and Illness Summary. Economic News Release*, November 7. (http://www.bls.gov/news.release/osh.nr0.htm (accessed October 2014).

Vázquez-Castillo, Maria Teresa. 2012 [2004]. *Land Privatization in Mexico: Urbanization, Formation of Regions and Globalization in Ejidos*. New York: Routledge.

Vickerman, Milton. 2001. "Jamaicans: Balancing Race and Ethnicity," in Nancy Foner, ed., *New Immigrants in New York*, 201–28. New York: Columbia University Press.

Waldinger, Roger. 1996. *Still the Promised City? African-Americans and New Immigrants in Postindustrial New York*. Cambridge, MA: Harvard University Press.

Waldinger, Roger, Howard Aldrich, and Robin Ward. 1990. *Ethnic Entrepreneurs: Immigrant Business in Industrial Societies*. Newbury Park, CA: Russell Sage Foundation.

Walker, S. Lynne. 2003a. "Tension in the Air." *State Journal-Register* (Springfield, IL). November 9, pp. 1 and 6–8.

———.2003b. "Living a Lie." *State Journal-Register* (Springfield, IL). November 11, pp. 1 and 6–7.

Warren, Wilson. 2007. *Tied to the Great Packing Machine: The Midwest and Meatpacking*. Iowa City: University of Iowa Press.

Wasem, Ruth Ellen. 2010. *Diversity Immigrant Visa Lottery Issues*. Washington, DC: Congressional Research Service. http://digitalcommons.ilr.cornell.edu/key_workplace/822 (accessed October 2014).

Wasem, Ruth Ellen, and Karma Ester. 2004. "Immigration: Diversity Visa Lottery." Report, Immigration Law Worldwide. http://www.ilw.com/immigrationdaily/news/2005,0809 -crs.pdf (accessed October 2004).

Waters, Mary C., Philip Kasinitz, and Asad L. Asad. 2014. "Immigrants and African Americans." *Annual Review of Sociology* 40: 369–90.

West, Cathy. 1986a. "The Efforts Begin to Solve OM Closing." *Illinoian Star Daily*. October 3.

———. 1986b. "Walters: Main Goal to Find a New Employer." *Illinoian Star Daily*. October 3.

———. 1986c. "Officials Optimistic about OM Sale." *Illinoian Star Daily*. October 4.

———. 1986d. "Cooperation Is Key to Easing the Effects of an Oscar Mayer Closing." *Illinoian Star Daily*. October 9.

Williams, Charlotte, and David L. Ostendorf. 2011. "From the Editors' Introduction to Special Issue on Food Justice." In *Race/Ethnicity: Multidisciplinary Global Contexts* 5 (1): vi–1.

Wilson, David, and Faranak Miraftab. 2015. "New Inequalities in America's Rust Belt." In *Cities and Inequalities in a Neoliberal and Transnational Era*, edited by Faranak Miraftab, David Wilson, and Ken Salo, 28–48. London: Routledge.

Winick, Norm. 1995. "A Gathering of the Klan: A Report of a Ku Klux Klan Rally Held Saturday, October 14, 1995 in Fulton County, Illinois." *Zephyr*, October 19. http://www .thezephyr.com/.

Wolpe, H. 1972. "Capitalism and Cheap Labour-Power in South Africa: From Segregation to Apartheid." *Economy and Society* 1 (4): 425–56.

Wood, Andrew Grant. 2013 "Mexicans in the United States: A Longer View." In *Latin American Migrations to the Heartland: Changing Social Landscapes in Middle America*, edited by Linda Allegro and Andrew Grant Wood, 25–41. Chicago: University of Illinois Press.

World Bank. 2011. *Migration and Remittances Factbook*, 2nd ed. Washington, DC: The World Bank.http://siteresources.worldbank.org/INTLAC/Resources/Factbook2011-Ebook.pdf (accessed December 2014).

Wright, Erik Olin.1989. "Rethinking Once Again the Concept of Class Structure." In *The Debate on Classes*, edited by Erik Olin Wright, 269–384. New York: Verso.

Wright, Ross B. 1973. Wright, Ross B. Interview and Memoir. Interviewed by Brian Alexander. Oral History, University of Illinois at Springfield; Norris L Brookens Library Archives/Special Collections. 1 tape, 30 minutes, 8pp.

Yeates, Nicola. 2004. "A Dialogue with 'Global Care Chain' Analysis: Nurse Migration in the Irish Context." *Feminist Review* 77: 79–95.

Yeboah, Ian E. A. 2008. *Black African Neo-Diaspora: Ghanaian Immigration Experiences in the Greater Cincinnati, Ohio, Area*. Lanham, MA: Lexington Books.

Yunez-Naude, Antonio. 2003. "The Dismantling of CONASUPO, a Mexican State Trader in Agriculture." *World Economy* 26 (1): 97–122.

Zeleza, Paul Tiyambe. 1998. *African Labour and Intellectual Migrations to the North: Building New Transatlantic Bridges*. Santiago, CA: University of California.

———. 2009. "Diaspora Dialogues: Engagements between Africa and Its Diaspora." In *The New African Diaspora*, edited by Isidore Opkewho and Nkiru Nzegwu, 31–58. Bloomington: Indiana University Press.

Zúñiga, Elena, Paula Leite, and Rosa Nava. 2005. *The New Era of Migrations 2005: Characteristics of International Migration in Mexico*. Mexico: National Population Council (CONAPO).

Zúñiga, Victor, and Ruben Hernández-León, eds. 2005. *New Destinations: Mexican Immigration in the United States*. New York: Russell Sage Foundation.

INDEX

FARANAK MIRAFTAB is Professor of Urban and Regional Planning at the University of Illinois, Urbana-Champaign. Her interdisciplinary work in critical planning, human geography, and transnational studies concerns the grassroots struggle for dignified livelihood and citizenship and is empirically based in marginalized communities of Latin America, Africa, and North America. Her most recent publications include *Cities and Inequalities in a Global and Neoliberal World* (edited with David Wilson and Ken Salo, 2015); and *Cities of the Global South Reader* (edited with Neema Kudva, 2014).

CPSIA information can be obtained
at www.ICGtesting.com
Printed in the USA
LVHW041455150819
627778LV00012B/937/P